WHITHER THE U.S. CHURCH?

WHITHER THE U.S. CHURCH?

Context, Gospel, Planning

John A. Grindel, C.M.

ORBIS BOOKS

Maryknoll, New York 10545

The Catholic Foreign Mission Society of America (Maryknoll) recruits and trains people for overseas missionary service. Through Orbis Books, Maryknoll aims to foster the international dialogue that is essential to mission. The books published, however, reflect the opinions of their authors and are not meant to represent the official position of the society.

Copyright © 1991 by John A. Grindel
All rights reserved
Published by Orbis Books, Maryknoll, NY 10545
Manufactured in the United States of America

Library of Congress Cataloging-in-Publication Data

Grindel, John A.
    Whither the U. S. Church? : context, gospel, planning / John A.
Grindel.
        p. cm.
    Includes bibliographical references and index.
    ISBN 0-88344-776-2
    1. Catholic Church—United States—History—20th century.
    2. United States—Church history—20th century. I. Title.
BX1406.2.G75   1991
282'.73'09049—dc20   91-19427
                                                              CIP

CONTENTS

LIST OF ABBREVIATIONS

CD   *Christus Dominus/Decree on the Pastoral Office of Bishops in the Church* (Vatican II, 1965)

CP   *The Challenge of Peace* (National Conference of Catholic Bishops, 1983)

DH   *Dignitatis Humanae/Declaration on Religious Freedom* (Vatican II, 1965)

EJ   *Economic Justice for All* (National Conference of Catholic Bishops, 1986)

EN   *Evangelii Nuntiandi/On the Evangelization of Peoples* (Paul VI, 1975)

GS   *Gaudium et Spes/Pastoral Constitution on the Church in the Modern World* (Vatican II, 1965)

HP   *The Hispanic Presence: Challenge and Commitment* (National Conference of Catholic Bishops, 1983)

JW   *Justice in the World* (Synod of Bishops, 1971)

LG   *Lumen Gentium/Dogmatic Constitution on the Church* (Vatican II, 1964)

MM   *Mater et Magistra/Christianity and Social Progress* (John XXIII, 1961)

OA   *Octogesima Adveniens/A Call to Action* (Paul VI, 1971)

PP   *Populorum Progressio/On the Development of Peoples* (Paul VI, 1967)

SRS   *Sollicitudo Rei Socialis/On Social Concern* (John Paul II, 1987)

INTRODUCTION

Where is the U.S. Church headed? Does it have a plan? What should be its primary goals and its strategies for achieving these goals? All modern organizations have come to understand how critical planning is for success today in view of the complexity of the modern world and the rapid changes taking place in that world. The Church as an institution is not exempt from this need for planning. Without a national plan the best intended initiatives of the Church, including those of the National Conference of Catholic Bishops (NCCB) and the United States Catholic Conference (USCC), will be disjointed and unrelated, and attempts to implement them will be ineffective.

A national pastoral plan is needed to give direction to those who do ministry in the Church in the United States and to provide direction for making decisions on the use of Church resources: people, talent, money, land, and buildings. Without such a plan the energies of the Church will be uncoordinated and significantly less effective than if orchestrated toward common goals and objectives. Also, until such a national pastoral plan is formulated, local churches will not be driven to formulate their own pastoral plans.

In formulating a national pastoral plan it is important to recognize the various roles played by the Church. There is, first of all, the *sacramental* life of the Church that is expressed above all in its celebration of the Eucharist. The Church also has the role of *comforter, counselor, and supporter* for those who are hurting and those in need. There is the *teaching/preaching* Church that has the responsibility for handing on the faith to its members and challenging them to live that faith. There is the *missionary* aspect of the Church where it attempts to bring the Gospel to those who have not yet heard it. There is the *public* Church that plays a role in the broader life of society.

Each of these aspects of the Church has its own inner life and dynamic, and it is not easy, perhaps impossible, to bring all these aspects of the life of the Church under one focus or common orientation. The comforting, counseling, supportive role of the Church especially has a life of its own that is dependent upon the immediate needs of the people who come to the Church for help. However, it seems to me that most of the other aspects of the life of the Church can be brought together, to some degree or

1

another, under a common focus. It is that focus — the need for direction — that we will be searching for in this book.

The origins of this book are complex and begin with my experiences in 1980 as a representative of the Conference of Major Superiors of Men at the Fourth Interamerican Conference of Religious in Santiago, Chile. The theme of the conference was the relationship of religious to the local Church. During this meeting we religious from the United States were hard pressed to explain our relationship to the Church in the United States because there was no clear understanding of the mission of the Church in the United States. I left that conference concluding that dealing with the question of the mission of the Church in the United States was one of the most urgent issues we needed to face in this country. It was also at this time that for the first time I saw with my own eyes the plight of the poor in Latin America and the impact of U.S. foreign policy and the transnational corporations on the people of Latin America. An extended return visit to Latin America in 1983 brought home to me even more what was happening there.

My experiences as a provincial superior of the Province of the West of the Vincentians from 1978 until 1987 reinforced my conviction regarding the urgency of coming to terms with the question of the mission of the Church in the United States. During these years I found myself reflecting again and again on the direction of the province and the Church in view of what was happening in the world. Several events in particular forced me to clarify my thinking about the mission of the Church in the United States. First, there was the experience of listening to the narration of the painful experiences of my confreres from the Third World during our General Assemblies in Rome in 1974, 1980, and 1986. Then in the early 1980s, I was involved in sending several men from the province to Burundi to begin a mission there. Burundi is one of the poorest countries in Africa. Before we were forced to leave Burundi, four years after we started, I visited Africa twice. I was overwhelmed by the poverty I saw there, especially in sub-Saharan Africa, and again I became aware of the impact of U. S. foreign policy and the transnational corporations on life in the Third World. Making the decision to withdraw from the mission in Africa and then beginning a new mission in Central America forced me to reflect even more on the Church's mission in the United States. I also faced the need to deal with personnel issues, formation issues, and the closing of apostolates brought on by a depletion of our numbers and individual confreres rethinking their own commitments in a changing Church. These experiences gave a focus to my reflections upon the Scriptures which I continued to teach in a graduate ministry formation program. In these reflections, especially upon the Hebrew prophets, I found myself coming to a growing conviction that something was terribly wrong with the foreign policy as well as the domestic and economic policies of the United States and that the Church should be addressing these problems.

While attempting to sort out the direction of the province, I discovered in myself a growing sense of frustration with the absence of any clear national pastoral plan for the Church in the United States. By a national pastoral plan I mean an agreed-upon plan of action that will, in the first place, give an overall direction and focus and provide priorities for the pastoral activities of the National Conference of Catholic Bishops (NCCB) and the United States Catholic Conference (USCC). Second, such a plan could offer some direction and priorities to the pastoral activities of individual dioceses and other ecclesial organizations. Such a plan should be developed in dialogue with the members of the Church in the United States by the process used in shaping the U.S. bishops' letters on disarmament and the economy. Such a plan should have clear goals and objectives as well as a clear set of strategies for achieving these goals and objectives.

Several presuppositions underlie this book. While all of them will be dealt with at greater length in the following chapters, I believe that it is important for the reader to know from the beginning what these presuppositions are.

First, the Church, as an instrument for making the Reign of God a reality, must be involved in the work of transforming the society in which it finds itself. For the Church in the United States that means that it must be about the transformation of U.S. society. Given what is happening in the world today, this aspect of the life of the Church takes on a special urgency.

Second, the concrete circumstances and needs of the area or country in which the Church finds itself must always play a significant role in determining the structure, role, and response of the Church in that context. If the Church does not adapt to the context in which it finds itself, it will be an irrelevant voice. Pope Paul VI, in his 1971 apostolic letter *Octogesima Adveniens*, in discussing the wide diversity among the situations in which Christians find themselves, made a very important observation:

> In the face of such widely varying situations, it is difficult for us to utter a unified message and to put forward a solution which has universal validity. Such is not our ambition, nor is it our mission. It is up to the Christian communities to analyze with objectivity the situation which is proper to their own country, to shed on it the light of the Gospel's unalterable words and to draw principles of reflection, norms of judgment and directives for action from the social teaching of the Church. (OA 4)

A third presupposition was stated by the bishops of the United States in their pastoral letter *Economic Justice for All*: "the obligation to provide justice for all means that the poor have the single most urgent economic claim on the conscience of the nation" (EJ 86); "as individuals and as a nation, therefore, we are called to make a fundamental 'option for the poor' " (EJ 87). Being called to make a fundamental "option for the poor" does not mean that the United States is to reach out in a paternalistic way to the poor people of the world and simply do things for them. Rather, the call is, above all, for the United States to stand in solidarity with the poor and to help them help themselves.

Because of the "global village" in which we now find ourselves, the United States cannot be viewed as an entity in itself but always as part of a global community. The issues and problems that we face today are global issues, and the solutions and responses must come from a global perspective even if they are more localized in their application. This is true for all aspects of U.S. society, including the responses of the Church.

In addition, the United States has a special responsibility to help to correct the injustices and inequities that have been created by the colonial domination of the Third World since the sixteenth century because the United States above all has inherited the wealth that was originally gained from this colonial domination by the Western European world. It is clear that there is a need today for a vast and radical transformation of the prevailing economic and political structures of society on a global level to ensure the human development of peoples. In other words, capital and modern technology must be used to serve basic human needs and fundamental human rights, rather than to develop profit. The overwhelming drive for profit and monetary success found in our society today leads to an oppression of the poor around the world—but especially in the underdeveloped countries—that cannot be justified in the light of the Gospel. As members and citizens of a superpower that is responsible for continuing the oppression of the poor through its foreign policy and transnational corporations, the members of the Church in the United States have a special responsibility to transform this society into an instrument of liberation on a worldwide scale.

It is not my intention to call people to help the poor nations of the world out of guilt for the past. The basic reason for helping poor individuals and poor countries must be a moral one. We must reach out because it is a moral duty to help those in need. At the same time, however, we cannot run from the responsibility of the past.

In view of the above stated concern for liberation it might be worthwhile to comment that, while much can be learned from Latin American liberation theology and many of its insights, it is not necessarily valid to apply it to the circumstances of the Church in the United States. The situations here and in Latin America are quite different. Liberation theology developed on the basis of a social-political system that differs from that in the United States. In Latin America there is no large middle class. The United States, on the other hand, is predominantly middle class. Because of its size the middle class in the United States has the potential for setting the direction of the U.S. Church. The middle class can exercise its potential both through the ballot box and through the way it decides to spend its dollars. In the United States one does not find the extreme situations of poverty and oppression that exist in many places in Latin America. The political structures of the United States and Latin America are also very different. Even in the most democratic country in Latin America there is neither the experience nor the capability of exercising democratic control as in the United States; these political systems that Latin American liberation theology opposes are thus different from that in the United States.

Even more important is that as a result of its lifestyles, its consumerism, its transnational corporations, and its government policy, the United States shares some responsibility for the structures and the situations of oppression in Latin America with which liberation theology is attempting to deal. In other words, the beginning and the basis for liberation theology come from the perspective of the periphery, of the underdeveloped countries that have been ravaged in the name of God and civilization to support the center, the first-world countries. However, the Church of the United States is at the center and must face the exploitation of the underdeveloped countries from the perspective of the center and as a Church of the center. Even though the Church in the United States may want to deal with many of the same issues that the Church in Latin America must confront, the two churches come at these issues from totally different perspectives.

The first part of the book will attempt to analyze the socioeconomic, cultural, and political realities in the United States as these pertain to the mission of the Church. This section also contains an analysis of the Church in the United States. Of necessity this picture will be painted with broad strokes. It will be an interpretative picture flowing from and dependent upon the primacy of justice and peace and the need for as well as the belief in the possibility of love and trust not only among peoples but also among nations. The second part contains a theological reflection on the reality of the United States with an eye toward developing a concept of the mission of the Church in the United States. The third part contains reflections on the mission of the Church in the United States and on possible strategies to achieve this mission.

In the second part of the book I refer extensively to documents from the Second Vatican Council, as well as to other pontifical documents, and to the recent pastoral letters of the U.S. bishops. I do not use these documents simply to make an argument from authority; rather, I use them because, to a great extent, they express the results of corporate reflections upon the biblical tradition and make that tradition real for today. To a greater or lesser degree, these documents have developed out of a reflection that begins with contemporary experience. If we are attempting to understand ourselves as a U.S. Church, then we should take special note of what our own bishops have said. The broad dialogue and discussion that lie behind the recent pastoral letters of the U.S. bishops add to their cogency and relevance for today.

The book is addressed, then, to all those who have an interest in the mission of the Church in the United States but especially to those who are responsible for pastoral planning. It is addressed to bishops, either individually or corporately, as well as to major superiors of religious men and women, administrators of Church organizations and their boards on all levels of Church life, planning offices, and individual ministers. Answers regarding the mission of the Church on both national and local levels must ultimately emerge through the corporate reflection of the people who are intimately involved in the life of the Church. Such answers are not to be dictated either by a leader or writer with a particular vision, no matter how sound that vision might be. The purpose of this book is not to say what must be the mission of the Church but rather to provide background for those who wish to deal with this issue and to put forth one possible direction for the Catholic Church in the United States.

Finally, something should be said about the obviously derivative character of parts of this book. My area of expertise is Scripture, especially the Hebrew Scriptures. I am not an expert in the areas of sociology, economics, or theology. And so I have turned to authorities in these other areas to help me with both social analysis and theological reflection. I happily and gratefully acknowledge my dependence upon such authorities as Robert Bellah, John Coleman, Brian Hehir, Charles Curran, Joe Holland, Peter Henriot, and many others. However, I believe that the final synthesis and conclusions of this book are uniquely my own and I take full responsibility for them. Throughout I have intended to use my sources prudently and intelligently.

In writing this book I have become very aware of the complexity of all the issues involved, both the socioeconomic and political issues as well as the theological issues. The temptation has been to give up the project because of this complexity. Moreover, the rapid changes in Eastern Europe and the growing tensions in the Near East that have arisen after the first draft of this book was finished have tempted me to give up. I have continued in the hope that the book might provoke discussion on what I see as a very important topic and help others to focus more clearly on the issues involved. I make no claim to having all the answers, if any. What I have attempted to do is to paint a broad picture that will make people aware of the basic global and national issues that must be considered in looking at the mission of the Church in the United States. Other people might paint different pictures but the basic elements in the picture would remain the same. Hopefully, the book will encourage those more competent than I to further the discussion of this topic.

PART 1

THE CONTEXT

1

SOCIAL ANALYSIS: A TOOL FOR CHURCH PLANNING

Before looking specifically at the global and national context of the Church in the United States, a few words on method are in order. In this chapter I present an overview of the method to be used and address the task of social analysis in particular. In a later chapter I will deal more specifically with the task of theological reflection.

The method underlying this book is an inductive process that begins with experience — lived reality — rather than with theological norms and principles. It is a process that is intended to lead toward pastoral planning, which in turn gives rise to more experience and further reflection. The process is best represented by the pastoral circle:[1]

DIAGRAM I
THE PASTORAL CIRCLE

Social Analysis

Theological
Reflection

EXPERIENCE

Insertion

Pastoral
Planning

At the center of the circle is "experience." Experience is what roots and grounds one in the process.

The first moment in the pastoral circle is "insertion," that is, insertion into the experience — the lived reality — of individuals and communities that are being studied. Primary data involves what people are feeling and thinking, what they are undergoing, how they are responding. It is important that pastoral responses are always rooted in the lived experiences of individuals and communities. In this book I will begin with the global, national, and ecclesial realities in which we live.

The task of "social analysis" is to understand experiences in all their richness and with all their interrelationships. Social analysis examines causes, probes consequences, delineates linkages, and identifies actors. It helps make sense of experiences by putting them into a broader picture and drawing connections between them. In this book I attempt to uncover, through analysis, the core issues that underlie the global, national, and ecclesial realities that we live in and that we need to deal with.

The third moment in the process is "theological reflection." Theological reflection is an effort to understand better the analyzed experience in the light of living faith, Scripture, Church teaching, and the resources of tradition. As the Word of God is brought to bear upon the situation, it raises new questions, suggests new insights, and opens new responses. What gives direction to this reflection are the core issues uncovered in the process of social analysis.

Since the purpose of the pastoral circle is decision and action, the fourth moment in the circle is crucial, namely, "pastoral planning." This step involves drawing out the responses called for by individuals and communities considering the experiences that have been analyzed and reflected upon. This step also involves designing the response in such a way that it can be most effective, not only in the short term but also in the long term. In this step of the process I will attempt to draw out the mission of the Church in the United States and suggest some strategies for achieving this mission.

Because this process is a circle, it is clear that this is a continuing process that must be gone through again and again. Every time a pastoral plan is developed and implemented it gives rise to another set of experiences which once again must be analyzed and reflected on in order to do further pastoral planning. Since experience is so complex one will continuously uncover more and more in it. Hence, each time the circle is traveled a clearer understanding of the root issues is achieved. This is also true regarding the mission of the Church in the United States. There will never be one clearly defined mission for the Church in the United States that will be valid for all ages.

In terms of the pastoral circle, this first part of the book involves "insertion" and "social analysis." Here insertion will be a process of describing the present situation in which we are living globally, nationally, and ecclesially. Each of these descriptions will be followed by a social analysis. What is involved in this analysis?

Social analysis is a tool one uses to get below the surface issues to the underlying causes of situations—why things are the way they are. Unless the underlying causes of situations are dealt with, any pastoral plan will be only the application of a bandage rather than a real solution. Underlying social analysis is the presumption that social problems and issues are linked together in a larger system and are parts of a whole. Social analysis is an attempt to go beyond the anecdote, the individual event, and respond to that larger picture in a more systematic way.

Social analysis can focus on reality from a variety of perspectives. It can focus on an isolated issue, such as unemployment, or the policies that address an issue, such as job training, or on the broad structures of the economic, political, social, and cultural institutions that have given rise to specific issues and policies. Where one starts depends upon one's purposes in using the process. Ultimately, social analysis attempts to go beyond the issues, policies, and structures to focus on systems. Again, these systems have many dimensions. We can speak of a social system's economic design, of its political order, and its cultural foundation. Social systems can also be viewed from the perspective of different levels such as primary groups, local communities, nations, and even the world's system.

The social system must be analyzed both in terms of time (historical analysis) and space (structural analysis). Historical analysis studies the changes in a system over a period of time. Structural analysis provides a cross section of a system in all its complexity at a particular moment in history. Both dimensions of analysis are necessary for a complete picture.

It is also important to distinguish between the objective and subjective dimensions of reality. The objective dimension includes all the organizations, behavior patterns, and institutions that make up a social system. The subjective dimension includes the values and ideologies that provide the assumptions operative in a system.

There are limits to social analysis as a pastoral tool. First, social analysis is not designed to produce immediate action plans. Social analysis is a way to diagnose a problem by unfolding the context within which a pastoral plan will have to be designed. Second, social analysis is not an esoteric activity intended only for the use of experts. It is a tool that everyone can and does use every day whenever they decide to do one thing rather than another. The process being explained here is intended simply to make more explicit and detailed the kind of analysis that goes on implicitly. Third, social analysis is not value-free. As will be seen, an individual's biases and values come into play at all stages in the process.

Social analysis is difficult for various reasons. The social system today is very complex and rapidly becoming more so as all the nations on the globe become more interrelated. The very fact of rapid change in society in every area — economic, political, social, and cultural — makes it difficult to do valid analysis. Finally, to do analysis is to enter the realm of the controversial. This is because no social analysis is value-free and so any analysis is implicitly linked to some ideological tradition. Identifying oneself with one particular vision of society is bound to bring one into conflict with those who hold very different visions of society.

The first step in the process of doing social analysis is what Joe Holland and Peter Henriot call "conversion." In this step one attempts to make explicit the values that one brings to the task. In other words, one attempts to get in touch with the perspectives, biases, and stances which influence the way one looks at life. In social analysis one does not come to a purely "objective" view of reality. Certainly one should try to be clear, precise, reasoned, and logical. However, a person needs to realize that their choice of topics, their manner of approach to an issue, their degree of openness to the results of analysis are all deeply affected by values and biases. Hence, a person needs to be aware of what their values, biases, and stances are so as to accept them or challenge them. I have attempted to spell out for the reader my basic presuppositions in the introduction.

This step is especially important if one is doing social analysis in a group. In this context the participants need to share with one another where they are coming from so that the group can clarify the commonalities and the differences that will influence its later decisions. If this is not done the process will "crash" at some point because there will be differences of opinions on issues in the group, and these differences will be rooted in the different values and biases of the members. Unless a group is aware of where it agrees and where it does not agree on values and biases, it will have no way of dealing with these differences.

The second step in the process of social analysis is to make a general description of the situation being studied. In this step it is important to remember that one is only describing a situation. One is not yet attempting to understand all the interrelationships of the situation nor is one making any evaluation or reaching any conclusions at this time. The point of the description is to help one get into the picture, to get in touch with the experience of the situation.

In doing a description one can take an impressionistic approach to the task or a more systematic approach or a combination of the two. In the impressionistic approach one gathers facts through brainstorming, telling stories, listening to the stories of others, and getting in touch with the experiences of others. Photographs, recordings, art, music can all play a role here. In a systematic approach one gathers all the pertinent information in a very orderly fashion. A person can go to almanacs and scientific studies for information about such things as population growth, per capita income, ethnic composition, and so forth. In other words, one gathers together all that will be helpful in describing a situation, given the resources and the time available.

The next step is the analysis itself. The analysis is "the effort to obtain a more complete picture of a social situation by exploring its historical and structural relationships."[2] One accomplishes this by working through a series of questions.

1. What is the main line of history of this situation? Some questions to ask here are the following: What have been the major stages through which

the situation has moved? What have been the patterns of development? What have been the key turning points in the development of the situation? What have been the major events that have influenced the course of history of this situation? This study of the history of a situation is an attempt to see where we are coming from. It places current events and challenges into a perspective. A historical consciousness helps people to see that present situations are the result of specific historical events and not of some invisible forces. Hence, through other events people can become agents of change in the world.

2. What are the major structures that have influenced this situation? There are many ways in which society is organized, and very often several structures will have an impact upon a particular situation. The goal here is to find out which structures have been operative in this situation. Some of the main structures that one will want to look at are economic structures, political structures, social structures such as family, neighborhood, education; and cultural structures such as religion, myths, art, lifestyle. One must also examine institutional alliances between various structures. For instance, what is the relationship between the economic power of the transnational corporations and the dominant political power in some developing countries, for example, military dictatorships?

3. What are the key values operative in this structure? By values here are meant the goals that motivate people; the ideologies and moral norms that guide; the aspirations and expectations that people have; the social emphases that are acceptable and accepted.

4. What is the future direction of this situation? The futuristic exercise of imagining "scenarios" is very important and can provide some important insights into the dynamics of what is occurring now. Here one would ask: What will the situation be in five years or ten years if things continue to go as they are now; what are the most important trends that can be seen now; and what are the sources of creativity and hope for the future in the present situation?

It is important not to look at a local situation in isolation; rather, it should be analyzed against the background of the larger regional, national, and global context, since in the world today almost everything is interconnected, even on a global level. One cannot study a particular situation divorced from larger regional, national, and global realities. It is for this reason that I will begin this analysis with a look at the global situation.

The final step is to pull all of this material together and to isolate the "root" elements in a situation. "Root" elements are the basic causes, the answers that finally turn up when one continually asks the question, "Why?" The completed analysis will have opened up a variety of factors. The purpose now is to discern the most important elements in the situation, the "root" elements. To get to these "root" elements one ranks within each analytical category (history, structures, values, direction) the most significant factors influencing the situation. Then one takes a further look at these ranked factors and asks: 1) What are the two or three root elements most responsible for the current situation? and 2) In whose interests do these root elements operate?

The conclusions drawn from a social analysis depend on a variety of factors, including the relative complexity of the situation being studied, the accuracy and adequacy of the data available, the rigor of the questioning, the criteria that influenced judgments, and so forth. Even if an individual or a group does not have all the possible data, or overlooks a significant fact, this process will still be valuable because it begins to open an issue and to reveal causes, consequences, linkages, and trends. We must first uncover the "root" elements since they will provide the focus for theological reflection.

2

THE GLOBAL CONTEXT

We live today as part of a global community in which each nation is related to all the others through complex sets of relationships. Nothing that any one nation does or does not do can be viewed only in terms of the effects of that action or nonaction on the individual nation. Rather, the actions of each nation affect in some way all the nations on the globe. This is as true for the United States as for other nations and even more so in most cases. When we look at the United States, we must see it as part of this global community.

Since World War II the United States has been a dominant power on the world scene and interrelated to other nations primarily in the three areas of foreign policy, economics, and communication/culture. While these three areas can be spoken of separately, they are in many ways interrelated with one another.

FOREIGN POLICY

United States foreign policy has gone through a series of changes since World War II.[1] During the twenty-five years after World War II this foreign policy was a policy of containment, the containment of Soviet power. It was this policy that led to both the Korean and the Vietnam wars. In turn the prolonged agitation around the Vietnam War led to a thorough questioning of the international role of the United States and gave birth to new models of American foreign policy.

Under Richard Nixon and Henry Kissinger this policy became one of détente. Whereas the United States had hoped for some kind of decisive victory over Russia, now it would attempt simply to maintain a balance of power. Whereas the United States had been ideological in its foreign policy, now it would accept that it was Soviet power that threatened the United States and not communist ideology per se. In the past the United States had reacted indiscriminately to challenges. Now the United States would distinguish between the essential interests it had in the security of Europe,

15

Japan, and the Persian Gulf, and the peripheral interests that could be left to others to deal with. It was also recognized that the United States could not rely solely on power in dealing with the Soviets but must combine power with diplomacy. Finally, the linkage between issues was accepted and it was recognized that everything might affect everything else. Nothing could be compartmentalized. In this context a premium was put on secrecy, on freedom from congressional restraints, and on circumvention when necessary. The quest for stability was seen as having a moral precedence over ideological claims of individual rights and national self-determination.

The Carter model of foreign relations developed in response to the Kissinger/Nixon model and differed from it in several ways. First, United States and Soviet relations would not occupy such a dominant place in foreign policy; rather, North-South questions—the relationship of the United States to the developing countries—would take on a real importance. Linkage was not a dominant concept and regional conflicts would be approached in their own terms. In other words, regional conflicts would not be viewed primarily in terms of the rivalry with the Eastern bloc. American foreign policy would be guided by a commitment to human rights. Finally, there would be a sustained effort to reduce the growth of armaments.

The foreign policy of the Reagan administration was a return to the policy of containment. For the Reagan administration the contest with the Soviet Union and its totalitarianism overshadowed all other issues. A return to military might and a manifest willingness to use it became axiomatic and the first priority was to build up American military strength. The Reagan policy was ideological as well as bipolar, that is, the conflict with the Soviets was presented as an ideological conflict. While the issue of linkage was not applied consistently, it was applied in a virtually unqualified way to the revolutionary turbulence in Central America. The administration did not believe that successful left-wing revolutions anywhere could be isolated from the basic East-West struggle. Not even the remnants of Carter's human-rights policy were allowed to interfere with military assistance to right-wing allies in Central America. In his latter years, the ideological tone of Reagan's foreign policy softened, together with the overriding emphasis on the buildup of military strength. However, the bipolar and linkage aspects of the policy did not change.

In view of "perestroika," the receding threat of communism, and the birth of new democracies in Eastern Europe that took place in 1989 and 1990, the foreign policy of the Bush administration has moved away from the shrill anti-communism of the Reagan administration. The policy for dealing with a new post–Cold War world is one of "idealism plus realism" rather than "idealism versus realism."[2] The intention of the Bush administration is to remain involved overseas and not retreat into isolationism as the threat of communism recedes and new democracies begin to emerge. The Bush administration sees its role as that of providing leadership in building up the new democracies. The Bush administration is also distancing itself from the Reagan administration's sustained United States military and political support for guerrilla movements battling communist regimes. Instead, the Bush administration is seeking to support democracy, in the form of elections, as a primary tool for resolving conflicts around the world. It is also clear, especially from the recent Gulf war with Iraq, that the Bush administration is not afraid to use the big stick to achieve its priorities and to establish what is being called a "new world order."

Behind these changes in United States foreign policy since World War II has been the uneasy relationship in the Northern hemisphere between the two blocs of the East and the West. This relationship to a great extent has been marked by continuing tension. The Eastern bloc has been dominated by Soviet Russia while the Western bloc has been dominated by the United States. In origin the opposition between the two blocs is ideological. In the West a system exists that is inspired by the principles of liberal capitalism while in the East there is a system inspired by Marxist collectivism. Each of the ideologies proposes, on the economic level, antithetical forms for the organization of labor and the structures of ownership, especially concerning the means of production. Behind each of the ideologies are two very different visions of the human being and the freedom and social role of that person. This ideological opposition has developed into an opposition that is political, economic, and military in nature.

This opposition is first of all political in that each bloc identifies itself with a system of organizing society and exercising power that presents itself as an alternative to the other. Today this opposition between the two blocs is more and more economic in nature as they compete for economic dominance and control. Both sides need to protect their economic interests that include, above all, access for themselves and their allies to needed resources, primarily oil and other raw materials, and to manufactured goods. These interests also demand access to the trade routes necessary for shipping these materials.

It was inevitable that these ideological, political, and economic tensions would bring about a growing military opposition between the East and the West. This military opposition has given rise to two blocs of armed forces that have been suspicious and fearful of one another. Tension between these two blocs has dominated international relations since the end of the Second World War. Sometimes this tension has taken the form of "cold war," at other times of "wars by proxy," through the manipulation of local conflicts. Throughout all these years there has been, in greater or lesser degrees, the threat of open and total war between the two blocs. While such a threat has lessened recently, the suspicion of the other side's motives continues to affect relations between the two blocs.

Growing out of this tension between the two blocs has been an exaggerated importance placed on national security. In the United States this concentration on national security has come to have a significant impact on the way the United States as a country has come to look at morality and the use of force. The need to defend national security gave birth to a vast new apparatus of power that radically transformed the United States government, giving rise to what Bill Moyers has called "the Secret Government."[3]

The foundation of this secret government was the National Security Act of 1947. That act established the National Security Council and the Central Intelligence Agency that have become the major actors in this secret government. The struggle for national security has required a mentality of permanent war, a perpetual state of emergency. In this context people are always looking for threats to security and for ways of orchestrating society in order to oppose those threats. The result has been that national security has become the primary motivator of U.S. activity on the international level.[4]

A morality has also developed from this mentality among many in defense and intelligence agencies, namely, that anything goes. It is a morality of the end justifying the means no matter how immoral or illegal the means may be. This morality has manifested itself especially in the police actions of the United States in Korea and Vietnam and it is also seen in the various covert operations of the United States in Central America and in other conflicts going on in many parts of the world. As Moyers points out, "We're never really sure who is exercising the war powers of the United States, and what they're doing, what it costs, or who is paying for it. The one thing we are sure of is that this largely secret global war, carried on with less and less accountability to democratic institutions, has become a way of life."[5] All the above came very much to the forefront in the Iran-Contra hearings with their stories of deceit, lying, misleading Congress and ignoring the Constitution by the highest leadership in the executive branch of government.

This tension between the East and the West in the Northern hemisphere has also governed the relations of the North with the countries of the Southern hemisphere, the developing countries. In many ways these developing countries have been used by the Northern powers to further and defend their own interests. In the process the developing countries have often become nothing more than cogs in a wheel caught up in the tension and competition between the developed countries of the East and West in the Northern hemisphere. In fact this conflict in the North between the East and the West has been an important cause of the stagnation and retardation in overcoming the conditions of underdevelopment in the Southern hemisphere.

This conflict and tension with the East has led the United States to enter ever more deeply into the life of the developing countries of the South so that it can defend its own interests. These interests arise from economic considerations and the need to preserve a balance of power with the East. This involvement has taken various forms, including the support of repressive dictatorships, as in South Korea, Argentina, South Africa, El Salvador, Guatemala, and the Philippines. The United States has not hesitated to use its power, either military or economic and sometimes both, to force those dependent upon it to do its will, as in Nicaragua, for example. The United States has also been blatantly involved in the internal life of other countries. This involvement was instituted to effect changes in these governments that would be more to its liking, as in Iran, Chile, Vietnam, Guatemala, Grenada, and Panama, to name but a few. In all these activities, out of an excessive concern for security and stability, there has been a growing premium put on secrecy, freedom from congressional restraints, and circumvention of law and even the Constitution. As Peter Steinfels observed, "The quest for stability had to be seen as having moral precedence over various ideological claims, whether those of anti-Communism or the liberal principles of individual rights and national self-determination."[6]

In all of these actions the United States has been involved in and at least partly responsible for the taking of thousands of innocent lives and the continuing oppression of millions of poor people. At the same time it has been involved in breaking the laws of other countries. We have also witnessed, on the part of some individuals, a blatant disregard of the laws and Constitution of the United States itself. These individuals have even been celebrated as heroes for their actions. Finally, this "imperial overreach" on the part of the United States is contributing to its own economic decline as it continues to maintain too great a global military role in the face of ebbing resources.[7] All this has been approved or rationalized on the basis of national security.

This involvement of the United States in the affairs of other countries, especially those in the Western hemisphere, is not a recent phenomenon. Such interventions have been going on for a long time, going back at least to the Monroe Doctrine of 1823. From the earliest days the United States has had definite imperialist and expansionist tendencies. These tendencies surfaced in the Indian wars, the forcible annexation of territory, and interventions in the Caribbean and Central America. They can be traced back to an early sense of the United States being exceptional and better than other countries because it was a nation chosen by God.[8] From its beginnings, the United States has seen itself as an exemplar for others and a bringer of order in the world.[9]

What is hard to understand is why the United States, which itself was born in revolution—a revolution seeking freedom and the right of self-determination—has become such a staunch opponent of revolution in other parts of the world. Certainly part of the reason is that often these revolutions are seen as posing a threat to the self-interests of the United States. Part of the reason is also connected with the tendency in U.S. foreign policy to deduce intentions from organization. In other words, the United States assumes that it knows how a country will act once it knows how the government of the other nation is put together. The most obvious example of this tendency has been the U.S. long-standing misunderstanding of international communism. From the beginnings of the Cold War the United States has taken the view that adherence to the principles of Marxism-Leninism marks a government as internally repressive and a threat to established international order, even a puppet of Moscow. There has never been very good evidence to support such assumptions,[10] yet these assumptions have come into play concerning almost any revolution that the United States sees as Marxist.

The continuing tension between the East and the West has also been responsible for a terrible arms race between the superpowers.[11] The 1980s witnessed a significant acceleration of the arms race in terms of both nuclear and conventional weapons. The justification for this arms race was defense of national security through deterrence, not just through a balance of power but even a superiority of power. The arms race has contributed to a rapidly mounting national debt and a cutback in social programs that serve the poor, as well as assistance to developing nations. Most people in the United States, though at times manifesting uneasiness over the arms race and its consequences, have generally supported a strong military defense as a means of preserving their present way of life. The end of the 1980s witnessed a pulling back from the ever mounting arms race and a willingness, on the part of the superpowers, to reduce both their conventional and nuclear arms. Hopefully, these cutbacks will continue and grow in scope. Another critical issue, however, is how the superpowers will use the funds gained from these cutbacks, the so-called "peace dividend."

Finally, these same forces of national security, together with a desire for profit by many people, have involved the United States in the international arms trade. Often this trade is to support nations friendly to the United States. At times this trade is for the purpose of bringing other nations under the arm of the United States. In other circumstances this trade is used as part of an overall strategy in the tension with the Eastern bloc. Too often these arms are sold to developing countries that use capital lent by the developed countries to purchase the arms. These monies could well be used to better the lot of the people of these countries rather than for the purchase of arms. As Pope John Paul II has pointed out: "We are ... confronted with a strange phenomenon: while economic aid and development plans meet with the obstacle of insuperable ideological barriers, and with tariff and trade barriers, arms of whatever origin circulate with almost total freedom all over the world" (SRS 24).

I would hope that the world is now on a path toward achieving real peace. Further developments toward real international peace will depend upon several factors: a growth in trust that is translated into greater cooperation between the East and West; a significant cutback in arms, especially nuclear arms; a genuine concern for the Southern hemisphere for its own sake by both the United States and the Soviet Union; and a respect for the autonomy and right to self-determination of all nations.

ECONOMICS

Underlying Reality

From an economic perspective the major reality today is the growing disparity between the North and the South, the developed and the developing nations. The hopes for the economic development of the South that flourished in the 1960s and into the 1970s have not been realized. Rather, the gap between the North and the South has been widening as the pace of development in the South has lagged significantly behind development in the North. Differences in culture and value systems have contributed to a widening of the gap between the North and the South that is not only reflected by economic indicators but can also be seen in such factors as illiteracy, the inability to share in building one's own nation, and various forms of exploitation, oppression, and discrimination. At times even nations are deprived of sovereignty over their own economic and development policies because of the dictates of the Northern powers.

As a result, the developing countries find themselves being forced more and more into a relationship of dependency upon the industrialized nations. It is the developed countries that set (1) the prices at which developing countries must sell their commodity exports and purchase their food and manufactured imports; (2) the rates of interest they must pay and the terms they must meet to borrow money; (3) the standards of economic behavior of foreign investors; (4) the amounts and conditions of external aid, and so forth. Moreover, the developing countries find their own traditional cultures under attack from the aggressive cultural penetration of Northern advertising and media programming. At best they find themselves treated like junior partners.

In considering the economic relationship of the United States to the developing countries, it is important to remember an underlying reality: the prevailing world system, economic, political and social, is rooted in and has its origins in the colonial domination, from the sixteenth century on, of Latin America, Africa, and Asia by the Western European world. In fact, the original accumulation of wealth in Europe that came from the economic rape of the colonies allowed the Industrial Revolution to take place. Their raw materials and natural resources were literally stolen by the colonizers. Today, on the stock market in New York, stocks and bonds from all over the world are bought and sold on an international scale. The capital involved in these transactions was first amassed in Western Europe and England and later it passed to the United States and Russia. As Enrique Dussel says, "that money is stained by the blood of Indians and wrapped in the hides of blacks and Asians."[12]

This is the original sin of the present world order. All who have inherited this wealth, and what it can effect, share in some way in this original sin. As a result those who have inherited this wealth have a responsibility to correct the injustices and inequities within the world created by the original rape of the colonies. This responsibility today falls in a special way upon the United States, since it has inherited so much of this wealth. The United States shares responsibility for the continuing oppression of the former colonies through its foreign policy and the actions of its transnational corporations and banks.

For example, by the mid-1960s there was a monopolization of Latin American economies by U.S. corporations to the extent that the Latin American countries had become economic vassals of the United States. This monopolization took place at the same time that Latin America was witnessing the rise of dictatorships, U.S. counterinsurgency training for Latin American military, and an increase in loans for arms purchases. The military dictatorships were justified as a means to protect "national security" and "profit and stability" in the global war between communism and the West. All who questioned the repression that took place were accused of being communists and violently put down.

Global Poverty

The gap between the North and the South and the need for action on the international level to correct the inequities that exist come home very strongly when we consider the critical problem of world poverty today. It is projected that the world's present population will double before 2020, with 90 percent of this increase taking place in Africa, Asia, and Latin America. However, even today it is estimated that nearly one out of every four people on this globe (mostly in the Southern hemisphere) lives in subhuman conditions of hunger, sickness, illiteracy, inadequate shelter, and unsafe drinking water.

> Half the world's people, nearly two and a half billion, live in countries where the annual per capita income is $400 or less. At least 800 million people in those countries live in absolute poverty, "beneath any rational definition of human decency." Nearly half a billion are chronically hungry, despite abundant harvests worldwide. Fifteen out of every 100 children born in those countries die before the age of five, and millions of the survivors are physically or mentally stunted. (EJ 254)

What makes this situation even worse is the high level of unemployment and underemployment in the Third World. It is estimated that in 1975, 35 percent of the labor force in the Third World was underemployed. Thirty-six million new jobs a year are needed between now and the year 2000.

Some would suggest that because of the rapidly growing populations and deepening poverty in the Third World some sort of population control is needed because the world will soon not have sufficient resources to support itself. However, with regard to basic food supplies, there is no real shortage of food in the world; the issue is that of proper distribution of the food supplies that do exist. Moreover, birth rates are not efficiently reduced through forms of birth control but through improving the living standards of people. As living standards rise, populations stabilize. The only way to deal with the stresses on global food supplies, resources, and the environment is through the economic development of the Third World in which ecologically sound technologies of production are used.[13]

U. S. Aid

Today the United States, through trade, investments, aid, and monetary arrangements, is involved in the life of all but a few nations of the world. While it can no longer be said that "when the United States sneezes, the rest of the world catches pneumonia,"[14] it can be said that when the United States sneezes, the rest of the world catches a cold. It is also important to remember that today when the rest of the world sneezes, the United States is likely to catch a cold.

This heavy involvement with the rest of the world on an economic level is the result of several factors. The significant contribution of the United States to the rebuilding of Europe and Japan after the Second World War was vital. There have also been its considerable relief and development aid to the developing countries since the 1950s. The United States has also been generous in its assistance to other nations in times of crises such as droughts and famines.

While the United States can be proud of much of what it has done through its economic assistance programs, the programs have also had their negative side. Significant in this regard is the way in which development monies have at times been turned more to the interests of U.S. corporations than to significant development of the developing countries. For example, the Agency of International Development (AID) was converted into a money tree for U.S. corporations in the 1960s. By the end of that so-called "decade of development" some $2 billion per year in U.S. exports were being financed by the foreign aid program. An incredible 99 percent of the loans made by AID to the Latin American countries was spent in the United States for products costing 30 to 40 percent more than the going world price.[15]

The United States today remains an important donor country to the Third World, though no longer the largest donor country. The Japanese have outstripped us even in this regard. However, the annual share of the U.S. gross national product (GNP) devoted to foreign aid is now less than one-tenth of that of the Marshall Plan which helped rebuild Europe after

World War II. Moreover, the United States is almost last among the seventeen industrialized nations in the Organization for Economic Cooperation and Development in its percentage of GNP devoted to aid (see EJ 266). Where does the money go that once went to aid? It goes into arms production. For example, in 1985 the United States budgeted more than twenty times as much for defense as for foreign assistance. Nearly two-thirds of that assistance took the form of military assistance (including subsidized arms sales) or went to countries because of their perceived strategic value to the United States (see EJ 289).

Moreover, as the U.S. Bishops point out in their letter *Economic Justice for All*: "In recent years U.S. policy toward development in the Third World has become increasingly one of selective assistance based on an East-West assessment of North-South problems, at the expense of basic human needs and economic development. Such a view makes national security the central policy principle" (EJ 262). In view of the recent significant lessening of tensions between the East and the West, there is now the real possibility that the industrialized nations of the North will have little interest in the Third World. Given that the nations of the Third World are no longer needed as pawns in the East-West struggle, plus the overwhelming social and economic problems of these countries, the North may simply be indifferent to them. Such a response, however, would neither be humane nor sensible. Eventually, the deprivation and suffering of these countries will, in one way or another, come back to haunt the North.

U.S. Dependence

An important reality today is the growing dependence of the United States on other economies of the world not only for resources and markets, but even for technology and capital and goods. The United States depends upon other countries for many of its goods because the United States is no longer the industrial power it once was. What brought this dependence home to most people in the United States for the first time was the rise of OPEC and the oil crisis in the early 1970s.

At the same time as the United States has become more dependent on others, many of the developing countries, encouraged by the initial successes of OPEC, have developed a sense of power over their resources and have attempted to protect themselves. While initial moves in this direction have not all been successful, it should not be presumed that the developing countries have given up in this regard. The growing push for changes in trade policies by the developing countries is related to this issue.

The level of U.S. interdependence with other nations becomes clear when one looks at a few facts. Today well over 25 percent of the GNP of the United States is accounted for by exports and imports. It is estimated that one of every six jobs in the manufacturing sector is due to export-related work and that one-third of the farm acreage in the United States is involved in the production of export-related materials. In fact the United States is the major supplier of food to the hungry nations of the world. If it were not for the ability of the United States to sell agricultural products overseas, its balance of trade deficit would be even worse than it is now. At the same time, in 1985, the United States had to import 25 percent of its machinery. Hence, the U.S. economy is increasingly vulnerable to international competition.

Over the past decade the United States has moved from being the world's largest creditor nation to being the world's largest debtor nation. While in 1980 the United States had a trade account surplus of $166 billion, in August 1987, the United States was in debt to foreign countries by $340 billion. Moreover, U.S. indebtedness is projected to exceed a trillion dollars by 1992.[16] Such a transformation has been due to the need of the federal government to borrow huge sums of money at high interest rates to fund tax cuts, the defense buildup, and 1981–82 recession spending. The slide into debtor status was intensified by the devaluation of the United States dollar from 1985 to 1987.[17] This debtor status has made the United States even more dependent upon other nations.

The consequence of this interdependence for Americans is a growing sense of vulnerability and apprehension regarding the rest of the world. The instinctive response has been to develop forceful military-political ties, relying on strategic alliances for controlling resources and markets. This trend is partly responsible for many U.S. actions in Central and Latin America as well as the Near East.

Transnational Corporations

This economic interdependence with other nations is taking place today on a global level. Every nation is becoming more and more integrated into a world economy that is under the control of neither governments nor international authorities. The major actor in the process of global economic integration is the transnational corporation.

Transnational corporations are conglomerates that have holdings in many countries, are highly diversified, and operate from a global perspective. They are firms that plan and produce with an international horizon, allocating production and sales in a way that takes advantage of the lowest costs and the best markets. To maximize global profit, the transnational breaks the production process into its components and then locates each part of the process where it can be done most cheaply. The sale of such goods is then focused on the countries that represent the richest markets. So, for example, there is a transistor radio whose parts are made in Hong Kong, South Korea, or Singapore, assembled in Mexico, and sold in the United States—by a Japanese manufacturer. The transnational corporations are the first human institution with the vision, technology, and experience to plan on a global scale. What has made them possible has been the growth of modern rapid transportation, instant global data retrieval, and highly organized systems of production and distribution.

At least two-thirds of the top 100 U.S. corporations are transnational corporations. Though the movement toward internationalization of production is not just a U.S. phenomenon, American transnationals account for 300 of the world's 500 largest corporations.

The spectacular rise of the transnationals is seen in the fact that in 1950 the value of United States foreign direct investment (U.S.-owned plants and equipment) came to $11 billion. In 1985 that total was over $210 billion. This latter sum reflects only the value of the American dollars invested abroad and does not include the value of foreign capital that is controlled by these dollars. If the value of this foreign capital is included, then the value of American overseas productive assets may be as large as $300 billion. Something between a quarter and a half of the real assets of the largest U.S. corporations are abroad.

The value of the output that is produced overseas by the largest U.S. corporations far exceeds the value of the goods they still export overseas from the United States. In 1985, the sales from the foreign branches of the 150 largest multinationals amounted to over $415 billion. In the same year, the total exports of merchandise from all U.S. firms came to only $207 billion.

The transnationals are changing the face of international economic relationships. Significant in this regard has been the shift away from exports to international production. This shift has introduced two important changes into the international economic scene. First, there has been the movement of foreign investment away from its original concentration in underdeveloped areas of the world toward the richer markets of the developed areas. Up to fifty years ago most of the capital leaving one country for another flowed from the rich countries to the poor ones. This foreign investment was largely associated with the creation of vast plantations, the building of railroads through jungles, and the development of mineral resources. There has been a significant shift away from investment in the underdeveloped world to investment in the industrial world. Almost three-fourths of the huge rise in direct investment during the 1960s and 1970s was in the developed world and the vast bulk of it was in manufacturing rather than in plantations, railroads, or minerals. This shift becomes clear when we see that in 1929 47 percent of U.S. foreign direct investment was in Latin America. In 1982 this figure was down to 14 percent. In the same period of time investment in Europe went from 18 percent to 45 percent. In Asia, Africa, and the Near East, U.S. investment went from 8 percent in 1929 to 17 percent in 1982. In recent years there has been a highly visible thrust of transnational corporations in manufacturing facilities into a few poorer nations, such as Mexico, Hong Kong, Taiwan, Singapore, and South Korea. However, these investments are much smaller than the investments in developed countries.

The second change has been a shift away from heavy technology to high technology industries. In other words, there has been a shift away from enterprises in which vast sums of capital were associated with large, unskilled labor forces, as in the building of railroads. Rather, the emphasis has been on industries that concentrate on research and development by a skilled technical work force with sophisticated management techniques.

There is no question that transnational corporations have made positive contributions to many of the third-world countries. These contributions have involved transferring technology to the Third World and training at least some of the native population in needed technologies and skills. Moreover, the transnational corporations are a major source of order in the world today. For all their progress the transnationals have also caused many problems.

The transnationals have added considerably to the problem of controlling domestic economies through the international movement of capital. Decisions made by government planners and authorities can be thwarted because of the actions of transnationals who operate on a much larger scale.

Serious international tensions between nations can also arise because of the actions of the transnationals. These tensions result from the conflict between the desire of nation-states to retain national control over productive activity within their borders and the desire by the transnationals for new markets. Most of these tensions are the results of resentments and different cultural values between the nation-states and the transnationals. For example, the transnationals can often win hard bargains from host countries because of their new technologies and management techniques and because of the contribution that they can make to the local economy. If a country refuses to give in to the demands of the transnational, it will simply move elsewhere and leave the country the loser. However, the transnational can also become a hostage of the host country once it has settled in. A good example of this is the transnational having to do things that are foreign to it because of the culture or accepted practices of the host country. For instance, in Japan it is an unwritten law that workers for giant corporations are never fired. This practice can be difficult for foreign companies to accept. Another possibility is that because of a fall in demand, a transnational must cut back on the volume of its output. This may well demand the closing of a plant. However, closing the plant for economic reasons may bring very serious economic repercussions on the host nation. The host nation may threaten political action to stop such a closing.

All the above issues become even more significant when one looks at the impact of the transnationals on the underdeveloped or developing countries. Because of the move of the transnationals to developed countries, a smaller percentage of foreign investment dollars is available for the developing countries, especially for urgent internal needs such as health care, sanitation, water, literacy programs and schooling, food production for local consumption, and roads. With the move to high-tech production, fewer jobs are made available. It is also difficult for the local country to do serious economic planning for development since its plan can be spoiled by a board of directors in the First World that decides to cut back on production or even to close plants for reasons that have nothing to do with the host country. The developing countries are then in a weak bargaining position because of their need for the technology, expertise, and economic contributions that the transnational can provide, and they can easily be taken advantage of regarding wage scales, working conditions, prices for their raw materials, and so forth. Too often they are also made the dumping ground for goods that are of such low quality or are so dangerous and toxic that their sale is not permitted in the developed countries. A good example of this last point is the marketing in developing countries of dangerous pesticides that have been banned in the industrialized nations. Moreover, because it has become more difficult to find places in the United States to dispose of trash and toxic ash from trash-burning incinerators (because of environmental issues), attempts have been made to dump them in the developing countries.

Even more significant for underdeveloped and developing countries, however, is that the process of industrialization has disrupted traditional lifestyles and cultures of peoples and has forced foreign cultures, customs, and languages upon them. As the wave of industrialization moves across parts of the Third World, people have been forced off their land. They cannot afford to stay because alternate uses of the land such as industrialization or mechanized agriculture for export are more profitable. Also, too often the profits from the new economic enterprises are not shared equitably with the people of the host countries. Rather, a large amount of the profits generated is removed from the country by the transnationals. At times repressive local governments are also supported through the combined efforts of the transnationals, the banks, and first-world governments in order to maintain stability for the sake of investors. Thus, the needs of the host countries and the human development of its peoples often take a back seat to the needs of the corporations implanted there. As a result the people are too often repressed and denied basic human rights; they become poorer and end up in a worse condition than prior to industrialization.

Associated with the move of the transnationals into the developing countries has been the stress put on exports as the means toward internal development in the developing countries. In other words, the developing countries are encouraged to generate the capital that they need for a suitable infrastructure of schools, roads, health care, and so forth, through developing their exports. The increasingly heavy reliance on exports is a striking characteristic of the development model now found in many places. Hence, between 1973 and 1980 the value of world industrial production increased two and a half times. World trade increased four and a half times in the same period.

This export model poses various difficulties for the developing countries.

The brightest and most energetic workers are put to work making goods for export rather than developing a domestic market. Scarce resources such as electric power are diverted from rural development to subsidize the manufacturing of export goods, and people are put to work for less than subsistence wages to create goods for the consumer society in developed countries at an affordable price. As a result, local governments usually have to subsidize many of their exports, thus contributing to their foreign debt position. Finally, pressure to export leads to quotas, protectionism, and outright rejection of proposals to open the markets of the developed countries to many of the developing nations. Meanwhile, the developing countries must continue to import machinery and consumer goods without a suitable market for their exports that would allow them to pay for their imports. This again contributes to the problem of global debt.

What is alarming about the transnational corporations and banks is that there is no international agency to govern and regulate their international activities. They operate without any significant controls over them, other than the mechanics of the marketplace. They are not in business to benefit humanity but to make a profit. The result is that decisions are often made and actions taken that significantly affect whole countries or regions; the people who are affected the most have no say in these decisions. A good example of this point is the production technologies that have been introduced since World War II. While these technologies have been responsible for the tremendous development of the industrialized countries since World War II, they have also been responsible for the present, excessive levels of environmental pollution in the world.[18] While the harmful effects of many of these technologies are now known and other safer technologies are available, they continue to be used and are even being introduced into the developing countries. Meanwhile those people who have been and will be affected by the harmful impact of these technologies are not given a voice in their use.

The transnational corporations often dictate policy to governments, including first-world governments. In fact, if one looks closely, one finds that most U.S. government officials, especially the appointed ones, come from the ranks of the transnational corporations and banks. This is not surprising and clearly demonstrates the close relationship between the interests of the transnationals and the interests of the federal government. Finally, it is the transnationals that own and control much of the media.

Since over half of the transnational corporations are based in the United States and are U.S. corporations, it is important for citizens of the United States to understand their role in the world today and accept responsibility for much of the inequity and injustice in the world that flows from the operation of these transnationals. This is especially the case when the U.S. government is found intervening in the internal life of other countries to defend the economic interests of U.S. corporations planted there.

National Security State

The rise of the transnational corporations and the internationalization of capital has also given rise to what is known as the "national security state." The key to understanding the "national security state" is to realize that global capital, and hence the transnational corporations, go wherever the return is greatest. This has put an enormous pressure on national governments, which are now expected not only to regulate the economic environment within their own boundaries, but also to streamline their national system for efficient transnational competition. Corporations no longer compete with one another in the marketplace; countries compete with one another for the attention of the transnational corporations.

To compete efficiently in the world market, countries need to accomplish several objectives. They must provide cheap labor for the corporations. This demands wage restraints and the destruction or crippling of unions. The nations must also provide low taxes for the corporations, which demands a curtailment of social services. There is a need to increase governmental authority by coercive methods to suppress internal dissent and to achieve competitive goals. This latter development is best witnessed to by the rise of military dictatorships in the 1960s and 1970s in the developing countries. Often enough the United States was directly involved in this development. This involvement was either through the efforts of the CIA (Chile) or indirectly through counterinsurgency training of the local military forces and an increase in loans for arms purchases. While this development can lead to dictatorship, it can also take more moderate forms, but even these will involve some curtailment of democracy. Along with all these developments of the national security state, one finds increased militarization, such as countries building up arms as a means of protecting access to their international resources and defending their foreign investments. We can see these trends also affecting developments within the United States.

Global Debt

One of the most significant economic issues today is the growing problem of global debt and its impact on the people of the Third World. Loans that were originally intended to contribute to development have turned into a counterproductive mechanism. So that the debtor nations can service their debt, they must export capital needed for improving or maintaining their standard of living. It is becoming more difficult for them to get further financing.

The total external debt of the developing countries now approaches $1 trillion, or more than one-third of their combined GNP. This total doubled between 1979 and 1984 and continues to grow. On average, the first 20 percent of export earnings goes to service the debt of these countries without significantly reducing the principal. In some countries debt service is nearly 100 percent of export earnings.

The historical roots of this complex debt crisis go back to the rapid industrialization in the 1960s, through importing machinery and developing high energy dependence. This situation was then compounded by the astronomical rise of energy costs in the 1970s. Between 1973 and 1979 oil prices rose eightfold and OPEC deposited its profits in commercial banks in the North. These banks then pushed larger and larger loans on third-world borrowers who needed funds to purchase more and more expensive oil. In some instances, corrupt governments invested in grandiose projects with little or no assistance to their people or sent millions into private Swiss bank accounts. Sometimes they simply invested their new money in the very banks from which it was borrowed. With a second doubling of oil prices in 1979 the borrowing countries were forced to refinance their loans and borrow more money at escalating interest rates. The global recession that began in 1979 caused the prices of third-world export commodities to fall and so reduced their ability to meet their rapidly increasing debt payments.

The debtor nations have been allowed more than once to refinance to avoid bankruptcy. They have also been forced by lending banks and the International Monetary Fund (IMF) to undertake austerity measures as a condition for new loans and for rolling over existing debt. The IMF has demanded such measures as the devaluation of currency and the abandonment of government welfare, job creation programs, price controls, and subsidies for basic needs. As a result living standards have been cut back even further and wages cannot keep up with inflation. Debt rescheduling— the postponing of interest payments—has offered short-term relief but has also helped to solidify the legal exploitation of the poor by the rich.

The global debt crisis must be seen as a symptom of the wider economic and development crisis involving Southern and Northern nations. It should not be regarded simply as a problem of indebtedness and financial flow. It is becoming clear that many of the debtor nations will not be able to pay off their debts and that at least some of the debts will have to be forgiven. One group called the Debt Crisis Network has suggested that the two groups who were the primary beneficiaries of the debt crisis should bear the brunt of the losses that result from nonpayment of the debt.[19] These two groups are the commercial banks in the industrialized world and the governments and elites in the developing countries. None of the burden, they argue, should be borne by those people who are already suffering and had no say in accruing the debt.

The argument regarding the banks is that there is increasing evidence that the debt has already been repaid through such mechanisms as increased interest rates, rescheduling fees, capital flight, and declining terms of trade. It is now clear that U.S. banks have sharply reduced their exposure in debt-ridden third-world nations and are no longer seriously threatened by the possible failure of loans to developing countries. Robert

L. Clarke, comptroller of the currency, told the House Banking Committee in January 1989 that the banks have steadily improved their financial standing since the debt crisis began in 1982. They will survive even if many of their loans to foreign nations are never repaid. Also, L. William Seidman, chairman of the Federal Deposit Insurance Corporation, reported that the nine largest money-center banks would remain solvent even if they had to write off all their loans to the six largest borrowers. The debt situation, he said, "poses no immediate discernible threat" to the federal insurance fund.[20]

Transformation Needed

It is becoming ever clearer today that a vast transformation of global economic structures is needed.[21] Present global economic structures have led not to progress for most poor people in the world, but to a world development crisis that involves incredible suffering for millions of people. The old models of growth—based on export-oriented development and the belief that if production is increased the benefits will "trickle down to the poor"—have been discredited. Many of the developing countries have been pushing since the early 1970s for comprehensive global negotiations regarding North-South economic issues. A New International Economic Order (NIEO) is imperative.

The basic goal of the NIEO is to move from dependent to interdependent economic and political structures. The General Assembly of the United Nations resolved at a 1980 special session that a round of global negotiations should be launched to promote international economic cooperation for development. However, nothing has happened due to the lack of support for such negotiations by the Northern economic powers, including the United States. In some ways this is another example of North-South issues being decided by East-West tensions. According to Dussel, it is also the result of the fact that the center (the first-world countries), since the end of World War II, "has closed in on itself, leaving no room for any other nation because, if the underdeveloped nations were allowed to come in, the high standard of living of those within the center would be lowered considerably."[22] For many people in the third-world countries, the pain is too great and the need for change too urgent for them to settle for a slow, long-term process, while the North changes its values. They feel an acute need to change economic and political structures now.

Ultimately, the issue of development today is no longer one of further capitalization or even better distribution of goods. Rather, what is called for is a vast and radical transformation of the economic and political structures of society on a global level, a transformation that will ensure the human development of people. In other words, capital and modern technology must serve basic human needs and fundamental human rights rather than simply to develop profit. Surely, the profit motive will always play an important role in an economy; however, the profit motive needs to be balanced by a concern for the common good and development of people. At the present, improvement in the lives of people is blocked by individuals and groups who benefit from the present concentration of power. On the international level there are unequal trade arrangements, monetary manipulations, and investment policies by the transnational corporations that benefit the first-world powers. On the national level, wealthy elites in both the developed and developing countries support one another in reinforcing their dominance over most of the people. What is needed is a redistribution of power and a change of policies that focus on the quality of the growth that is occurring and not just on the quantitative aspects of economic growth.[23]

The international institutions established by the Bretton Woods Conference in 1944 to oversee the global system of finance, trade, and development—the International Monetary Fund (IMF), the International Bank for Reconstruction and Development (the World Bank), and the General Agreement on Tariffs and Trade (GATT)—do not adequately represent third-world debtors and seem incapable, without significant changes, of helping the debtor nations. They were established without any input from the developing countries of the South. Many of these new countries in the South came into existence only as the result of the process of decolonization that took place after the Second World War and so were not in existence in 1944. It is not surprising that these developing countries of the South mistrust the present international economic order and the dominant ideological position of free trade present in this economic order. Moreover, their practical experience has been that too often aid from the established countries, in whatever form, is just a new form of colonialism and a way to keep the South in a state of dependency vis-à-vis the North. This is the reason that the developing countries have called for a new international economic order.[24]

The necessary transformation must also include a transformation of the production technologies introduced since the Second World War because of their harmful impact upon the environment. As Barry Commoner points out:

> We must recognize that the assault on the environment cannot be effectively controlled, but must be prevented; that prevention requires the transformation of the present structure of the technosphere, bringing it into harmony with the ecosphere; that this means massively redesigning the major industrial, agricultural, energy, and transportation systems; that such a transformation of the systems of production conflicts with the short-term profit-maximizing goals that now govern investment decisions; and that, accordingly, politically suitable means must be developed that bring the public interest in long-term environmental quality to bear on these decisions. Finally, because the

problem is global and deeply linked to the disparity between the development of the planet's northern and southern hemispheres, what we propose to do in the United States and other industrial nations must be compatible with the global task of closing the economic gap between the rich north and the poor south—and indeed must facilitate it.[25]

It is clear that the United States is shifting from being an isolated, virtually self-sufficient national economy to being part of an interdependent global economy. It is only one of a group of economically strong countries, not the dominant force. This trend is not going to change. We are deep into a process of global redistribution of labor, of production, and of wealth. What is demanded of the United States, as of all countries, is at least greater cooperation in the economic order. All nations need to recognize that they are not alone in the world. While "cooperation" falls short of "coordination" and "harmonization," it is more than "consultation," which may mean no more than that other interested parties are kept informed.[26] As Henry Wallich points out, the growing world interdependence is not yet matched by a growing ability or willingness to cooperate in dealing with the results of such interdependence. The present low level of cooperation is due not to a lack of instruments, but of will. Wallich asserts that "the existing structure of institutions is quite capable of sustaining a higher level of international cooperation."[27]

COMMUNICATION

The third area where the United States impacts the international scene is in the area of communication. Today there is no place on the surface of the planet that is isolated from the electromagnetic environment. We live in space that is permeated by millions of electromagnetic information carriers. All that is needed to retrieve the information is the proper technical equipment, such as a radio or TV set, that can be obtained for a very few dollars. We are living in the midst of a microelectronic revolution. According to Alvin Toffler, the microelectronic revolution is only the third major technological development in all human history; the other two were the agricultural revolution and the Industrial Revolution.[28]

The impact of this pervasive presence of electronic information is enormous.[29] As the family, religion, and school were at one time the primary instruments for the socialization of youth, now it is increasingly television that plays this role. With this mass media has come constantly changing fashion that touches on everything from expected behaviors to styles of music and literature. The mass media has a potential for a conscious, systematic, strategic destruction and re-creation of the symbolic culture, images, values, centers of concern, and behavior patterns of a society. It is very possible for the few thousand people who decide on programming, the reporting of news, and the determination of editorial policy to set the agenda of public concern and the range of acceptable ideological commitment. As the result of global communication satellites, the future homogenization of world culture is possible.

The ones who will set the agenda for this world culture will be those nations and/or transnational corporations who are wealthy enough to launch and program the satellites. The United States and its technological elites are now in control and will be for the foreseeable future. Today the United States is the most powerful communications center on the globe with satellites sending constant messages, good and bad, to the entire planet; U.S. culture sets the pattern for the rest of the world.

Modern culture has arisen out of the Reformation, the rise of the nation-state, the Enlightenment, liberal democratic revolutions, the industrial capitalist revolution, and later communist political and economic revolutions. As Joe Holland points out, while this modern culture did not begin in the United States, it has found in the United States its most unfettered expression and its global center.[30] In fact the cultural power of the United States has increasingly penetrated all global culture, even where its political power is fought against. Holland proposes that the positive side of this culture is that its innovative spirit has shown a remarkable openness to enrichment from other cultures. What is distinct about the United States is that it is a continuing creation of all of the world's cultures. The negative side of this culture, that is, its powerful techno-scientific commitment to autonomous definitions of freedom and progress, may be destroying the ecological, social, and religious foundations of the life system on planet earth. As Holland says, "The global culture may be emerging only to face the death of all life at every level from the womb to the planet. In the meantime, American culture seems to be propagandizing the world with a trivialized definition of sexuality and massive celebration of violence."[31] A heavy responsibility lies upon the United States to use this power in a way that will lead to the betterment of the human race and the planet and not to its destruction.

A corollary of this communication/culture issue, which will be dealt with later, is that U.S. Catholicism has become a central place for debate over the path of global Catholicism and global evangelization.

ANALYSIS

History

As we look back over these areas of international involvement by the United States, certain events emerge as having been most influential. Without doubt World War II forced the United States onto the international scene as never before in its history. Following its victory in that war the United States became engaged in a widespread program of rebuilding those nations that were allied with it, whether formerly friend or foe and began to offer assistance of various kinds to other nations in Africa, Asia, and Latin America. The spread of communism and the establishment of the Eastern bloc of nations after the war, because of the fear it aroused in the United States, gave a focus to its rebuilding and assistance programs. The same circumstances gave rise to a morality where the end justified the means if the end would curtail and eventually overcome communism.

The internationalization of capital that developed rapidly after the war, aided by improved communications and rapid transportation around the world, gave birth to the transnational corporations. The emergence of the transnationals has changed the face of the globe both politically and economically. The new technologies centering on nuclear physics, rockets, and communications, which had their origins in World War II, have given rise to present technologies, especially in the area of communications and weapons. OPEC made most Americans aware for the first time of how interdependent they are on other nations, politically and economically.

The more recent moves of developing countries, such as those in Central America, to set their own agendas and directions, have brought on blatant interventionist tactics by the United States acting to protect its own interests. For the most part these actions by the government have received the support of the citizens.

Finally, the recent moves toward perestroika in the Soviet Union, toward democracy in Eastern Europe, and toward cutbacks in arms are positive signs that there is hope for the future.

Values

The values of the United States that have been dominant in these areas over the last forty years have been national security, preservation of a way of life, protection of access to resources, and profit, especially short-term profit. Too often behind these values lie a sense of superiority regarding our own political, social, and economic systems and almost a messianic drive to impose such structures upon the rest of the world. A deep mistrust of communism, especially as it is embodied in Soviet Russia, and other forms of socialism also plays a significant role. Because of the need to use power to achieve its goals, arms have become more important than butter. Moreover, a sense of truth and honesty has been clouded in pursuit of secrecy for the sake of national security. The United States often verbalizes that its motives on the international level are the well-being of other nations and the promotion of global peace and justice and human rights. The reality is that U.S. foreign policy is dictated by national interests which are narrowly interpreted in terms of military security and economic prosperity. Foreign assistance is used to stabilize friends of the United States, promote its own exports and help its domestic business interests. Peter Henriot maintains that "the human rights program is seen in a utilitarian framework, meaning that countries which are our 'friends' and of military-strategic importance should not be pushed too hard regarding human rights violations, lest 'subversive' elements create instability in them."[32]

Several structures have supported these developments. The economic structures include capitalism supported by the World Bank and the International Monetary Fund, the transnational corporations, and banks. The political structures have been the legislative and executive branches of government together with the military, the CIA, and the National Security Council. Social and cultural structures comprise the media giants as well as the scientific, technological community together with the mainline churches to some extent, and the fundamentalist churches to an even greater extent. Lastly, the basic myths of origin and the themes of U.S. civil religion, with their combined sense of moral superiority, have provided the moral support for many of these developments.[33]

Richard Dickinson makes the following frightening observation about the future:

A future simply extrapolated from the present, without significant changes in economic, political and cultural relationships between nations, will produce a world in 1990 or 2000 even worse off than today. This is likely to be the kind of world we will have, unless there is significant change, generated from both the richer and poorer countries. The record of the past two decades does not generate much hope. It is a record marked by increasing polarization between rich and poor countries, and between the rich and poor within countries — a polarization which makes the victimized ever more ready to use violent means to overcome the oppressive system which dominates them, and a parallel readiness on the part of incumbent political and economic authorities to reinforce themselves through centralization of power and intensification of "security" measures.[34]

The world is very unsettled at the present moment. The decisions that will be made in the capitals of the world in the near future will be crucial for future relations between nations. Not for a long time have the nations of the world had the kind of opportunity that now exists to choose a world of peace based upon justice. However, such a world will call for a radical transformation of the economic and political systems as well as of many of the present production technologies that have proven to be so harmful to the environment. If the United States continues along the same lines that it has been heading it is going to edge closer and closer to financial ruin. This ruin will result from an ever-growing national deficit fueled by a continuing arms buildup together with more local wars (declared and undeclared) and regional involvements to protect its interests around the globe. The consequences will be a growing inability to hear not only the cries of the poor in its midst but even more so the needs and demands of the peoples of the Third World. The result will be even more poverty and hunger in that part of the world. Almost certainly all this will demand ever greater secrecy in government because of an unwillingness to be accountable to the people. This will lead to a gradual destruction of both the intent and the fact of the Constitution.

Hopefully, the above scenario will never occur. However, its prevention will happen only if steps are taken now to transform the social, economic, and political systems that control the world.

3

THE NATIONAL CONTEXT

In the previous chapter I looked at some of the issues that form the global context in which the United States finds itself today. The purpose of this chapter is to look at the more important national issues that the United States needs to deal with. It is important to remember that these national issues must always be viewed against the background of the larger global context in which we now live. None of these issues affects only the United States. They also impact and are related to the larger global issues presented in the previous chapter.

If we are to understand ourselves as a people and the tensions that exist among us, the best place to begin is with a look at the civil religion that sustains our identity as a people and the myths that support it. Against this background I will then take a look at more specific issues that challenge the United States. As will become clear, many of the issues that face the United States today are rooted in the imperfections inherent in the original vision of our founders, or in later corruptions of that vision, or in the great chasm between high American ideals and actual moral performance.

CIVIL RELIGION AND ITS MYTHS

Robert N. Bellah defines civil religion as that religious dimension found in the life of every people through which it interprets its historical experience in the light of transcendent reality.[1] "Myth" in this context does not mean a story that is untrue, but rather a story that has the power to transform reality so that reality can provide moral and spiritual meaning to individuals or societies. There are several myths that underlie civil religion in the United States. The following seem to be the most important.[2]

First, there is the myth of origin. This is a somewhat complex myth with several aspects to it. The Declaration of Independence and the prologue to the Constitution express very clearly the goals of the revolution and those ideals that permeate our life as a people and form the core of our self-understanding. These goals and ideals include justice, freedom, independence; the equality of peoples; that all people have been endowed by the Creator with certain inalienable rights, which inhere in the person prior to any act of the government, among which are life, liberty, and the pursuit of happiness; and the understanding that government derives its just powers from the consent of the governed. These values are the core of our self-understanding and give focus to the various elements of the myth.

From the time of its discovery there was a sense of newness about America, newness bestowed by the hand of God; it was the last remaining remnant of the primordial state of the world and of the human race. This sense of newness remains even today. As Bellah points out, "If it gives us a sense that we come from nowhere, that our past is inchoate and our tradition shallow, so that we begin to doubt our own identity . . . it also gives us our openness to the future, our sense of unbounded possibility."[3]

The Bible above all has provided images by which Americans from the very beginning have understood themselves. However, it is important to remember that the original use of these images was shaped by expectations springing from the Protestant Reformation. While the Reformation began as a reform of the Catholic Church it soon led to a stress on the reform of the individual and carried overtones of apocalyptic expectation. For many the Reformation was an event that foreshadowed the end of time and the birth of a new heaven and a new earth. It is not surprising, then, that the New England founders saw themselves on a divinely appointed "errand in the wilderness" and believed that in the wilderness of the new world God was most likely to begin the new heaven and the new earth.

It was John Winthrop, the first leader of the Massachusetts Bay Colony, who in 1630 expressed the biblical ideals that would give a sense of identity to the new foundation. In a sermon delivered onboard ship before the colonists landed, he compared the ocean-crossing to the crossings of the Red Sea and the Jordan River and expressed the hope that the Massachusetts Bay colony would be a promised land. The agreement that the colonists had made, even before leaving England, is presented as a new covenant with obligations to both God and one another. Their success in their venture is related to the blessings and curses which Moses proclaimed to the Israelites in the desert (Dt 28). In these passages the success of Israel in the new land is said to depend upon the fidelity of the people to the covenant. As for Israel of old, biblical faith was to inform both the religious and the political structures of the colonists.

Coming out of the Calvinist tradition, it is not surprising to find among the early New Englanders not only a strong sense of the dignity and responsibility of the individual but also a strong social, communal, or collective emphasis. This collective emphasis was derived from several sources: the classical idea of the "polis" as responsible for the education and the virtue of its citizens; the Old Testament notion of the covenant between God and a people who were collectively responsible for their actions; and the New Testament notion of community based on love and expressed in membership in one common body. The basis of civil society was the national covenant to which all New Englanders were understood as belonging or at least to which they were subject. Hence, conversion was never an act of purely private piety but always carried a strong social responsibility.

Another important source of myth and symbol for the founders was ancient Rome. Modern political theory from Machiavelli to Montesquieu had been preoccupied with understanding the rise and fall of the Roman empire and especially with the history of Roman liberty. Moreover, in America, as in Europe, Latin literature was at the core of humanistic education. It is not surprising that the history of Roman liberty dominated the minds of educated Americans in the late eighteenth century and that Roman classicism dominated the surface symbolism of the new republic. As Bellah points out, "Its very terminology was latinate, the words 'republic,' 'president,' 'congress,' and 'senate,' being Latin in origin and clearly distinct from the terminology for their British counterparts."[4] The architecture and much of the art of the early republic period was dominated by Greco-Roman classicism.

However, on a deeper level the Roman attribute that captured the imagination of the founders was "republican virtue," especially as this was interpreted by Montesquieu.[5] According to Montesquieu each type of society has its own principle of social life that provides the spring of action for its members. So, for example, for despotism that principle is fear; for monarchy, it is honor. For a republic, however, especially in its democratic form, the principle of social life is virtue. The point is that in a democratic republic the will or motive to see that the laws are obeyed and that justice is done must come out of the will of the people to act on behalf of the greater community. This quality is the meaning of virtue and is what makes things work in a democracy. James Sellers comments that virtue "conveys the idea that the citizen of a republic finds the beginning of his participation in governance in his own inner spirit, but that this spirit takes the form of action, and especially that kind of action that expresses willingness: initiative."[6]

As John A. Coleman points out, classical republican theory has lapsed as a separately vigorous tradition of public philosophy, at least since the mid-nineteenth century. The tradition of public virtue is no longer a living part of the texture of American public discourse. However, Coleman says, "The importance of classical republican theory is that it served to reinforce biblical religion in stressing love and sacrifice for the common good and the need to found the health of public life on virtue and a morally good citizenry."[7]

According to Bellah the American Revolution and the establishment of a new civil order succeeded principally because of the convergence of the Puritan covenant pattern and the Montesquieuan republican pattern:

Both patterns saw society resting on the deep inner commitment of its members, the former through conversion, the latter through republican virtue. Both saw government as resting on law, which, in its positive form, was created by the active participation of those subject to it, yet ultimately derives from some higher source, either God or Nature.[8]

However, from the very beginning of the new republic there was tension between this concern for a public good and an emphasis on a utilitarian, individualistic concern.

This individualism entered the colonies in the eighteenth century as part of the public philosophy of the Enlightenment, especially as developed by Thomas Hobbes and John Locke. The essence of this philosophy, as developed by Locke, is that the individual is prior to society and that a society comes into existence only through the voluntary contract of individuals trying to maximize their own self-interest. The state can only be justified in terms of its utility to the individual and social concord is based on self-interest alone. This philosophy is totally void of any notion of God or the good that transcends the individual. It is a radical theoretical individualism that is purely utilitarian in its considerations. By the time of the post–Civil War era, liberal Enlightenment philosophy had become the overwhelmingly dominant force in American culture.[9] The result is the individualism that is so prevalent in our society today.[10]

Another important myth that sustains U.S. civil religion is the sense of chosenness. The idea that the Americans are a people specially marked and chosen by the hand of God can already be found in the seventeenth century. William Lee Miller would trace this sense of chosenness back to a view of England's role in carrying out the purposes of God in this world. As he says:

This sense of a nation's dramatic particularity in God's reforming purposes, a "special" Providence, a covenant nation, was transmitted in concentrate to the New World, and entered into that sense of a particular relationship to God and his purposes, especially his reforming purposes, that certainly has become a part of American culture.[11]

As a chosen nation Americans understood themselves as called to take the lead in the redemption of the world. As Herman Melville said in his earlier years (he would later change his mind):

And we Americans are the peculiar, chosen people—the Israel of our time; we bear the ark of the liberties of the world. ... We are the pioneers of the world; the advanceguard, sent on through the wilderness of untried things, to break a new path in the New World that is ours. ... the political Messiah had come. But he has come in us ..."[12]

We can see in such a statement the origin of the idea of the manifest destiny of the United States to share its experience and way of life with the rest of the world so that the world can also be saved, even if this involves forcibly imposing American values and systems on others. It is this type of thinking that has led to the self-righteous domination and oppression of others around the globe that was discussed earlier.

In its more positive form, in its origins, this sense of chosenness meant that the United States had the role to set an example for oppressed peoples of the world. This sense of chosenness did not include forcing others to accept American ways through some sort of political or economic power. In its origins, this notion of chosenness was not absolute but conditional and involved a choice. The chosenness was understood to be dependent upon fidelity to the covenant that God had made with the people. However, divine judgment would come upon even an elect people if they did not choose fidelity to the covenant. This is not to justify this sense of chosenness but to point out that, at least in its origins, it did not involve the absolute self-righteousness that has too often been at work in the United States' dealings with other nations. It is this sense of chosenness that has too often led to an uncritical acceptance of U.S. social, political, and economic structures as God-given and hence beyond criticism.

This sense of chosenness also led to what Bellah calls the primal crime on which American society is based, that is, the failure of the early settlers to see the Native Americans in their own terms and, later, their depriving them of land, livelihood, and even life itself.[13] To this sin was added the forcible transportation of African blacks from their own land and their enslavement in America. The basis of this mistreatment of both American Indians and blacks was the sense of chosenness by the new settlers and their descendants.

While this sense of chosenness, at least in its origins, was understood to be dependent upon fidelity to the covenant, the sins that were denounced by the early preachers were, for the most part, the conventional sins of Protestantism. Sabbath-breaking and profanity were more apt to be mentioned than anything to do with the treatment of the Indians and the blacks. While there was concern about slavery at the time of the Revolution, the new nation became so preoccupied with the creation of a viable national structure and its defense against foreign incursion that the issue of slavery never fully emerged. Only the intense revivalism in the first part of the nineteenth century, known as the Second Great Awakening, and the push for social change and reform that accompanied it, gave birth, from 1830 on, to the antislavery movement. However, even the freeing of the slaves as the result of the Civil War and the establishment of the Fourteenth Amendment, which guaranteed the natural rights of all people, gave them equal protection under the laws, and authorized Congress to enforce these rights, did not really deal with the issue. As Bellah points out:

> For all the vitality of the antislavery movement and the living heritage
> that it bequeathed us, its success was only partial and much of what

was gained legally was quickly lost socially and politically. . . . The antislavery movement was a drama in the white soul. The black American scarcely emerged on the public stage. . . . The whole epic struggle, as far as most white Americans were concerned, was one of sin, judgment, and redemption in the white soul. . . . Thus fundamental aspects of the American self-picture went unchallenged. For 50 years after the Civil War that picture was more self-congratulatory than it had ever been before. . . .[14]

America as an asylum for the oppressed is one of the oldest elements of the American myth. The image of America as being open to and receiving the afflicted of the world has deep roots in U. S. history. Immigrants were supposed to find an open society with equality of opportunity for all when they arrived. When compared to European societies of the time, there certainly was more openness in America and for some there was true equality of opportunity. However, for the most part, most immigrants found that America was the domain of a particular ethnic group, that is, the white Anglo-Saxon Protestant. White Anglo-Saxon dominance has declined in all areas of American life over the last century. However, it is important to see what lay at the root of this dominance, since it explains much of U.S. history and present attitudes.

Among the early Puritans there was a strong sense of the difference between the saved and the reprobate, the saints and the sinners. As the result of the fear of contamination, sinners were separated from the saved or there was external repression of the sinners. Originally none of this had anything to do with the relations between ethnic and racial groups. However, it was not long before certain characteristic traits of sinners were projected onto whole groups of people. Indians and blacks were seen as prone to every kind of sinful impulse, and, as a result, they had to be separated from the righteous, the white Anglo-Saxons, and even destroyed. In this perception of reality can be seen the roots of the racial segregation that has stained U.S. history and continues to affect North Americans' perceptions of those with a different color of skin. In this perception of reality can also be found the origins of the wars to wipe out the American Indians and U.S. savagery in wars against those with a different colored skin, such as in Hiroshima, Nagasaki, My Lai. This same racism stands behind North American attitudes toward black, yellow, or brown people in the Third World. It also plays a significant role in the basic disregard by the United States of the Third World and its problems. To some extent the same dynamic of the sinner and saved also explains present U.S. dealings with Russia, and the so-called "Marxist" governments of Central and Latin America and Africa. The classical American must overcome evil where evil is defined as those with a different skin or language or customs or beliefs who in some way threaten the American way of life.

This sense of the saved and reprobate has been operative in U.S. society not only in terms of external groups but also for internal groups that are seen as sinful. In this latter circumstance stringent controls, such as rigorous policing and occasional mob violence in order to force such sinners to conform, have not been unheard of in U.S. history. Yet groups considered morally upright in the United States have been allowed extraordinary freedom to effect their will in society. In the nineteenth century moral uprightness came to be more and more identified with secular and especially monetary success. The successful, often the white Anglo-Saxon, determined who were the sinners in society and who was to be controlled. This dynamic was evident in the treatment of the Irish and Italian immigrants in the nineteenth century and continues to manifest itself in recent times, as in the 1968 police action in Chicago at the time of the Democratic convention, Selma, Birmingham, and so forth.

The final myth has to do with the issue of success and salvation in America.[15] People have come to America for various motives; normally these motives were either finding salvation or getting rich or, suggests Bellah, often for both reasons in some combination that was perhaps unclear to the people themselves. Bellah sees these motives as versions of the same mythic archetype: the quest for earthly paradise either now or at some future time. Eventually, however, salvation and success in America became identified. This identification developed out of the fact that the original Puritans placed a high value on work. It was believed that good Christian work would not go unrewarded. Hence, by the nineteenth century, as the result of a practical rationalism that concentrated on worldly practical achievement, success, which meant money, became the all-important reality. Such success then became identified with moral goodness and was evidence of moral virtue and religious salvation. This has continued to be the case until the present. Belief in the myth continues — especially if one is a white Anglo-Saxon male — if one works hard then the American dream will come true and salvation will be won. The flip side of this myth is that the poor are listless, lazy and immoral, and responsible for their own plight. If they worked harder, all would be better. A consequence of this myth is that for many Americans there is no need for a transformation of the systems, only hard work.

An interesting absence in the United States is the lack of any significant socialist movement. Socialism arose in Europe early in the nineteenth century as a critique of industrial society. A significant socialist movement can be found in almost every industrial nation in the world but the United States. In fact socialism has been viewed as taboo in the United States while capitalism has been sacrosanct. The question is, why?

The idea of socialism came to the United States at the same time as individualism, in the first half of the nineteenth century. Individualism immediately resonated with much that was latent in American ideology and became popular. Socialism, its opposite, was rejected after an initial flurry of interest. As capitalism in the United States became ideologically self-conscious, it was associated with individualism and eventually both were identified with the American form of government. Thus, by the mid-twentieth century it could be said that our "private enterprise system and our American form of government are inseparable and there can be no compromise between a free economy and a governmentally dictated economy without endangering our political as well as our economic freedom."[16]

However, the U.S. aversion to socialism goes even deeper. Socialism has always been seen as a foreign ideology and un-American. More specifically, the ideology of socialism was associated with the French Revolution. In the United States there had been a deep revulsion against the excesses of the French Revolution, which was contrasted to the moderate and humane character of the American Revolution. Hence, any ideology associated with the French Revolution was rejected as foreign. That later socialist ideologists were frequently immigrants only added to the foreign image of socialism. In addition, atheism and materialism, along with an abusive tone about God and religion, characterized at least the most influential strand of socialism, Marxism.

However, the central negative image of socialism was the attribute of collectivism or statism connected with it that contrasted sharply with peoples' understanding of American individualism. As Bellah notes, this image involved a double distortion: "For one thing there were religious, democratic, and humanistic forms of socialism emphasizing individual dignity that Americans almost entirely failed to see or appreciate. For another the American tradition itself was not one-sidedly individualistic but always involved a balance of concern between the individual and his community."[17] Finally, in American eyes, the Russian Revolution symbolically linked socialism with foreign revolutionaries.

To conclude this section on U.S. civil religion and the myths that support it, something should be said regarding the issue of separation of Church and state. The concept of the separation of Church and state is deeply rooted in the American mentality. In its origins, as embedded in the First Amendment, it referred to the nonestablishment of any religion by the state and the free exercise of religion. However, especially during recent decades, the idea of the separation of Church and state has come to be understood in the popular mind as the noninvolvement of the Church in matters of state so that there should be "no politics from the pulpit." This has been part of the growing privatization of religion in U.S. society. It is important to realize, though, that it was never the intention of those who framed the First Amendment to divorce religion from politics in such a way that religion should have no influence upon government and political decisions. Those who fought for the separation of Church and state supported religion; they saw religion as necessary for fostering the morality, the public virtue, or common good that was necessary for the continuance of the republic.[18] Moreover, the United States has a long history of Church involvement in social reform movements, from the abolition movement in the nineteenth century down to the civil rights and anti-Vietnam movements.[19]

This attempt at a summary of the major tenets of the civil religion of the United States recalls what we have believed about ourselves as a people and what we would most likely explain, in some form or another, to an outsider who might ask us who we are as a people. Whether we believe today every element of this vision of ourselves as a people is another issue. Our behavior as a nation over the last several decades seems to suggest that perhaps there are some elements of this vision that we would not accept today. As already pointed out in the foregoing discussion, there are also certain imperfections inherent in the vision that we have inherited.

PLURALISM OF U.S. SOCIETY

When we look at our reality as a nation today the first thing that strikes us is the pluralism of our society, especially its multicultural and multiethnic composition. People from all over the globe—North, South, East and West, black, brown, yellow, red, and white—can be found here. They speak numerous languages and dialects and look at reality and deal with it from very different religious, ethnic, and cultural perspectives. Some of these people, such as the American Indian, are indigenous to the land. Others are descendants of the original colonists or the black slaves that were imported onto these shores from the early seventeenth century on. The families of others came as part of the great wave of immigrants in the nineteenth and early twentieth centuries; still others have entered more recently from the South and the East. While many have prospered, many others have not or have lost an earlier wealth.

Some of the more recent immigrants are here by choice, while others have been forced by political and economic situations to take refuge here. Some have come with proper documentation while others lack such documentation and live in fear of being discovered. While many Americans welcome new immigrants with open arms and support, others fear them and find them to be a threat to their jobs and neighborhoods. Meanwhile, most of the population, unsure of what to do, stare at this phenomenon of a new wave of immigrants in silence and harbor apprehension and expectation that these newcomers will become "American" as soon as possible by learning English and adapting "American" ways. In some places, older inhabitants find themselves a new minority as waves of new immigrants from the Spanish-speaking South enter the cities and proudly retain their language and culture while also learning the ways of the United States.

In the midst of such pluralism one finds racism in various forms that continues to present basic and continuous challenges to our national cultural ideals of liberty, justice, and equality for all. This racism takes the forms of discrimination, social distance, and subtle and not so subtle forms of prejudice. As was seen earlier this racism has deep cultural roots in U.S.

society flowing from the sense of chosenness on the part of the early settlers and the need to separate the sinners from the saved. Studies have shown that the basic attitudes of American whites toward blacks and other people of color have improved dramatically since World War II. However, changes in economic structures that would ensure economic equality have not kept pace with this change in attitudes. In other words, while legal and social restrictions on political involvement and civil liberties have been removed, "yet it still remains the case that economic structures allow that blacks — as a racial class despite the individual exceptions — statistically remain the last hired, the first fired."[20] In fact, as Coleman points out, "many of the most potent political issues of our day are directly or indirectly related to racism," for example, affirmative action programs, the minimum wage, compensatory justice, school busing, attitudes toward welfare, neighborhood decline, homelessness.[21] Racism today is especially evident in the marginalization of a permanent underclass where a group of people is ignored and is isolated from the political and economic mainstream.

Aside from racism one also finds sexism in the United States as women struggle for equality within society. In the first phase of the women's movement (1840–1920), women gained their basic rights to a college education, to own property in their own name, and to vote. Their agenda now, according to Mary Burke, involves

> empowerment, enabling women to take control of their own lives and to function effectively in the public arena. Integration of women into public life, including public decision making, is another. Economic equality is a third. Recognition of women's gifts, talents and needs is another.[22]

The women's movement is not unique to the United States; however, it has been most visible here because more and more women are entering the work force. What is desired most is that women be treated as members of the human family with full and equal human dignity. As with racism the transformation of economic and social structures has not kept pace with the aspirations of women and the greater desire within society as a whole for total equality.

INDIVIDUALISM

When one looks at U.S. society as a whole, however, what is especially obvious, across almost all lines, is a pervasive individualism. Many people have commented upon this individualism, but the book that has best traced this phenomenon in the United States is *Habits of the Heart* by Robert Bellah and his associates.[23]

The main thrust of this American individualism is that the ultimate goals of life are matters of personal choice. That is, the meaning of one's life for most Americans is to become one's own person, almost to give birth to oneself. Much of this process is negative and involves breaking free from family, community and inherited ideas. U.S. culture does not give much positive guidance about how to fill out the contours of this autonomous, self-responsible self. However, it does emphasize two important areas of life. First, there is work. Men and women are supposed to stand on their own two feet and be self-supporting in the occupational world (utilitarian individualism). People are also supposed to find a group of sympathetic people, or at least one such person—what *Habits of the Heart* calls the lifestyle enclave—with whom they can spend their leisure time in an atmosphere of acceptance, happiness, and love. In this lifestyle enclave, modes of relating are highly therapeutic. The ideal relationship is one in which everything is completely conscious, and all parties know how they feel and what they want. The only morality that is acceptable is the purely contractual agreement of the parties; whatever they agree to is right (expressive individualism).

The means to achieve the individual choices involved in this approach to life depend on economic progress and success. For most people being a success in this society means to advance up the hierarchy of the corporation. In this context people are normally unconcerned with the wider political and social implications of their work. All that is important is their own economic progress that allows independence.

There is a great concern for freedom in this approach to life. Freedom means being left alone by others, not having other people's values, ideas, or styles of life forced upon one. It should not be surprising to find that where people wish to be free of others' demands, it becomes hard to forge bonds of attachment to, or cooperation with, other people.

Justice in this context is a matter of equal opportunities for every individual to pursue whatever he or she understands by happiness. Such equal opportunities are to be guaranteed by fair laws and political procedures. Private property is seen as an absolute right, and a role of the state is to help one to hold on to that property. The problem with this way of thinking about justice is that it contains no vision of the ideal distribution of goods in a society.

The result of such radical individualism is that the larger society is left to look after itself. The center of reality is the autonomous individual who owes no one anything and hardly expects anything from anyone. The radical individualist forgets ancestors and descendants and becomes isolated in his/her own lifestyle enclave. While U.S. society has become vastly more interrelated and integrated economically, technically, and functionally, this is a society in which individuals can only rarely and with difficulty understand themselves and their activities as interrelated in morally significant ways with the activities of other, different Americans. Lost is the sense of a common good, of values that transcend the individual, of goals that are common to a people as a group and transcend private interests.

As a nation it would appear that the only thing holding United States society together today is its concern for the economy; "we the people" are an economic "special interest group." Such a radical individualism has a very detrimental effect on the well-being of community life and leads to a lack of concern for the plight of the helpless, the oppressed, and the poor within society.

It is important to realize that individualism lies at the very core of American culture. As a people we believe in the dignity and the sacredness of the individual person. We always have; this is what has made us great as a country. Modern individualism, now running rampant in U.S. society, has its philosophical roots, as we saw earlier, in the public philosophy of the Enlightenment, especially as developed by Hobbes and Locke. This philosophy emerged over three centuries ago in Europe from a struggle against a monarchical and aristocratic authority that seemed arbitrary and oppressive to citizens who wished to govern themselves. William Miller suggests that another important source of this individualism can be found in the Protestant religion so influential in our beginnings. More specifically, its insistence on "every man his own priest," and "Scripture alone," and the consequent development of so many sects and denominations, make it a contributing force. As Miller points out, a pietist-Protestant form of religious liberty was not just a corollary of individualism but its essence.[24] Miller also points to the practice of adult baptism, "baptism at the age of discretion, when the converted one is old enough to have made his or her own decision," as something that very much heightens the distinct and separate place of each individual, and correspondingly diminishes the place of the continuities of institutional life.[25] Miller continues,

> Implicit in conversion and revival, in gathered churches, adult baptisms, congregational polities, and homiletical services was the image of the powerful role of the free decision of the individual, and that image carried over into society at large. . . . In order to hold to a high view of the "dignity" and "worth" of the individual, it is felt, one must also hold to a large view of his importance in making himself, mastering nature, and determining history.[26]

Modern individualism has long coexisted with classical republicanism and biblical religion.[27] The conflict in their basic assumptions regarding the relationship of the individual and society was initially muted. All three perspectives, in the forms commonest in America, stressed the dignity and autonomy of the individual. However, as modern individualism has become more dominant, some of the difficulties in it have become apparent. These difficulties are its stress on the absolute priority of the individual over society and its lack of a sense of the common good as the reason for a society and the responsibilities that flow from that common good.

There are both ideological and sociological reasons for the growing strength of modern individualism. Above all, modern individualism has pursued individual rights and individual autonomy in many different areas. In so doing, it has come into confrontation with those aspects of biblical and republican thought that have accepted, even enshrined at times, unequal rights and obligations, such as the relations between husbands and wives, masters and servants, leaders and followers, rich and poor, clergy and laity. As the absolute commitment to individual dignity has condemned those inequalities, it has also seemed to invalidate the biblical and republican traditions. However, in undermining these traditions individualism also weakens the very traditions that give content and substance to the ideal of individual dignity in the first place. The question, then, according to Bellah, is whether the older civic and biblical traditions have the capacity to reformulate themselves while simultaneously remaining faithful to their own deepest insights.

ECONOMIC SITUATION

From an economic perspective the American Dream (a new car, one's own home, and college education for the children) has always been a significant motivation for the typical American. At bottom this Dream is based on two articles of national faith: each generation will live a bit better than the preceding one and build a still better life for its children; and the nation will slowly but steadily progress toward greater equality. These two pillars of belief have helped to create the political and social stability and economic dynamism that have characterized the United States for more than a century. During the 1950s and 1960s the Dream seemed to be coming true. However, during the 1970s the fortunes of different income groups diverged, and this divergence has skyrocketed through the recovery that followed the 1981-1982 recession.

Income Trends

From 1977 to 1988, the inflation-adjusted income of the families who make up the poorest 10 percent of the population declined more than 10 percent. The total number of people living below the poverty line fell from almost 40 million in 1960 to less than 23 million in 1973. Yet, by 1988 there were 32.5 million Americans (13.5 percent of the population) who lived under the poverty line of $5,800 or less for one person or $11,611 for a family of four. (Some would say that the actual number of poor in the United States is closer to 50 million people or one out of every five.) Meanwhile, between 1977 and 1987, the average family income of the top 10 percent of the population increased by over 24 percent and the income of the top 1 percent increased by 74.2 percent![28] To look at this in another way, the upper one-fifth of American families took 44 percent of the nation's total income in 1988, compared to 41.6 percent in 1980. The share of that national income for the top 1 percent of families climbed from 9 percent to 11 percent in the same period of time. Meanwhile, the poorest one-fifth of families received only 4.6 percent of the national income in 1988, down from 5.1 percent in 1980. The poor are indeed getting poorer, and there are more of them, and the rich are getting richer.

The disparity between the rich and poor is even more obvious when one considers that 26.9 percent of the nation's wealth is held by the top one-half of 1 percent of U.S. households and that the top 10 percent of households controls approximately 68 percent of the nation's wealth.[29] Between 1981 and 1988 the net worth of the Forbes 400 richest Americans roughly tripled.[30] As Kevin Phillips points out, among the major Western nations, the United States has developed one of the sharpest cleavages between rich and poor. The 1980s, in fact, witnessed a doubling of the number of millionaires and an increase in billionaires from a handful in 1980 to over 50 in 1988. This upsurge of riches was due to global and national economic restructuring, the stagnation of wages, and the increased income coming from rents, dividends, capital gains, and interest that took place in the 1980s due to tax cuts, high interest rates, and the bull market.[31]

To put the above figures into global perspective, it is important to realize that though the United States accounts for only 5 percent of the world's population, it consumes 25 percent of the world's annual production! Also, contrary to a lot of popular rhetoric, only a relatively small portion of "social spending" programs in the United States is devoted to the poorest members of society. For example, the total expenditures for Medicaid, food stamps, the federal part of Aid to Families with Dependent Children and other income security programs, excluding retirement and unemployment compensation, amounted to only 9.2 percent of federal outlays in the first half of the 1980s. In contrast, 27 percent of the federal budget was devoted to Social Security (essentially a working- or middle-class benefit) and Medicare (a transfer payment to all people above a certain age irrespective of their income and wealth) in the same period of time.

Of the 32.5 million Americans who lived under the poverty line in 1988, 40 percent were children under 18; these were one-fifth of all American children. In fact two-fifths of all the poor are children. The problem is particularly severe among female-headed families, where more than half of all children are poor. Two-thirds of black children and nearly three-quarters of Hispanic children in such families are poor.

The past twenty years have witnessed a dramatic increase in the number of women in poverty. More than one-third of all female-headed families are poor. Among black and Hispanic families headed by women, over 50 percent are poor. Moreover, racial minorities have the highest rates of poverty; while 10 percent of white Americans live in poverty, 33.1 percent of blacks and 28.2 percent of Hispanics are poor.[32]

Reasons for Poverty

There are essentially five reasons for poverty in the United States.[33] First, lack of adequate wages is the most direct cause of poverty. A growing number of jobs employing the poor and low-skilled or older workers pay wages that cannot sustain a subsistence living standard. Contrary to common belief most heads of poor families do work; the predominant cause of working poverty is not seasonal or less than full-time work, but low wage rates. The number of families who do work and are still poor has shown the largest absolute increase since 1979. At the present only 40 percent of the jobs in the United States pay enough to support a family. Moreover, in the first quarter of 1988 weekly wages were 2.4 percent below those in 1980, and they continue to fall more than 1 percent per year.[34]

Second, unemployment is a chief cause of poverty. Although unemployment has dropped from a high of almost 11 percent in 1982 to less than 5.5 percent in 1990, this figure is misleading. It fails to reflect those who have given up looking for work, those who work part-time instead of full-time, and the massive shift from well-paid manufacturing jobs to low-paid service sector jobs. Kevin Phillips points out that

> by the summer of 1988, 45.3 percent of New York City residents over the age of sixteen could not be counted as labor force participants because of poverty, lack of skills, drug use, apathy or other problems. Similar circumstances were reported in Detroit and Baltimore, while the ratio of uncountables for the nation as a whole was 34.5 percent.[35]

The third cause of poverty in the United States today has to do with trends in the U.S. jobs structure.[36] New jobs being created by the present economy are either in high-skill occupations or in low-paying "service" occupations. Between 1979 and 1984 the number of industrial jobs (manufacturing, construction, mining) decreased by 2.4 million, while service industry jobs grew by 4 million. Today about 70 percent of all employees work in some kind of service industry, such as a hospital, an office, or a fast-food operation.[37] However, since 1968 two-thirds of all new jobs created have paid a wage of less than $13,600 per year. Fifteen percent of all manufacturing jobs existing in 1980 disappeared by 1990, putting three million more people into other jobs or unemployment. New growth jobs between 1984 and 1995 are projected to be concentrated in low-paying service areas. The economic outlook became bleaker after the 1981–82 recession when 53 percent of all interrupted jobs were not restored. After previous recessions only an average of 36 percent of jobs was permanently lost.

Lack of education is a fourth cause of poverty in this country.[38] Inadequate education leads to low earnings. People with minimal training find low-paying jobs that typically have less on-the-job training than do higher-paying positions. The United States has 60 million people who are at least functionally illiterate. Hispanics are the most poorly educated segment of society with a median of 10.8 years of school completed. A college diploma is becoming a necessity just to avoid falling out of the middle class. A significant problem is the low quality of primary and secondary education currently available to low-income families in large cities.

The final cause of poverty has been the changes in national government policies. Between 1981 and 1984 programs primarily serving the poor were cut $57 billion. Nearly one-third of the dollar amount of federal budget cutbacks between 1981 and 1984 came from programs serving the poor, even though such programs constituted less than 10 percent of the federal budget. It is estimated that 2 million people became poor due to changes in the federal budget at that time.[39] Between 1981 and 1988 spending in domestic areas dropped 22 percent on an inflation-adjusted basis. The worst cuts were in housing where subsidies decreased from $24.8 billion in 1981 to $7.7 billion in 1988—a cut of 77 percent! Moreover, new housing for the elderly was reduced by 43.5 percent from 1981 to 1988. Funds for job training decreased from $7.8 billion in 1981 to $3.8 billion in 1988—a 63 percent drop in inflation-adjusted terms. Grants to furnish funds to states to reduce poverty and assist various nutrition and community programs dropped from $525 million in 1981 to $382 million in 1988. Food stamps for the poor were available to 1.9 million fewer people in 1988 than in 1981 even though the number of poor increased during the same period of time. Medicare for the elderly has suffered cuts of $35.9 billion since 1981. Moreover, as the result of tightened eligibility rules for Medicaid, the number of people with no medical insurance has grown by one-third to 35 million people.

The Middle Class

There is also a trend of downward mobility for the middle class who more and more find themselves caught in a squeeze. Median family income was about $30,850 in 1988, almost exactly what it was fifteen years earlier once inflation is factored in.[40] However, today, for many families, it takes two jobs to get by. Since 1979 the incomes of married-couple families without a wage-earning wife declined by 4 percent. Hence, it is not surprising that in 1987 65 percent of all mothers, including 51 percent of those with infants under the age of one, were either holding jobs or looking for them. Many women work because they want to. However, an even larger number of mothers feel driven to take jobs by sheer economic necessity, though they would prefer to stay home and raise their children. Families hurting the worst are those headed by a person between 25 and 34 years old. Such families had 12 percent less income than such a family in 1973.[41]

The middle class especially feels the squeeze in the area of housing. Between 1980 and 1988 home ownership declined for the first time since 1940. The fall has been sharpest for young families.

In 1980, 21.3 percent of people under twenty-five owned their own homes. By 1987 that rate was down to 16.1 percent. Among those between twenty-five and twenty-nine the rate fell from 43.3 percent to 35.9 percent. For persons between thirty and thirty-four the decline was from 61.1 percent to 53.2 percent. And among those thirty-five to thirty-nine the drop was seven points—from 70.8 percent to 63.8 percent.[42]

The reason is that middle-class salaries fall far short of the inflation in housing costs. The average home buyer today has to save 50 percent of a full year's income just to make the down payment, as opposed to 33 percent in 1978.

The cost of a college education for the children is also getting farther out of reach for many middle-class families. According to the Senate Education Subcommittee, the full annual costs at a private college came to $12,924 a student in 1985. That represented approximately 40 percent of a median family's total income.[43] The annual costs for a public college were $5,823, or almost 20 percent of a median family's income. At the same time student loans have become harder to get. The significance of these facts becomes clear when one recognizes that in the early 1970s a thirty-year-old male college graduate could expect to earn at least 15 percent more than a thirty-year-old with a high school diploma. By 1986 the gap had grown to 49 percent. To remain in the middle class a college diploma has become essential.

New Stage of Industrial Capitalism

All this raises the question of what is creating all these problems? Ultimately the same drive for profit and security that operates on the international scene is at work also on the national scene.

It is important to realize that we have entered a new stage of industrial capitalism. Joe Holland and Peter Henriot speak of this stage as the stage of National Security Industrial Capitalism.[44] As they see it we are entering an era in which life will be quite grim on all levels because of changes in the areas of capital and technology.

The first change is that capital is becoming increasingly transnational—the networks and criteria for the movement of capital are no longer national but transnational. The dominant features of economic life are now the transnational corporations and the transnational bank. The impact of this change is brutal since it allows transnational capital to increase its control over national economies in a number of ways.

First, the conditions that allowed the national corporations to cooperate with labor (the unions) and bend before workers' demands no longer exist. The United States must compete with advanced industrial bases in Europe, Japan, the Third World, and the communist states. U.S. corporations will be undercut by their international competitors if they give in to labor. Second, global capital will flow where the return is greatest, and returns will be greatest where wages are restrained and taxes kept low. This circumstance gives a competitive advantage to those authoritarian states that repress their workers and provide few social services and is one cause of the crisis of democracy worldwide. Transnational capital outflanks national workers' movements so that if workers in one country develop a strong labor movement, capital simply moves elsewhere. However, transnational capital outflanks workers by not only geographic diversification, but also by industrial diversification. Because transnational conglomerates are highly diversified, with holdings in various industries, they can subsidize the losses from a labor strike in one industry with the profits from its other industries. As a result, they are no longer as vulnerable to labor's classical weapon, the strike.[45] Moreover, it is often difficult for labor to get a fair hearing, since the transnationals also dominate the media.

The other major change in this new stage of industrial capitalism is the even greater use of technology. Technological change has always been a reality in the U.S. economic experience. However, in recent decades the pace of such change has accelerated and the complexity of rapidly expanding technology has increased to the point that the most brilliant individual or committee cannot keep pace with all of it or comprehend it in all of its forms. While not denying the real values of such technology, one must also look to the human consequences of such development. Workers especially must constantly adapt to the changing demands of such technology or simply be left behind and marginalized. Those above all who are being marginalized by such technological advances are the aged, the minorities, and the uneducated. What is also significant about this technological development is that technology is becoming more capital-intensive, as it uses less labor in relation to capital. In other words, industry is using more machinery, computers, and energy, and less of society's labor supply since this makes for more efficient and cheaper production. Not to move in this direction would mean the loss of the competitive edge that a nation needs to compete on the international scene.

One impact of these technological developments on labor is "structural unemployment" or permanent "marginalization" from the main economy. Another consequence of this phenomenon in the United States has been plant closings and capital flight. Capital flight involves corporations simply packing up and moving their operation from a particular area to an area where cheaper labor is available. This normally happens without any consultation with the people involved and no real regard for their future. Whole areas of the country (Appalachia), cities (Youngstown), and neighborhoods (South Bronx) have been sloughed off in this process for the sake of better profits. Another consequence is the development of a permanent underclass in United States society, a class that will never enter the mainstream of productive life in contemporary society.

The use of these new technologies has also had a very harmful impact upon the environment. In fact it is the production technologies that began after World War II and brought about a massive transformation in agriculture, transportation, and power production that are responsible for the high levels of environmental pollution that we experience today. As Barry Commoner points out, this technological transformation for the most part did not produce different kinds of goods, it only introduced a new way to produce the goods.[46]

> Before 1950 crops were grown without chemical nitrogen fertilizer or synthetic pesticides; now these chemicals have become a major element in crop production. Before 1950 American cars were small and driven by low-compression engines; now they are larger, heavier, with higher engine compression ratios. Before 1950 beer and soda were sold in reusable bottles; now they are sold in containers that are used once and then converted into trash. Before 1950 cleansers were made of soap; now over 85 percent are synthetic detergents. . . . Before 1950 all these goods were shipped from farm and factory to distant cities by rail; now highway trucks have taken over most freight hauling. Before 1950 meat was wrapped in paper and taken home in a paper bag; now it is encased in plastic and carried home in a plastic bag. Before 1950 college cafeterias and fast-food restaurants used washable plates and utensils; now everything is "disposable," which means that used once, it becomes trash.[47]

At the present time the United States is having difficulties adapting to this new stage of industrial capitalism.[48] A very significant problem in this regard has been the failure of American industry to invest in enough modern capital equipment to stay abreast of its international competitors. There are several reasons for this failure. First, Americans concentrate too much on short-term profits whereas European and Japanese managers think in terms of long-range growth. In the area of steel, for example, U.S. steel companies trail the entire world in converting their steel plants into continuous casting. This is at least partly due to the steel companies using their profits to acquire businesses in other areas, for the sake of short-term profit, while foreign competitors have been plowing their earnings back into steel. While leveraged buyouts and corporate restructuring over the last several years have made a few people a lot of money, mergers do not create new assets and have not contributed to the long-range growth of the United States economy. It is the same short-term profit motive that has also been responsible for the introduction and retaining of the modern production technologies in spite of their known, harmful impact on the environment.[49]

Another reason for this failure of United States industry to invest in modern capital equipment has been the lack of available capital. This is partly due to the fact that Americans typically save only 5 percent of their income whereas West German families save about 15 percent of their income and the Japanese save about 20 percent. Even when corporate savings are included, in the United States only about one seventh of all income is available to replace old capital and to form new capital. In West Germany and Japan, the availability of total savings is about one and a half to two times as great as ours.[50]

Another reason for the inability of the United States to keep up with its foreign competitors in this new age of industrial capitalism has been the lack of effective business-government coordination. In Japan, certainly, and in a lesser fashion in some Western European nations, one finds today close coordination between the activities of government, the big banks, and the largest corporations. Such coordinated effort does not exist in the United States due to the suspicion of Americans of government regulation and involvement in the "marketplace." The rapid move toward deregulation (fewer governmental restraints on economic activity) in the 1980s reflects that suspicion. However, it has now become clear that the pace and extent of this move toward deregulation has raised safety issues in such areas as the airline industry, and favored prosperous individuals and financial institutions. Such deregulation has also contributed significantly to the horrendous savings and loan crisis.[51] The new global setting for industry demands greater coordination and cooperation between business and government.

As Benjamin Friedman points out, America is not investing in its infrastructure or in education any more than in business capital formation in the conventional sense.[52] In the 1980s, the share of federal spending, outside of defense, in such projects as interstate highways, airports and harbors, research laboratories, weather stations or information transfer facilities has fallen to 1.2 percent. This is the lowest since World War II. The decline has been even more substantial at the state and local level of government. Hence, spending on elementary and secondary education has fallen from a high of 4.4 percent of the nation's total income to 4 percent in the 1980s.

Consequences

Many other consequences flow from the transitions going on in industrial capitalism and put in context much of what is happening in U.S. society today. There is a shift from upward mobility to downward mobility for most of the population together with a loss of the possibility of achieving the American Dream. Central to this shift is a condition of permanent inflation that is rooted in increased military spending,[53] the high cost of present technologies in the basic needs areas (such as food, housing, medicine, and health care), price fixing by the transnational corporations, and restraints on the growth of the public service area.

A second consequence is seen in the recent tax cuts and the cutbacks in the social welfare programs pointed out earlier. Cutbacks in the social welfare programs are a consequence of the tax cuts. These tax cuts had a primary purpose of making U.S. industry more competitive in the world market by lowering their tax burden. As the result of 1986 legislation, the corporations are only required to pay a minimum of 15 percent and a maximum of 34 percent on corporate profits. Also, 1986 legislation lowered top-scale individual tax rates to 28 percent and 33 percent. Previous to 1971 these rates were 70 percent! According to a Congressional Budget Office study, only the top 10 percent of the population received a significant net tax cut between 1977 and 1988. Most of the other 90 percent of the population, because of increases in the Social Security tax, paid a higher share of their incomes in taxes. At the extremes, the richest 1 percent got a net tax savings of 25 percent; the poorest tenth of workers saw 20 percent more of their incomes swallowed by taxes. Moreover, the surge in savings that was supposed to flow from these tax cuts—savings that would be available for development of new industrial capital—did not materialize.

A third consequence has been the calm acceptance of a normal unemployment rate that, at times, may be as high as 6 or 7 percent. This is part of the structured unemployment spoken of above. It also results from a deliberate decision to solve the inflation problem. Keeping inflation under control demands that a certain fraction of the labor force be unemployed. This is achieved through restrictive monetary and fiscal policies. A significant unemployment rate also makes for a more controllable work force. When a nation moves toward full employment its labor force may become more militant, since people are not afraid of being fired for their activities when other jobs are available. However, when jobs are not as plentiful, labor is more willing to give in to industry's demands. Also, one of the things that attracts investment capital is a controlled labor force.

A fourth consequence has been the failure of the government to deal effectively with the environmental issues. Undeniably the only effective way to deal with pollution is to prevent it by dealing with its root causes rather than by attempting to control it.[54] However, corporate America has been unwilling to change its production technologies that are the primary cause of the present excessive pollution levels. Corporate America has also been able to pressure the federal government out of imposing significant preventive measures. As a result our response to the pollution problem has been to spend billions of dollars on basically ineffective control strategies. Real change will come only when it is seen that pollution is not cost-effective.

An added issue that helps us understand what is happening in the U.S. economy today is the development in major urban areas of what is known as FIRE—*F*inance, *I*nsurance, *R*eal *E*state. As heavy industry has moved out of the United States, the urban areas have turned to finance, insurance, and real estate as the basis of their economy. The centers of large urban areas doing well today are filled with banks, insurance companies, and real estate concerns. Around them are being built condominiums to house the executives. The support system for FIRE is composed of the middle-class people who live in the suburbs. Formerly, they were involved in heavy industry as professionals and support personnel; now they must travel into the center of the city each day. They are not organized and wages are kept low. They are part of the growing service industry in the United States today and unless circumstances change radically they will become a whole new class of poor. All this, of course, is part of the fallout from the increased use of technology and the need for cheap labor in order to be competitive in the world market.

Another side to this is the claim of Naisbitt and Aburdene that we are about to enter an era of full employment.[55] This is because the new economy flowing from the microelectronic revolution is creating millions of new jobs, and the number of people entering the work force is declining dramatically.

This should make the job market a sellers' market and work to the advantage of women, older people, and the poor and disadvantaged.

However, important issues will be the ability of such people to organize and the level of wages that the new economy will be allowed to pay. Before the underclass will be able to benefit from this development, something drastic must be done about the quality of public education to prepare these people for this opportunity.

At the present the most immediate threat to U.S. prosperity is the huge federal budget deficit. When the federal government spends more than can be paid for by taxes, it must borrow the difference through Treasury bonds. These bonds are the safest credit instrument available, and the Treasury will price the bonds at whatever levels are required to sell them. As a result the federal government always gets first crack at the nation's savings. All other borrowers—states and localities, businesses, households—will have second crack at these savings and if the total demand for all savings is greater than the supply of savings, then those other borrowers may be "crowded out." Moreover, the interest rates on what funds are available will be high.

With the continuous high federal deficits of the 1980s, roughly two-thirds of the total net new capital available for investment in the United States is currently being used to finance the federal budget deficit. One result of this has been to raise the cost of capital for private purposes and so inhibit the capital growth of businesses. However, such expansion is needed for greater long-term production growth and higher income levels and employment. Moreover, the country was saved from the possibility of "crowding out" in the 1980s only because foreign investors bought up a considerable amount of Treasury bonds. As a result, for the first time in this century, the nation's debt is no longer merely an internal obligation, as a significant part of the federal debt is owed to foreigners. In fact, over the decade of the 1980s the United States went from being the world's largest creditor nation to being the world's largest debtor nation. As of January 1989, the indebtedness of the United States to foreigners came to approximately $500 billion. Related to this development has been the increase in foreign direct investment in United States corporations and real estate. Such direct investment has risen from $83 billion in 1980 to $304 billion in 1988. Moreover, as of 1988, foreigners owned 12 percent of America's manufacturing base and nearly 20 percent of bank assets in the United States.[56]

The major ramification of the above developments is that our children will have to accept a lower standard of living. This is due to several factors. First, a portion of American wealth will have to be transferred to non-Americans to service the foreign-owed debt.[57] In addition, a significant amount of the profits generated by foreign-owned firms will be sent home from the United States to the parent company. Our ability to compete successfully in foreign markets will be hindered by our failure to have invested in enough modern capital equipment to stay abreast of our international competitors. The reality is that in terms of international purchasing power, the United States even now is only the ninth wealthiest country in terms of per capita GNP.[58] While this situation will mean more austerity—especially for the middle class and working class—the poor will suffer the most from this situation. The bailout of the savings and loan industry, now projected to cost from $500 billion to $1 trillion dollars over the next thirty to forty years, will make circumstances even worse.[59]

Closely related to the deficit problem is the need to reduce the balance of payments deficit and increase trade without resorting to an inappropriate and potentially even more explosive protectionism. While this issue, like all the issues surrounding the U.S. economy today, is complex, it is very clear that solutions to these problems will force Americans to address squarely their own consumerism and desire for economic success.

What we are witnessing in the United States is the end of the golden era of continuous economic growth. This growth was the cornucopia from which came the material abundance to satisfy the rising expectations of all classes of Americans. With this growth severely constrained not only diminished expectations but also fears of disentitlement are occurring. As a result those who have are attempting to protect the privileges and powers they have achieved. Those who seek for more justice can only take from those who already have. Those who have seek more emphasis on law and order and the development of the mechanisms of social control over the oppressed such as the police, the military, and the power of the state.[60]

Part of the difficulty in dealing with these problems in a healthy way as a country is the absence of any national consensus on what tradeoffs should be acceptable to achieve justice and economic stability.

In spite of the many problems that face the U.S. economy today, and so also the world economy, it is amazing how persistent the American Dream is in the consciousness of Americans who are unwilling to give it up and accept the realities of the present context. To a great extent this is because of the absurd promises and posturing of national politicians regarding the American Dream. Instead of holding out unreal promises to gain election, they need to honestly face the issues and what will be involved in dealing with them. They should then begin to create a vision and consensus among the people for putting into place the necessary measures for coping with the problems.

Arms Race

In connection with the issue of the economy it is important to say a few words regarding the economic impact of the arms race. As noted earlier, U.S. foreign policy has gone through a series of changes since World War II. The policy for the 1980s was a policy of deterrence based on a balance of power—if not actual supremacy—in relationship to the Soviet Union. This policy led, over the last decade, to an attempt to regain nuclear supremacy and an arms buildup of both nuclear and conventional weapons, tactical as well as defensive. A recent thawing in relations between the United States and the Soviet Union has led to an agreement on the mutual destruction of some nuclear weapons, as well as proposals for further cutbacks of both conventional and nuclear arms, and proposals for significant cutbacks in the overall defense budget. This trend hopefully will continue but whether it will is not yet clear.

The amount of money allotted for military purposes in the United States alone is staggering, around $300 billion a year. The amount that is spent solely on arms on a worldwide basis comes to around $550 billion a year. This is an amount equal to the annual income of the 4 billion people who make up the poorer half of the world's population. It is estimated that 400 nuclear warheads would constitute a more than adequate deterrence capability for the United States. In 1988 the United States had well over 20,000 such warheads and was heading toward 30,000 by the year 1990. The United States also had at least 22,000 tactical nuclear weapons designed for use in conventional wars.

The economic impact of this arms race, especially on the poor, is staggering. As President Eisenhower already said in 1953: "Every gun that is made, every warship launched, every rocket fired signify, in the final sense, a theft from those who hunger and are not fed, those who are cold and are not clothed." In sheer tonnage there is more explosive material on earth than there is food. The world has been spending money to prepare for war at the rate of one million dollars every minute. Four hours of such spending could eradicate malaria from the earth; less than ten hours of such spending would solve the entire world's hunger problem. In 1985 the United States budgeted more than twenty times as much for defense as for foreign assistance. Nearly two-thirds of the foreign assistance offered by the United States took the form of military assistance (including subsidized arms sales) or went to countries because of their perceived strategic value to the United States. Here at home one need not stretch the imagination too far to realize how even a fraction of the money spent on arms could relieve the present housing shortage and provide the monies for needed improvements in the education of our young people. One hopes that the so-called "peace dividend" promised from cutbacks in the defense budget in this period of lessened tensions will be spent to deal with such human needs.

It is not only the poor in our society who are affected by the arms race. The entire U.S. society is affected. Huge military spending has contributed significantly to both the national debt and continuing inflation. Monies that go into arms do not return to the mainstream of the economy as a good to be consumed that bolsters the economy. This loss in turn demands a policy of structured unemployment so that inflation is kept in check. Moreover, we have found that we cannot afford both "guns and butter" in our society. Hence, paralleling the significant buildup in defense spending over the last decade was a concomitant drastic cutback on the amount spent on human resources. Whereas the amount spent on human resources (excluding Social Security and Medicare) declined from 28 percent to 22 percent of all federal outlays between 1980 and 1987, the amount spent on defense went up from 23 percent to 28 percent.[61] One final impact of the arms race is that it consumes some of the finest talent in the United States.[62] Engineers and scientists who could be working at building a vibrant economy and developing technology for the benefit of the human race are instead involved in developing and building instruments of destruction.

It is important to keep in mind that simply doing away with nuclear arms will not relieve the economic condition in the United States and the rest of the world. In fact, it will worsen it unless nations learn to trust one another. The point is that the superpowers have depended so heavily upon nuclear weapons in their policy of deterrence because this is the cheapest way to go. As one economist puts it "nuclear arms provide a large bang for the bucks."[63] To get the same power of deterrence from conventional arms would require an even larger defense budget. The issue is much larger than just a consideration of nuclear weapons. A context in which nations can trust one another and therefore not feel the need to have such strong deterrent power is necessary. This demands a conversion not only of political leaders but of the people themselves. Present developments in the world hopefully will bring all peoples closer to such a conversion.

System of Corporate Industry

It is important to be aware of the impact on American values and constitutional order of the system of corporate industry that has grown up in the last century. The issue here is power, the power that large-scale business corporations have today on the economic, political, and social levels of American society.

If one looks only at the industrial sector of the American economy, over 200,000 manufacturing firms will be found operating in the United States today. However, only 500 of these firms account for 80 percent of the nation's industrial profits, 80 percent of its industrial assets, and 80 percent of all industrial employees. If all sectors of the economy are considered, one can count about 2.5 million companies in the United States. Again, however, the 500 largest of these have sales equal to about 80 percent of the United States gross national product; they employ about 20 million people and have assets valued at about $4 trillion. It is clear, then, that the bulk of the economy is under the private control of a relatively small number of corporations.

These relatively few corporations have massive dimensions. For example, Exxon had sales in 1982 of close to $100 billion. The budgets of only eight nations in the world are larger than this! In the same year, General Motors employed about 700,000 people. Only thirty nations had more people involved in manufacturing. The 500 major American corporations each have annual revenues of over $1 billion and almost all of them operate all over the globe, often overshadowing the economies of the host countries.[64]

The giant corporation, then, is an intrinsic and all-pervasive component of developed contemporary economies. Because they are so large, the giant corporations have widespread effects on their natural and social environments. These effects range from the crippling layoffs and pollution of the environment to influences on the political system and social structures of society.

Looked at in itself, the giant corporation is the necessary concomitant to the phenomenal productivity of modern societies. Moreover, as Velasquez points out, "the corporate organization is thus the institution through which modern man and woman continuously and abundantly respond to the command of God to be productive; to produce from the earth's resources the goods that can meet human needs, the goods that feed, clothe, house, culture, transport and promote health."[65] At the same time, however, the very size and division of labor that enable the corporation to multiply its productivity are also the bases of its tendency to waste resources, to continue to use environmentally harmful technologies, to produce socially useless commodities, and to take little account of worker frustration, job satisfaction, worker safety, worker autonomy, or work variety.

The giant corporation wields significant power both externally on society and internally on its workers. In exercising this power the corporation often fails grievously by affecting the right to self-determination of people in the broader society as well as of its workers. In doing so they undermine essential American values and constitutional order.[66]

The founders of our country believed strongly that private productive property was the essential economic base for a free citizenry. If citizens were going to be equal and free to express their own opinion then they must be economically independent. It was this thinking that led to the constitutional guarantee of the right to property. However, from a nation of individual property holders the United States has become a nation of wage earners, dependent on vast institutional structures that the people do not control. Today 60 percent of the ownership of the means of production is concentrated in the hands of 1 percent of the population. With the decline of private property has come a great concentration of political power in corporate hands, a power not easily brought to account by any form of democratic process. Decisions that in their general implications are profoundly political are made based on economic considerations and decided by the balance of private economic power. Private profit outweighs public order and public good. Moreover, the present economy can only survive through constant expansion. But, as Robert Bellah says, "how many more belts of uncontrollable economic expansion will we be able to absorb before the social and ecological consequences totally undermine our democratic society?"[67]

Nor is it possible to overlook what the present form of the economy is doing to public morals. Every religion and philosophy known to the human race denies that happiness is attained by limitless material acquisition. Yet this message is preached incessantly on every American television set. Few societies could imagine themselves surviving very long if one of their central institutions advocated unrestrained greed.

We have become accustomed to think of the economic realm as autonomous and subject to no external controls but the pressures of the marketplace, "the Invisible Hand" of Adam Smith. However, it is important to understand that today the freedom of the "free market" is significantly restrained, not by government, but by the market power of the large industrial corporations. Monopoly and oligopoly in almost all areas of manufacturing, retail trade, and financial services occur more and more often. This is especially true with the giant mergers that have been taking place over the last few years. Whatever the cause of all this, the welfare of the society is at great risk. It is important to realize that the economic realm is not autonomous; it also comes under the realm of God and must be understood in the light of higher values than those of self-interest, profit, or efficiency. Economic decisions must also be made in light of ethical criteria and be subject to the values and ideals that stand behind the establishment of our country, to say nothing of justice and charity.

POLITICAL CONTEXT

The political mood in the United States during the decade of the 1980s had a decidedly conservative stance due to a breakdown of consensus among the people on the direction of U.S. society. The geographical and economic frontiers of U.S. society have been closed and no longer allow a continually expanding society; large bureaucratic structures and growing centralization have undercut small, self-sufficient communities; and deep divisions based on race, sex, and class run through the citizenry with a concomitant breakdown of consensus. In this kind of context, says Peter Henriot, "the liberalism of expansive pluralist competition gives way to the conservatism of limits, cautions and retreats, especially in the areas of social welfare and governmental action."[68] As Robert Bellah has pointed out, "If the culture of individualism has difficulty coming to terms with genuine cultural or social differences, it has even more difficulty coming to terms with large impersonal organizations and institutions."[69] It is not surprising then that Americans have real difficulty piecing together a picture of the whole society and how they relate to it. Nor is it surprising that they lack a way of making moral sense of significant cultural, social, and economic differences between groups as well as a means for evaluating the different claims such groups make.[70]

At a time of enormous expansion of government programs and functions, especially since World War II, there has been a significant decline in popular political activity. While in the 1960 presidential election 62.8 percent of the eligible voters actually voted, in 1980 only 52.3 percent of the voters voted and in 1988 only 50 percent voted. The turnout in nonpresidential year elections has been significantly lower. Moreover, blacks and Hispanics do not exercise an influence comparable to their numbers. Those who do vote are disproportionately the rich and upper middle class. The diminution in voter participation may be caused by a cynical perception that government and politics are not oriented to the best interests of the people and so voting is seen to lack any real import.[71] As a result those who have been making ballot-box decisions are those who have been profiting from the present economic situation. In this "politics of interest," as Bellah calls it, in which politics means the pursuit of different interests according to agreed-upon neutral rules, politics is often seen as a kind of necessary evil.[72] Since one enters this "politics of interest" for reasons of utility—to get what one or one's group wants—it is viewed by many as not entirely legitimate. This perspective is strengthened by watching powerful special interest groups exert significant influence in the political arena; thus political power tends to mirror economic power. Decisions that are profoundly political in their general implications are based on economic considerations and decided by the balance of private economic power.

As Henriot points out, "In the face of corporate power centers, counterbalancing citizen groups have not been particularly strong."[73] This is due to "single-issue" politics, economic constraints, and the fact that the ordinary citizen feels lost in the face of modern technical issues such as nuclear power and environmental standards. Moreover, geographic mobility with a consequent lack of rootedness affects people's willingness to get involved in a community in order to effect change.[74] Henriot finds signs of hope in the efforts of community organizations and in the building of a few national movements such as Common Cause, Network, Bread for the World, and so forth.

John Naisbitt sees things from a different perspective.[75] He agrees that people are not voting because they do not put much stock in either political office or the people filling it, especially on the national level. At the same time, however, this represents no lack of interest in political issues. Indeed, a transition from representative democracy to participatory democracy is occurring. The people, better educated than ever before and as knowledgeable as their elected representatives on local issues, are deciding for themselves on issues that directly relate to their lives by voting through local initiatives and referenda. Naisbitt sees this as a movement bubbling up from the bottom that will eventually affect national politics also. For the present, however, it reflects an attitude that local issues are more important and that they should be decided directly by a vote of the people rather than by elected representatives.

From Bellah's perspective, administrative centralization is now an integral part of American life and will stay that way. We cannot, then, simply write off "big government" as the enemy.[76] While its powers should be reduced where appropriate and its authority decentralized as far as practical, for the future, the spirit of centralized administration needs to be transformed. Concomitant with this transformation there is needed a strengthening of those associations and movements through which citizens influence and moderate the power of the government. This strengthening is needed because when new visions have appeared in the United States, they have assumed the form of social movements that have taken their life from organizations, movements, and coalitions responsive to particular historical situations.

The move toward a more conservative stance in U.S. politics has provided the context in which the "New Right" has gained significant power and influence. The "New Right" evolved out of frustration with the inflation that followed Vietnam and the emergence of the OPEC petroleum cartel, a desire to return to traditional economic and cultural behavior, and a fatigue with overexpanded government.[77] This movement is a well-financed and well-organized group that has attempted to form a close alliance with certain Christian fundamentalists. It has built a strong constituency by catering to people's fears rather than focusing on the deep structural causes of people's anxiety. It promises to provide law and order, to defend the family, and to restore the American Dream. However, through its attacks on social welfare programs, labor unions, rights movements, regulations on business, and its support for hard-line foreign policies and expanded military spending, it is in reality undermining the values it is supposed to stand for. As Henriot observes, "By catering to fear, the New Right hopes to drive a strategic wedge between the middle class on one side, and labor unions and the poor on the other. Labor unions and the poor are being used as scapegoats for the social problems that are threatening the security of the middle class."[78]

Many people have been attracted to the message of the New Right. They are frightened that they will not be able to hold on to the American Dream in the midst of a changing economical environment. They are tempted to seize whatever means seems to preserve their present way of life, even if this is at the expense of those poorer than themselves. They often see the preservation of their present way of life as connected to the United States reasserting itself as the number one country in the world, and so they are willing to support the government taking stronger, belligerent stands and continuing a frightening arms buildup. For the sake of the arms buildup they are even willing to accept cutbacks in welfare programs and aid to the poor and the removal of government restraints and controls on the development of corporations.

However, a change seems to be taking place in the national attitude as we enter the 1990s.[79] The middle class is beginning to awaken to the fact that over the past decade, while the rich were becoming even richer, their own standard of living was often slipping significantly. People are now seeing poverty, hunger, and homelessness as the nation's most serious problems after drugs.[80] We need leaders who will have the courage to speak out candidly on the significant issues facing our country today. They must also be able to present a vision that considers the changing world in which we live and which can give people a sense of meaning and direction as a nation.

It is impossible to leave this political context without a word on the Watergate and Iran-Contra scandals and what they say about our present reality. Both of these scandals seriously threatened the Constitution. They also exposed another layer of government in the executive branch that Bill Moyers has called "The Secret Government" and one which the American people have not chosen.[81] These scandals arose out of a contempt for the law, the truth, the Congress, and the God-given rights of people, because those in the executive branch wanted things done their way and wished no outside interference. National security, as defined unilaterally by the executive branch, came to outweigh the balance of powers among the three branches of the United States government and the rights of individuals.

This concern for national security went so far that one president established a secret police operation in the basement of the White House, whose agents would bypass regular governmental, investigatory agencies and would break the law to achieve their goals. In another administration the executive branch was involved in matters that Congress had forbidden and then misled Congress regarding what was going on while also selling arms to terrorists. In the process many innocent lives were taken.

What has happened, suggests Moyers, is that the powers claimed by presidents in the name of national security have become the controlling wheel of government, driving everything else.[82] The frightening thing is that so many people saw nothing wrong in all this. Some even attempted to make the main agent of this secret government in the Iran/Contra deal a popular hero. The minority report from the congressional investigation of the Iran/Contra scandal dismissed everything as "mistakes in judgment" and called for increasing both secrecy and the power of the president. In this way debate, dissent, and scrutiny would be ruled out. Moyers adds,

Meanwhile, the public—that vast part of the public that no longer expects much from the political process anyway—grows more indifferent and cynical, while the highly vocal partisans, deluded by ideology and frustrated by democracy, scream for more of what has already led to unqualified disaster.[83]

MICROELECTRONIC REVOLUTION

Finally, something should be said about the impact of the microelectronic revolution on U.S. society. We already spoke of the impact of this revolution on the global level (chapter 2); so our concern here is to discuss its impact specifically on U.S. society. This area is so vast and complex that it is impossible to deal with all the issues involved. We will limit ourselves to a few generalizations.

Television and computers are two examples of the microelectronic revolution that most immediately affect the greatest number of people. Television began as a significant transmitter of electronic information soon after World War II. It is now found everywhere and allows people to be immediately connected to any part of their own country or to almost any place on the globe where there is a receiver. Its impact on society has been immense. Today television is one of the primary means by which electronic information is transmitted and it influences culture, social norms, and the expectations of people. Moreover, it provides a means by which a few can influence the masses, for good or ill.

As a primary source of communication within society it shapes peoples' perceptions and understanding of reality.[84] Like all communication, it tends to support existing institutions by uncritically passing on the assumptions and consensus of society. At the same time it has the ability to present a set of values, beliefs, and assumptions as common to society, whether that is or is not the case. This "persuasion by appearance" can become a powerful force for change and for developing a common culture. It also fosters a high mobility among people, since it allows one to encounter the same common culture wherever one travels.

The news presentations on television have a significant impact on the way people perceive reality. They do this by the way they must simplify complex issues into two-minute time slots. People accustomed to this kind of message no longer want to face complexity but prefer labels and summaries. Television, along with radio, also heightens people's sense of immediacy through live coverage but avoids in-depth reporting and facilitates a rapid shift of attention with its series of two-minute presentations. It also contributes to a sort of "loose listening" through constant repetition and instant replays. Because of its ability to create a synthetic reality, events are not real to many people unless they are reported or pictured. All this affects the way politicians, leaders, and industry communicate with the masses and allows them to have a substantial impact through the medium of the television set.

Computers have become part of almost every aspect of U.S. society from space and military equipment to health care, banking, factories, grocery stores, nuclear reactors, air traffic controllers, the office, and the home. U.S. society has become more and more dependent upon the computer and the ability to transfer information rapidly back and forth between computers. As a result American society is very vulnerable to any serious disruption of such information management as a result of war, natural catastrophe, or intentional sabotage. The computer enables the mind to do things it could not otherwise do. It also creates a growing sense of remoteness in society as the worker is pulled back and loses touch with the results of his or her efforts. This condition can also develop a lack of accountability by the worker for whatever her or his efforts contribute to producing. People may see only a dial or screen and have little understanding of the results of their efforts. Moreover, the fewer people who now have access to more and more information have more power. There has been such a shift in the power base that even the most powerful must depend upon the computer technician. The computer also contributes to the development of larger, more complex, more capital-intensive systems, such as industry, government, or the military, within society.[85]

The microelectronic revolution is having a significant impact upon the business environment in American society.[86] We have moved from a situation where most people worked to produce goods to a situation in which most people work with information.[87] Today over 65 percent of the people in the marketplace are involved in creating, processing, and distributing information. John Naisbitt contends that, as a result, there is now a shift from financial capital to human capital.[88] While the strategic resource in the industrial era was financial capital, in the new era—which he speaks of as the information era—the strategic resources are information, knowledge, creativity. However, the only way that the corporation can gain access to these valuable commodities is through the people in whom these resources reside. Therefore, it is important for corporations to foster the personal growth and development of its employees and to give them a voice in determining how the corporations will achieve their goals. Naisbitt also points out that as a result of the computer there is beginning a tremendous whittling away of middle management. The computer is replacing line managers who had the role of collecting, processing, and passing on information. The computer now gives top management immediate access to information previously obtained from middle managers.[89]

Naisbitt also claims that high technology will lead to people wanting to be with other people more (high tech/high touch) as a way of compensating for the impersonalism of increased technology.[90] This is the reason, as he sees it, for the popularity of the human potential movement. He says, "Our response to the high tech all around us was the evolution of a highly personal value system to compensate for the impersonal nature of technology. The result was the new self-help or personal growth movement, which eventually became the human potential movement." This fits in with the trend toward expressive individualism that was noted earlier.

In connection with the microelectronic revolution it is also important to be aware of the developments in biotechnology. As Naisbitt points out, the next twenty years will be the age of biology in the way the last twenty years spanned the age of microelectronics.[91] With recent developments in biotechnology there will be a growing capacity for human beings to master themselves technologically through such means as *in vitro* fertilization, cloning, increasing of the life span, chimeras (human/plant or human/animal hybrids), and cyborgs (the mating of the human brain with a machine body). This biotechnology revolution will also make available new drugs; enzymes that will produce more powerful chemical reactions and the ability to synthesize expensive natural products; new high-yield, disease-resistant, self-fertilizing crops; and substances to replace oil, coal, and other raw materials. The implications of these possibilities are beyond imagination at the present. However, they present a formidable challenge to society and call for norms to govern such developments.[92]

ANALYSIS

History

As we look at the United States of today we can see that certain past events have left their imprint on the nation and make us who we are. First, there was the American Revolution and its ideals of freedom, justice, equality, independence, inalienable rights, and government of the people, by the people, and for the people. Though perhaps the ideals behind the Declaration of Independence and the Bill of Rights and the Fourteenth Amendment to the Constitution, which guarantees all citizens equal protection of the laws, have not yet been fully implemented, these ideals have set the direction for much that has happened in this country and remain alive in some form in most people.

The Civil War was another pivotal point in the country's history. At war's end the great industrial expansion of the United States began. One of the victims of this expansion was the public virtue so important to the founders of our country; public virtue gave way to utilitarian individualism as economic success became the primary value in the lives of so many. With the loss of public virtue the sense of a common good also began to erode. From a social perspective, while the Civil War brought an end to the institution of slavery, it did not deal with the deeper issues of segregation, discrimination, and prejudice, which remained very much alive and in many ways unchallenged.

World War II gave birth to nuclear weapons and to the horror of living under the constant threat of nuclear extinction. The technological breakthroughs made during the war foreshadowed the staggering technological developments that have taken place since then as well as many of the ecological problems we now face. The immediate aftermath of the war gave birth to the national security state in the United States with the creation of the "secret government" and an overriding concern with national security. Out of the shambles of that war were also born the basic global economic structures that exist today.

As the nation entered the 1970s it began to experience the end of the continuous economic growth that had characterized it from the beginning. Our economic and political interdependence with all other nations also began to sink into national consciousness. Along with the social movements in the 1960s, the Vietnam War, and Watergate, there was a breakdown within our society of a consensus on the direction our country should take. With this breakdown there emerged a cynicism regarding government, especially the federal government, and its care for the people, and the New Right came into its own. Finally, the Reagan era of the 1980s witnessed a growing disparity between the rich and the poor as well as an alarming increase in the national debt and balance of trade deficit. At the same time there have been sweeping cutbacks in social welfare programs and the concomitant impact of these developments on everyone, especially the poor.

Values

When one looks at the values that are important in American society, the continuing impact of the religious values of the original colonists— though often in a corrupted form—is obvious. The myth of Americans as a chosen people with whom the Lord made a covenant and who crossed the sea to enter the promised land still influences us. Out of this myth has come Americans' sense of themselves as chosen ones with a manifest destiny to spread their way of life to the rest of the world. The sense of being "the saved" has also led the white person in the United States to fail to take the Native American and the Black on their own terms and to look down on anyone who has a different colored skin, different language, customs, or beliefs. The myths behind our civil religion have inspired much good in American history. However, ripped from their biblical and republican roots, these myths have also been responsible for much of which the country must be ashamed. The association of wealth and success with salvation lead many to look down on the poor and to see them as responsible for their own plight—when all the evidence points elsewhere.

The individualism that accompanied the philosophies of the Enlightenment has now become predominant within U.S. society. As a result each individual strives to become his or her own person, free of all restraints from the past and the present with success and worth equated with economic success. This individualism has been at least partly responsible for keeping before us as a people the sense of the dignity and sacredness of the individual. It has also inspired the struggle for individual rights and autonomy. However, because it has also been responsible for the continuing breakdown of the sense of a common good and of values that transcend the individual, it is difficult today for us to see ourselves as a people with common goals and aspirations.

A root metaphor that governs U.S. culture, like other capitalist societies, is the marketplace.[93] As a result the economic domain dominates the other domains of our society, such as the religious, social, political, and so forth. Life is seen as a race, a struggle in the marketplace, and success results from success in this arena. Economic codes of efficiency, maximal utilization of capital, and progress also influence the other domains.

National security has become almost a god as the United States finds itself caught in a web of international interdependency, and its lifestyle and standard of living are called into question by developing countries. In the midst of everything the American Dream remains a real hope for many, even though the evidence shows that they will never be able to achieve it.

Finally, as Coleman points out, we have never really abandoned "the essential postulate of eighteenth-century political science, i.e., the belief that political problems are best solved by technology and instrumental means rather than by education to virtue, communal self-sacrifice and restraint and a love for the substantively good society."[94]

Structures

The political structures underlying the present reality are controlled by concerns for economic prosperity and national security. Real political power is passing more and more into the hands of giant corporations and the secret government. Those who have political responsibility, meanwhile, are people who are long on technological expertise but short on vision in terms of who we are and who we should be as a people.

Concerning economic structures it is difficult to tell if the capitalist system is hitting its stride or suffering the breakdown foreseen by Marx. Basically the economy is controlled by national and international agencies working with the transnational corporations and banks of the First World. The ownership of the means of production is concentrated in the hands of a few. This situation confers immense power on a few and powerlessness on most. In the United States the economic evolution over the last several decades sparked the loss of heavy manufacturing and a turning to capital-intensive technologies and FIRE. This has led to the loss of many well-paying manufacturing jobs and an increase in low-paying, unorganized, service sector jobs together with structural unemployment and the development of a permanent underclass. The country is also experiencing a system of permanent inflation rooted in increased military spending, the high cost of present technologies in basic needs areas, and price fixing by the transnationals.

Sociologically, while the grip of the white, Anglo-Saxon Protestants on the social structures of the country has been broken, their values and myths continue to influence the white society. Racism, discrimination, and prejudice feed a deep structure within society and give rise to some of the most potent political and social issues of the day. As a result of individualism, the larger society is left to look after itself by a people who have turned cynical and are concerned with their "lifestyle enclaves."

The Future

At the present time the United States lacks a national vision that fully integrates it into the global reality and that would help the country to deal in a just way with the issues that confront it. The visions that do exist are too caught up in a concern for profit and national security. Such a situation does not speak well for the future. Lacking a sense of a common good and a vision of what a just distribution of goods in society should look like, the future will witness an even greater neglect of the plight of the poor, the helpless, and the oppressed. If the United States continues on the same path it now treads, the chasm between the rich and the poor in the United States itself will continue to widen. The numbers of those who are poor will witness a significant increase from the ranks of the middle class. However, even more important on a global level, the United States, as it becomes ever more preoccupied with itself, will pay even less attention to the developing countries and their needs. If budget deficits and balance of trade deficits are not dealt with soon, there is a danger that the U.S. and global economic systems could come tumbling down. Also, if the environmental issues are not squarely faced soon, the country and the globe will be even more seriously harmed. Finally, if the concerns for national security and the secret government that it has spawned are not controlled, the Constitution and the rights of individuals will be undermined to the point of collapse.

4

THE CHURCH IN THE UNITED STATES

Catholicism entered the United States with the Spanish conquest in the sixteenth century and the French and English settlements in the seventeenth century. The first parish was established in St. Augustine, Florida, in 1565. The United States received its first bishop, in the person of John Carroll of Baltimore, in November 1789, seven months after George Washington was sworn in as the first president. At that time there were about 35,000 Catholics in the United States.[1] These numbers swelled rapidly in the nineteenth century as the result of the large influx of Catholic immigrants. In 1820 there were 195,000 Catholics in the United States; by 1850 the number of Catholics amounted to 1,606,000 so that the Catholic Church became the largest denomination in the country. By 1860 the number of Catholics had doubled again to 3,103,000.[2]

Archbishop John Hughes of New York pointed out that, in the mid-nineteenth century in the United States the people came first and the Church followed. This makes the Catholic Church in the United States unique in the sense that the Catholic faith here is the result not of missionary activity but of Catholic people coming to these shores to seek a new life and new opportunities. The Church hierarchy then followed to serve its members.

Despite several waves of mistrust and suspicion over the next century, the Catholic Church continued to grow and prosper. With the election of John Kennedy in 1960, the first Catholic president of the United States, and the Second Vatican Council soon afterwards, the American Catholic Church entered a new phase of its history. With the election of Kennedy the American Catholic Church came of age politically; with the Council it came of age religiously. As George Gallup and Jim Castelli point out, "Today American Catholics no longer worry about being accepted—they worry about how to lead," because "In the quarter century since Kennedy's election, American Catholics have developed a stunning momentum—economically, socially, politically, spiritually—that ensures that they will have

75

a profound impact on the shape of American society a quarter century from now.[3]

PRESENT SITUATION

Today American Catholics number about fifty-two million and make up 28 percent of the United States population, an increase of almost half since 1947 when they accounted for 20 percent of the population. This rapid increase is due to the birth rate among American Catholics and a large Catholic Hispanic immigration during this period.[4] The American Catholic community is a young community with 29 percent of its members under thirty, 36 percent between the ages of thirty and forty-nine, and 35 percent over fifty. One in every five Catholics belongs to a minority group. Hispanics now make up 16 percent of United States Catholics while blacks account for 3 percent and another 3 percent, probably mostly Asian, describe themselves as nonwhites.

In general American Catholics are doing well financially and have become part of the middle class. Seventeen percent earn over $40,000 per year and 13 percent earn between $30,000 and $39,000 per year. These figures are related to the fact that the percentage of Catholics with a college education has more than doubled in the past twenty years; as of 1984, 17 percent were college graduates and another 24 percent had some college education.

Only 26 percent of American Catholics live in rural areas with 39 percent living in the inner city and 35 percent in the suburbs. Regionally, Catholics are concentrated in the Northeast and the Midwest. However, over the last twenty years there has been a substantial shift toward the Sun Belt so that today Catholics are 44 percent of the population in the East, 26 percent in the Midwest, 16 percent in the South, and 26 percent in the West.

While Catholics have historically favored larger families than other Americans, by 1985 Catholics had become part of the mainstream in considering two children the ideal number for a family. The percentage of Catholics divorced or separated doubled from 5 percent to 10 percent between 1976 and 1985. During the same period of time the number of those married dropped from 69 percent to 62 percent and the percentage of those who have never married rose from 19 percent to 22 percent.

In terms of their political self-perception, 33 percent of Catholics describe themselves as left-of-center, 12 percent as middle-of-the-road, and 55 percent right-of-center. In this respect they do not differ significantly from Protestants. However, there is a significant difference in American Catholics' self-perception concerning their values toward sex, morality, family life, and religion. In these areas 29 percent of Catholics, versus only 19 percent of Protestants, place themselves firmly in the liberal category.

Gallup and Castelli[5] propose five ways in which the American Catholic religious worldview differs from the Protestant worldview:

1. The Catholic worldview is intellectual; it is more likely to reconcile reason and faith than the Protestant worldview. Hence, Catholics do not believe that the Bible must be interpreted literally and they can reconcile the evolution of physical life with the creative power of God.

2. The Catholic worldview is accepting; it takes a more understanding attitude toward sinners and toward those who hold different religious views.

3. The Catholic worldview is pragmatic and earthy. Hence, Catholics give a higher priority to dealing with problems in this world than to personal salvation.

4. The Catholic worldview is communal. Hence, Catholics place a greater emphasis on social justice and love of neighbor as a dimension of faith and a corresponding lower priority on personal piety.

5. The Catholic worldview is private; it views religion as an individual choice and does not actively seek the conversion of others.

While weekly church attendance among Catholics declined dramatically from the 1950s to the late 1970s, it has been stable for a decade. Today, 71 percent of Catholics attend church at least twice a month and 78 percent attend at least once a month. There has also been a significant increase in religious activity outside of Mass over the last decade.[6] About half of "Core" Catholics (a term referring to non-Hispanic Catholics who are registered members of parishes) took part in at least one activity outside of religious rites.[7] The greatest percentage of those who took part in parish activities did so in social or recreational activities (22 percent). Sizable numbers, however, were also involved in liturgy, as planners or ministers (19 percent), in education (14 percent), in parish governance (12 percent), in personal or devotional renewal (6 percent), and in social action, welfare, or justice issues (4 percent).[8]

Concerning their Church, American Catholics have more confidence in the Church than in any other institution and overall are quite happy with it. White, affluent, middle-class families are especially happy with the Church. In fact college-educated Catholics are the Church's cutting edge; they are more involved in the Church and more satisfied with their involvement. However, the farther one moves from the category of the white, affluent, middle class, the greater grows the discontent with the Church. Nonwhite Catholics and those with incomes below $15,000 a year are considerably dissatisfied with the Church. As Gallup and Castelli point out, "the Church may be in danger in meeting the needs of middle-class families so well that it is losing its ability to serve Catholics who do not fit that mold."[9]

Catholics overwhelmingly (88 percent) approve of the job that priests are doing.[10] They are seen as understanding and able to appreciate the parishioners' practical problems and people generally like their homilies. While the Church gets high ratings for its handling of the needs of families, it gets low ratings regarding its dealings with singles and the youth. The worst ratings concern the Church's treatment of the separated, divorced, and remarried.[11] For the most part, Core Catholics are attached to and pleased with their parishes. They give the parishes high marks for meeting their spiritual and social needs.[12]

Many women are dissatisfied with the Church over its treatment of them and women in general "as women." However, the data suggest that while many women are not satisfied with the way the Church deals with them as women, they are more satisfied with the treatment they get as persons in their parishes. They desire a vast improvement in the Church's dealings with women.[13]

While Catholics would like more practical help from the Church in approaching moral issues and putting their faith into practice, they are not pleased with the Church's handling of political issues.[14] Catholics are evenly divided regarding whether the priest should discuss social issues from the pulpit. By a fifty-five to thirty-nine percent margin Catholics disagree with the bishops speaking out on social issues such as nuclear war and the economy. However, there are contradictions in these findings. Most Catholics would agree with the positions taken by the bishops on such issues as arms control, Central America, abortion, education, and economic policy. Yet they strongly resist the Church's involvement in the political arena. Gallup and Castelli suggest that the problem arises more from the style of the bishops' political involvement than the substance of the issues involved. In other words, the bishops have not articulated a clear, simple, convincing rationale for speaking out on public issues. They have not persuaded people that they know what they are doing and that they are not acting in a partisan manner. Finally, American Catholics are opposed to their bishops even remotely appearing to tell them how to vote. Core Catholics, in contrast to Catholics as a whole, strongly support the Church addressing major social and political issues; they also support the Church's right to lobby on such issues.[15]

Catholics most want help from the Church in becoming more effective parents. They would also like more frequent informal relationships between priests and laity and more small groups within parishes to encourage face-to-face relationships.[16]

Concerning leadership in the Church, only 32 percent of Catholics believe that the solution to the shortage of priests is to recruit more priests. Most Catholics (54 percent) believe the first priority should be to "think of new ways to structure parish leadership, to include more deacons, sisters, and lay persons." There is strong support for a married priesthood (63 percent are in favor and 34 percent opposed) and Catholics are evenly divided on the issue of the ordination of women.[17] While the Church receives high marks for the broader participation of lay people in church life, even more lay leadership is desired. Hence, Catholics support greater lay participation in parish decision making; more influential roles for women in parishes; allowing parishes to help choose the priests who come to serve them; full-time lay parish administrators; hiring full-time lay religious educators and liturgists; and hiring lay marriage or personal counselors.[18]

The reality today is that the American parish is returning to its lay roots.[19] As Gremillion and Castelli point out, "Throughout its time in the New World, the American Catholic laity has maintained a leadership spirit within the parish and the church community. That spirit has been overshadowed by other forces at various times ... but it has never disappeared."[20] Today's parishes are served not just by priests and religious, but by a corps of dedicated, serious, and trained lay people. Aside from the pastor, 83 percent of the leadership within the parishes, paid or unpaid, are lay people. Fifty-seven percent of the paid staff responsible for key programs are lay people. Of the unpaid leadership responsible for central parish activities, 94 percent are lay. In 64 percent of parishes, leadership involves a combination of pastor, religious, and laity. Ministerial teams are overwhelmingly lay and in an estimated 10 percent of parishes nonpriests are the central figures.

As Archbishop Weakland has pointed out, one of the greatest assets of the Church in the United States today is its well-trained laity.[21] No other group of Catholics in the world can boast of such a high degree of education. However, there are some negative aspects. First, Catholic social teaching from Pope Leo XIII to Pope John Paul II has not been assimilated by the Catholic population. It has not been part of Catholic education on any level and so was not formative of the thinking of a new and important generation of Catholics in the United States. It has been customary in religious education to keep to catechetical formulas that do not touch social and political issues but reflect the American view of religion as a private affair.

Also, the Catholic Church in the United States has had a tendency to assimilate the American political experience without critical judgment. This tendency came from American Catholics who wanted to be accepted and seen as thoroughly loyal Americans. Hence, Catholics enthusiastically supported all of the nation's policies and actions in the world. Their American political experience also deeply affected many U. S. Catholics in their attitude toward separation of Church and state. For both laity and many clergy separation of Church and state means a separation of political, social, and economic issues from religious and moral implications. People say that the clergy should speak about "spirituality," which for them means an inspirational faith that does not challenge them to social involvement. There is to be no politics from the pulpit.

Even though they have become entrenched in the middle class, American Catholics have remained liberal on economic issues and are in substantial agreement with the bishops on broad economic themes. First, they urge a strong role for government in economic matters. They support an activist government in its increased spending for social programs. Given a choice they would spend more for butter and less for guns and cut military spending before cutting social spending to reduce the national debt. American Catholics lean toward placing the major blame for poverty on circumstances rather than lack of effort by the poor, and they see the need for making the distribution of wealth and income in the United States more equitable than it is today. For this purpose they support a tax reform that would lower taxes for the poor and middle-income Americans and raise them for wealthy people and corporations. They remain supportive of labor unions, though not to the extent they did in the past. This is due, in the first place, to fewer American Catholics having contact with the unions today. Also, along with other Americans, they see labor leaders as one of a group of "special interests" who put parochial concerns ahead of the national interest.[22]

One of the most significant findings of the Notre Dame study is the growing emphasis in parishes on justice and peace issues and the acceptance by Core Catholics of the need for structural change.[23] While social action programs (efforts to change social structures and institutions to make them more just) in parishes were rare before Vatican II, 20 percent of parishes (27 percent in the suburbs and 29 percent in urban areas) now have such programs.[24] Thirty-seven percent of Core Catholics want more parish activity to "change unjust socio-economic conditions." What is very surprising is that 52 percent say they feel close to God while working for justice and peace. This ranked ahead of reading the Gospels, obeying church rules, and praying in a charismatic group. As Gremillion and Castelli point out, "The fact that half of Core Catholics feel closer to God while working for peace and justice indicates that the church's post-Vatican II emphasis on social justice is reaching into the consciousness of American Catholics."[25] The potential for involving Core Catholics in social action and promoting peace and justice seems to be significant.

Gallup and Castelli note that one of the most important findings in their study is the breadth and depth of Catholic dovishness.[26] As they point out:

> American Catholics, influenced by their church's leaders, their own experience with the Vietnam War, and security in their identity as Americans, are firm in their commitment to peace. They will be a major force for arms control, reduced military spending, and a prudent foreign policy for the foreseeable future.[27]

Eighty-four percent support a bilateral nuclear freeze and 68 percent want to cut military spending. However, this dovishness is not pacifism. Catholics still support a discreet use of force and will support new weapon systems if they believe these will reduce the risk of war.

Regarding current social issues Catholics take a conservative position regarding abortion, the death penalty, school prayer, pornography, busing, and the legalization of marijuana. However, they are clearly "liberal" when it comes to women's rights, gun control, civil rights for minorities and homosexuals, and the decriminalization of possession of small quantities of mari-juana.[28]

Gallup and Castelli conclude their book with some comments on the catholicization of American culture.[29] First, Catholics have helped other Americans become more tolerant of religious, racial, ethnic, and other diversities in American society. They have done this by their presence and their example. More than Protestants, they have supported women's economic rights. Catholics have also been responsible for bringing a communal dimension to American society and supporting an active role for government in meeting the needs of people. In addition, Catholics make up the most important swing vote in American society: "When traditional Catholic allegiance to the Democratic Party asserts itself, the Democrats win — or come very close. When the Republicans make substantial inroads into the Catholic vote, they win."[30] Finally, Catholics have emerged as the "peace church" in the United States. Catholic support for a verifiable bilateral nuclear freeze was a major factor in pushing the Reagan administration back to the negotiating table. Its strong opposition to a military solution in Central America may well have prevented the use of U.S. troops in Central America, especially in the early 1980s.

This rapid summary of the present situation of the Church in the United States brings home the reality that it has moved swiftly away from being an immigrant Church. However, to understand the present American Church it is important to realize that the ethos that went with the older immigrant Church has not yet died out. This ethos was characterized by four central traits: authority, sin, ritual, and the miraculous.[31] Many of the present tensions within today's Church become clear when seen against the background of this older ethos that dominated life in the United States Church until a few decades ago.

With the rise of modernity and its new sciences and technology in the nineteenth century, religion was pushed to the periphery of society. The reaction of the Catholic Church to this reality was at times extreme, especially in its assertion of its authority, now that it was being challenged. The high point of this reaction was the declaration of papal infallibility in 1870 by the First Vatican Council. This declaration resulted in the centralization of the Church around Rome and the papacy and increased the power of Church bureaucrats in the Vatican. Local bishops shared in this emphasis on authority, which made local pastors dominant figures in their parish communities. In this context the rights of the individual conscience were deemphasized as each person was expected to submit to the external authority of the Church. In such a culture Catholics were raised to be docile and submissive.

The second trait of the old Catholic ethos was its emphasis on sin, arising from the Augustinian tradition's pessimistic concept of the human being. Original sin was seen as undermining the strength of men and women. People had to earn holiness and salvation through a victorious struggle against sin. Because sin was so pervasive and powerful, peoples' evil inclinations had to be curbed; this was done through a multitude of laws and regulations. A culture of sin demanded a culture of authority. The emphasis on sin also put a strong emphasis on the importance of confession. Because of this emphasis on sin, attitudes toward the world or secular society were quite negative.

A third feature of the older Catholic ethos was its valuing of ritual. For Catholics, the way to the sacred was through ritual and the central ritual was the Mass. Next in importance were the sacraments and devotions to the saints with associated novenas. This emphasis on ritual and the many Church laws that were to be kept associated religion with the performance of certain external acts and the fulfillment of a series of obligations. It also fostered the notion of individual or personal salvation. Because the salvation of one's soul was the highest goal for Catholics, it was difficult for a social Gospel to get a hearing.

The final trait of the older Catholic ethos was its openness to the miraculous. A sense of mystery and of the holy is part of the mystical tradition of Roman Catholicism. The celebration of the Mass evoked this atmosphere of the holy as did many of the rituals. Even more telling was the popular belief in miraculous cures. This belief was reinforced by the elaborate network of saints and the use of sacred objects such as relics, rosaries, candles, scapulars, and holy water. The Catholic God was seen as a personal figure who listened to the prayers of people and would reach down and touch the lives of people when called upon. While a culture of authority and sin emphasized the dark side of the divine, the practice of ritual and belief in the miraculous underscored the bright side.

The Mass and sacraments—the public worship of the Church and the principal means by which people gained access to the supernatural—together with the emphasis on law and authority, enhanced the authority of the clergy and the institutional church. These perspectives supported a theology of priesthood that elevated the priest to a realm above and beyond that of the laity. Such a lofty view of the priest served to reinforce clerical control of the church.

A new Catholicism has developed during the last two decades that is in tension with the older ethos. One of the most striking features of this new Catholicism is pluralism—there are various ways of being Catholic, and people are choosing the style that best suits them.[32]

With the emergence of the new Catholicism, the immigrant Catholic ethos is changing. A new participative, collaborative model is replacing the old, monarchical, clerical concept of Church and authority. A new Catholic morality is replacing the traditional moral code with its exaggerated emphasis on sin and guilt. Ritual remains very much a part of the new Catholicism, but new rituals are taking the place of old ones. Most of the older devotions have disappeared and prayer is now more likely directed to Jesus. The sense of the transcendent, the miraculous, remains prominent, especially among evangelical, charismatic Catholics. The spiritual focus for the post-Vatican II Catholic is found in Sunday Mass, in receiving Communion, and in private prayer. Though the future shape of this new Catholicism remains uncertain, one thing is clear: the traditions of the past no longer work. The U.S. Church is in a period of transition and this is creating tension as one model of being Church is passing away and another one is taking its place.

Joe Holland points out that people are increasingly experiencing two great hungers in the post-modern world—the hunger for peace and justice and the hunger for meaning.[33] Many see that the present Church needs to be fundamentally transformed and that this is to be accomplished by tapping the tradition and recovering roots in a creative fashion. The spirituality connected with this movement emphasizes the need for both social and personal transformation. This spirituality is also communal, meaning that the small group is the mediator of the spiritual dynamics. There is a new model of evangelization emerging as well; namely, in the post-modern world the poor and oppressed are the sources of evangelization. The rich and the powerful, in order to be converted, need to hear the Gospel from the poor and oppressed. The face of God begins to appear in places people do not expect—in the face of the poor, the imprisoned, the tortured; in the face of the woman who labors under sexism; in the face of people of color who bear the burden of racism; in the face of the Third World and its massive poverty. This movement in the Church is what provides hope for the future, says Holland.

The overview of the present situation of the Catholic Church in the United States offered here is primarily an overview of the white, Anglo-Saxon Catholic Church. This will also be the case regarding the other issues and attitudes that will be presented in this chapter. Missing are the attitudes and data of minority members of the Catholic Church in the United States, especially the Hispanics. Given the rapidly growing number of Hispanics in the U.S. Church, this absence is more than regrettable. However, to a great extent, the data regarding Hispanics does not exist, at least not in the detail that it is found in the studies that I have been citing. The most thorough study is Gonzalez and LaVelle's *The Hispanic Catholic in the United States: A Socio-Cultural and Religious Profile.*[34] However, it is difficult to integrate this material into an overall picture of Catholics in the United States. A weakness of the Notre Dame study is the decision to exclude Spanish-speaking congregations from its in-depth analysis of thirty-six parishes. This decision was made on the basis of the distinctive character of Hispanics as a religio-cultural community, their history, and their continuing influx from Latin America.[35] However, the book *The Emerging Parish* does contain a chapter on "The Hispanic Community and the Parish." A difficulty, however, is that in those places with a high concentration of Hispanics, and even more so where they are not that numerous, Hispanics form one parish community with their white and black sisters and brothers. Hence, the picture of the parish community that emerges in these situations would probably differ in many ways from the picture presented in the Notre Dame study because of the mix of cultures and values and the tensions between them. Much more attention needs to be given to this reality. For the present we can only offer some data uncovered in the Notre Dame study and the study by Gonzalez and LaVelle as summarized by Gremillion and Castelli.[36]

The 1983 pastoral letter of the United States bishops on Hispanic ministry estimates that the total Hispanic population in the United States (including Puerto Rico and the undocumented) is at least 20 million.[37] As a result the United States ranks fifth among the world's Spanish-speaking countries (HP 6). It is further estimated that between 70 and 80 percent of these Hispanics are Catholic. While Hispanics are found in every state of the Union, over 75 percent reside in six states: California and Texas with about 5 million and 3.3 million respectively; New York and New Jersey with 2.3 million together; and Florida and Illinois with about one million Hispanics in each. Over 85 percent are found in large urban centers like New York, Chicago, Miami, Los Angeles, San Antonio, and San Francisco. The number of Hispanics is growing in places like Hartford, Washington, D.C., and Atlanta. Their numbers are growing due to both continuing immigration, especially from Mexico and Cuba, and to high fertility. As a result they will become an ever greater presence in the U.S. Church as well as in American society at large.

In general, most Hispanics in the United States live near or below the poverty level and are severely underrepresented at decision-making levels in the Church and society. Historically, unemployment has been higher among Hispanics than other nationalities. Well over half the employed Hispanics work at nonprofessional, nonmanagerial jobs, chiefly in agricultural labor and urban service occupations. Only 40 percent graduate from high school and educational opportunities are often below standard in areas of high Hispanic concentration.[38]

The U.S. bishops point out that Hispanics exemplify and cherish values central to the service of Church and society. Among these are:

1. Profound respect for the dignity of each person;

2. Deep and reverential love for family life, where the entire extended family discovers its roots, identity, and its strength;

3. A marvelous sense of community that celebrates life through "fiesta";

4. Loving appreciation for God's gift of life and an understanding of time that allows one to savor that gift;

5. Authentic and consistent devotion to Mary (HP 3).

The bishops further point out that the pastoral needs of the Hispanics are great. While their faith is deep and strong, it is being challenged and eroded by steady social pressures to assimilate (HP 4).

As Gremillion and Castelli demonstrate, the growing Hispanic presence in the U.S. Church poses both challenges and opportunities.[39] The Church must recognize that Hispanic Catholics are extremely diverse and come from a variety of ethnic and national backgrounds. They vary in their racial origins, color, history, and expressions of faith and they come from nineteen different Latin American countries, Puerto Rico, and Spain. The largest group is Mexican-American (60 percent). They are followed by Puerto Ricans (17 percent) and Cubans (8 percent). The Dominican Republic, Peru, Ecuador, Chile, and increasingly Central America, especially El Salvador, are amply represented. Hispanic Catholics are not well integrated into parish life and are the target of intense proselytizing efforts by fundamentalist Christians. Few Hispanics are becoming priests or religious and Hispanic clergy have not followed the immigrants. Moises Sandoval has pointed out that, "proportional to their numbers in the 1980s, there should have been at least 17,000 priests. Instead there were only 1,400. The same disparities applied to Sisters and Brothers."[40] This lack often creates a real leadership vacuum among Hispanics. Finally, Hispanics are not very familiar with Church developments since Vatican II. Fifty-five percent said that they had never heard of the Council, while 65 to 78 percent knew nothing of the lay apostolate or parish councils, liberation theology, or base communities. There is a clear need for an extensive education in the Hispanic community.

RELIGIOUS INDIVIDUALISM

Several significant issues face the U.S. Church today when looked at from the perspective of the mission of the Church in this country.[41] The first issue is religious individualism and the relation of the Church to society. Throughout the history of America religion has played an important role in the life of the country. Without attempting to present a full picture of this role, a few observations might be helpful.[42]

The original settlers of North America saw themselves on a religious mission when they came to these shores. In colonial New England, the roles of Christian and citizen were closely linked and the minister was seen as a public officer. The role of the minister was to be the keeper and purveyor of the public culture and the enforcer of the personal values and public decorum that sustained it. With the disestablishment of religion through the First Amendment, religion began to become more of a personal matter. In the early nineteenth century the political function of religion was no longer direct intervention in the public order but support of the mores that made democracy possible. Religion had the role of placing limits on utilitarian individualism by emphasizing proper concern for others. By the time one enters the twentieth century, because of the privatization of religion, institutional religion was no longer able to challenge the dominance of utilitarian values in American society. For the most part the impact of religion on society was now through societies and voluntary associations. In these societies and associations clergy and laity could now bring their concerns about social issues to the attention of their fellow citizens without disturbing the harmony of the local congregation. For by this time the local congregation had become a community of the like-minded, "protected and withdrawn islands of piety."[43]

Today, most Americans see religion as something that concerns only their own personal life. They do not see religion as having a public role. Because of this privatization of religion, most Americans, then, see religion as something individual,[44] and they believe that their personal relationship with God transcends their involvement in any particular Church. Belonging to a Church is much like belonging to any other organization. What people, including Catholics, look for in a Church body is primarily personal intimacy and support. As Bellah points out,

> The salience of these needs for personal intimacy in American relig-ious life suggests why the local church, like other voluntary commu-nities, indeed like the contemporary family, is so fragile, requires so much energy to keep it going, and has so faint a hold on commitment when such needs are not met.[45]

What is clear is that Americans, including Catholics, have a hard time thinking of their relationship to God as mediated by a religious community that existed before they were born and will continue after they die. They do not realize that their Church is a community of memory that passes on to them certain perceptions about God, life, and others, and provides mod-els for dealing with all of life. Rather, they see themselves and their beliefs as prior to the community, and they see themselves as members of this community because they have chosen to join it. It is not surprising, then, that if a local Church begins to proclaim an uncomfortable interpretation of the Gospel, especially a social message, some individuals will leave. They will go where they can find the support and intimacy they desire. Coming from a voluntaristic idea of Church, people do not have the same loyalties to a Church body as in the past. They feel free to leave and move on when they want to.

The Notre Dame study of Catholic parish life has confirmed this indi-vidualistic emphasis among Catholics.[46] In a study of "foundational beliefs"—the most deeply held values that shape all other beliefs, including religious ones—it was found that 39 percent of Catholics are exclusively individualistic in foundational belief. Eighteen percent of Catholics are exclusively communal in their foundational beliefs while 21 percent are integrated, defining their religious beliefs through both themes. Another 22 percent showed either anomalous patterns or could not think about their religion in the terms used in the study. As Gremillion and Castelli point out, the large proportion of Catholics with exclusively individualistic foun-dational beliefs is startling and sobering. It shows that the Church, which emphasizes communal symbols and values, faces constant tension with not only the individualistic impulses of American society, but with similar impulses among many of its own members. To some extent, this impulse toward individualism can be blamed on four centuries of catechesis that emphasized growth in personal holiness and the individualistic nature of sin, confession, and absolution.

Given this context it is difficult for the local religious community to move beyond an individualistic morality that concentrates on family and personal life to a concern with social, political, and economic issues. The split that results between religion, on the one hand, and social, political, and economic life on the other hand, strips religion of the possibility of having a significant impact on these public aspects of life. The founders of our country believed that our form of government was dependent on the existence of virtue among the people. As Bellah observes, "It was such virtue that they expected to resolve the tension between private interest and the public good."[47] Moreover, our country has been built upon biblical and republican traditions as well as the philosophies of the Enlightenment. If we are to correct the exaggerated individualism that has developed within our society, we must return more fully to biblical and republican traditions. The Church, as the carrier above all of the biblical tradition, must help people to regain a sense of public virtue and the common good. It must also show people, in a creative, meaningful fashion, how the biblical tradition pertains to the social, political, and economic context in which they live.

This mission pertains to the American Catholic Church as well. Through the entire period of immigration the Church was primarily concerned with the welfare of its own and not with affecting national policy. In this century, as the flow of immigrants from Europe died away, the Church was at first too insecure to enter fully into a discussion of national policies. However, with their recent letters on disarmament and the economy the American Catholic bishops have fully joined the discussion of national priorities. That the letters of the bishops have received such a mixed reaction, both from Catholics and non-Catholics, is not surprising, given the Church's history in this country and the present cultural climate of the United States.

U.S. CATHOLIC CHURCH AS A "PUBLIC" CHURCH

In his 1982 book *An American Strategic Theology* John A. Coleman, S.J., claims that the American Catholic Church now finds itself in a state of crisis in the sense that it has reached a decisive turning point in its history.[48] As he points out, the crisis cannot be blamed on Vatican II. While the Council may have precipitated the crisis, it was ready to happen. With the election of John F. Kennedy to the American presidency, the historic goals of the American Catholic Church had been achieved. The goals of the immigrant Church had included upward mobility and acceptance by American culture. In the process of achieving these goals, Coleman claims, American Catholics had been influenced by the American culture to a much greater degree than they had influenced it. However, the United States now needs to be challenged by what the Church has to offer, especially in the area of social teaching.

In 1986 J. Bryan Hehir maintained that through the efforts of the U.S. bishops the U.S. Church had become a "public church."[49] Hehir defines the role of such a public church as "less that of providing definitive answers to complex socio-political questions than it is to act as a catalyst moving the public argument to grapple with questions of moral values, ethical principles and the human and religious meaning of policy choices."[50]

This public role is not entirely new for the U.S. Church.[51] Throughout this century and especially during the Great Depression and the years immediately following, the National Catholic Welfare Conference (NCWC) played a crucial role in public policy by supporting New Deal legislation. Moreover, the institutional Church was at the forefront of the labor movement at the beginning of the century. The differences between the earlier version of the Catholic public Church and the present one center on the role of the bishops and how the Catholic community relates to other religious groups in the United States. Formerly, the bishops themselves were less directly involved in the public sector but left this to delegated NCWC officials. Also the tendency was to take action on an interreligious basis. In the present version the bishops are much more directly involved in the public sector and are inclined to go it alone.

This present entrance of the U.S. Catholic Church into the public sector raises a series of issues and questions. No attempt will be made here to deal with all of these.[52] In a later chapter I will look at these issues in more depth.[53] Here I will simply put the issues in context.

As has already been mentioned, the original vision of the founders of this country gave religious groups an important mediating role in our society. According to Hehir, the purpose of the separation clause in the Constitution is "not to silence the religious voice but to strengthen it, not to fetter the church but to free it to contribute to the public life of the nation."[54] John Pawlikowski points out that Catholic leaders "are convinced that the Catholic Community has every right, in fact has the obligation, to bring Catholic perspectives to bear on central public policy issues."[55] As Catholic leadership approaches further dialogue on the relationship of religion and politics, they have some clear convictions. As Pawlikowski observes:

> They include rejection of any notion that public morality must be shaped only by secular norms, a firm belief that the American vision involves meaningful cooperation between religious groups and the state in framing national morality, the belief that religious groups can never allow themselves to become single issue oriented, and the realization that Catholics must be prepared to accept only partial implementation of their particular moral vision in state legislation. What is

emerging is a definite rejection of a secular state idea that reduces religion to the realm of private morality.[56]

At the same time, however, there is definite disagreement among Catholic leaders on how to bring Catholic perspectives to bear on public policy and how far to go in voicing their opinions. As Coleman points out, "The problem for the Church is not whether it will be political or not but how to find the appropriate arena, style and stance where it can handle the political role it is most suited to play in society, a political role which is most consonant with its character as Church."[57] This, of course, is related to the broader question of the proper role of religious groups in shaping public policy, especially in a pluralistic society. This issue is also related to how one understands the very mission of the Church. The answer to this question depends upon to what degree one considers earthly progress to be of concern to the Reign of God. Another related issue is the role of Catholic politicians and their responsibility to bring the concerns of Catholic tradition to their conduct of public affairs.[58]

Another important issue concerns the need for the U.S. Catholic Church to work closely with other religious bodies in its attempt to affect public policy. In the earlier version of the U.S. Catholic public church (the first half of the twentieth century) the Church's efforts had a definite interreligious cast; this has not been the case recently. However, any successful attempt at bringing religious values to bear on public policy will have to be an interreligious affair involving not only cooperation with other Christians but also with Jews.[59]

AMERICANIZATION OF THE CHURCH

Jay Dolan has argued[60] that contemporary Catholics are now undertaking their third encounter with modernity. The first experiment took place from 1776–1800 under the leadership of John Carroll, the first American bishop. As Dolan points out, the American Revolution was an ideological revolution. Quoting John Adams, Dolan maintains that the real revolution took place "in the minds and hearts of the American people."[61] The Revolution fostered a new emphasis on equality and a spirit of independence and rugged individualism. The Revolution also affected the small group of Catholics who were part of the new nation. By 1790 a distinctive vision of the Church was taking shape in the United States under Carroll's leadership. This vision called for "a national, American church which would be independent of all foreign jurisdiction and would endorse pluralism and toleration in religion; a church in which religion was grounded in intelligibility and where a vernacular liturgy was normative; and finally a church in which the spirit of democracy permeated the government of local communities."[62] This was not so much an organized national program for reform but a new understanding of Catholicism.

The vision began to unravel in the 1790s. There were many reasons for this, such as the more conservative Federalist attitude that was sweeping the country, the destructive impact of the French Revolution on the Church, a desire for unity with Rome together with Roman pressure for centralization, and the Catholic tradition about the bishops' authority. Also significant was the influx of European clergy (because of a lack of native clergy) that led to a continental understanding of Catholicism. New bishops were also Europeans.[63] Concern with developing a specific American Catholicism remained in the background for almost a century because of the massive influx of European immigrants from 1820 on. However, people like Orestes Brownson, Bishop John England, and Isaac Hecker kept the issue alive.

The second encounter with modernity took place in the 1880s and 1890s with the Americanists. The roots of this new experiment were in the thoughts of Brownson and Hecker. While they saw the Church as ahistorical, transcending time and immune to change, they were also committed to a historical, developmental view of reality. They were convinced that the Church must adapt itself to a particular time and culture.[64] Their thoughts encouraged a new generation to search for ways to adapt the Church to the new age in which it found itself. The leader of this group of thinkers was John Ireland, archbishop of St. Paul. He pushed for a new crusade in which "the Church must herself be new, adapting herself in manner of life and in method of action to the conditions of the new order, thus proving herself, while ever ancient, to be ever new, as truth from heaven it is and ever must be."[65] Ireland's concern was not so much with what the Church is, as with what it does.

The basic ideas of this movement involved the adaptation of the Church to modern culture; the idea of God as one who acts in history and is revealed through it; the vision of the Reign of God as moving toward realization in history; the need for an active, energetic laity; a more tolerant view of Protestants; the superiority of this American version of Catholicism to that of the Old World.[66] It was this latter perspective that would eventually undermine the crusade of the Americanizers. When they took their crusade to Europe and presented these "American" ideas as the key to the renewal of the Church in Europe, they came into conflict with European ecclesial powers.

Conservatives in the United States, especially in the hierarchy, did not support the efforts of Ireland and his followers. These conservatives were hostile toward Protestants, wary of government reform efforts, and alienated from the progressive thinking of the times. For them the Church admitted of no modifications and was incompatible with modern culture. Hence, their crusade was to strengthen the Church so that it could withstand the attacks of the modern world.[67]

In 1899 Pope Leo XIII issued a letter, *Testem Benevolentiae*, in which he condemned a group of ideas that he labeled "Americanism." What triggered the writing of this letter was a French translation of a biography of Isaac Hecker and the ideas in that book "concerning the manner of leading a Christian life." The Pope condemned the idea that the Church ought to adapt its doctrine to the modern age. He also warned against the idea that the Church in America could be different from the Church in the rest of the world. He then listed as suspicious ideas such as the depreciation of external spiritual guidance and increased reliance on direct inspiration, the placing of natural virtues ahead of supernatural virtues, emphasis on active virtues rather than passive virtues, a lack of regard for the traditional vows taken in religious communities, and the desire for new ways and methods to seek converts.

While progressives denied that these ideas existed, conservatives expressed gratitude that the heresy had been exposed. While the Pope did not explicitly condemn Hecker, Ireland, or others, "the ideas he labeled as erroneous were ideas that these men had championed."[68] Hennesey quotes William Halsey as coming near the mark when he says that they "were accused of heresy for espousing the activist individualism, self-confident mystique and optimistic idealism of American civilization."[69]

Dennis McCann has proposed that *Testem Benevolentiae* was not about heresy at all. Americanism was never a challenge to Roman Catholic orthodoxy but rather "an emerging style of religious praxis nurtured by the experience of Catholic people in America." McCann's claim is that what was being condemned was the notion of a "certain liberty" in the Church. At stake in this "certain liberty" was the revolutionary American principle of "self-governing association" and its extension to all institutional sectors of society.[70]

The condemnation of Americanism, together with the condemnation of modernism less than a decade later, "brought an end to the American Catholic romance with modernity."[71] The romanization of the Church in the United States now begins, and the American Church becomes more closely bound to the Vatican and its way of thinking; the spirit of independence disappears. According to Dolan, "Rome had become not just the spiritual center of American Catholicism, but the intellectual center as well."[72]

Dolan argues that we are now in a period of the third encounter of American Catholicism with the modern world. American theologians began to strike out on their own, instead of following European theologians. It is a period in which the times of Carroll and the Americanists are seen as the best periods of United States Catholic history. This third encounter with the modern world is also found in the recent pastoral letters of the United States bishops on disarmament and the economy. That something new is afoot in these letters is supported not just by the bishops' struggles with knotty contemporary issues but even more by the process of public dialogue and broad consultation that formed the context for writing these letters. This is truly an American way of dealing with an issue and manifests a belief that the Spirit is present and operating in all members of the Church. As McCann points out, one can trace a relatively straight line from the Detroit "Call to Action" consultation in 1976 to the process of broad consultation of believers and others in the development of the pastoral letters.[73] Gradually, the bishops have been opting for a participative style of life in the Church. This participative style has its roots in the American principle of "self-governing association" that is at the basis of all other aspects of life in the United States.

As Coleman comments, the events of the 1960s and 1970s awakened Americans to issues such as race, war and imperialism, women's rights, the environment, and the government's misuse of power.[74] William McLoughlin has spoken of this period as another great awakening, "a transformation of our world view that may be the most drastic in our history as a nation."[75] Because this period coincided with the spiritual awakening of the Second Vatican Council, Catholics have been especially influenced by it. Several facts make this encounter with modernity different from the previous two, says Coleman. First, it is a worldwide phenomenon in Catholicism, as seen in the development of various local theologies. Second, American Catholics are no longer wedded to immigrant traditional cultures. Third, it is not limited to the clergy and an elite group of lay intellectuals but is widespread among the laity.

Where this new encounter will go is still an open question. However, realizing that the U.S. Church is going through another stage of experimenting with modernity helps to put into perspective much that is happening today. This realization clarifies both internal tensions and the tension it is experiencing with Rome. Joe Holland has suggested that the present tension between Rome and the U.S. Church originates from the fact that the United States has become the center for the global extension of modern culture through its communication system. This modern culture is very threatening to classical Roman culture, which for centuries has been the medium for the Church's global strategy of evangelization. To the extent that Catholicism becomes enculturated in this country, U.S. Catholicism becomes a significant threat to Roman Catholicism, especially since U.S. Catholicism will play a predominant role in future global evangelization efforts of the Church. Holland says, "American Catholicism thus becomes a central place for debate over the path of global Catholicism in its strategy of global enculturation. Is the inherited Roman culture of Europe to remain the cultural ground for global evangelization?"[76] That is the question and the real issue behind present tensions with Rome.

SELECTIVE CATHOLICISM

What finally brought an end to the immigrant Church was the massive entry of Catholics into the mainstream of the American middle class in the early and middle part of this century. With the rise of an educated and independent laity, together with the changes brought about by Vatican II, there has emerged what Andrew Greeley has called "selective Catholicism."[77] Greeley argues that perhaps four-fifths of the regular Sunday church attenders, while remaining loyal to the Church, ignore official Catholic teaching in those areas where they judge papal and episcopal leadership to be incompetent. This selectivity pertains especially to issues related to sex, above all birth control. These findings of Greeley are supported by the Notre Dame study, which shows that Core Catholics are no less likely than unchurched or nonpracticing Catholics to make up their own minds: "If they agree with the church on an issue, it is because the church position makes sense to them and they actively decide to agree. If a church teaching does not make sense to them, they will refuse to agree, no matter how often or how clearly or how authoritatively the church has spoken on it."[78]

According to Greeley, this selective Catholicism correlates positively with a shift in the religious imagination of ordinary Catholics. This shift is away from images and stories of God as the dispenser of just punishments and toward images and stories that envision God as a warm and loving spouse or parent.[79] Assured of God's love, these Catholics set their own terms of commitment and involvement in the Church.[80]

Because of these developments Greeley speaks of the communal Catholics:

> They are loyal to the Catholic collectivity and at least sympathetic toward its heritage. At the same time they refuse to take seriously the teaching authority of the leadership of the institutional Church. Such communal Catholics are Catholics because they see nothing else in American society they want to be, out of loyalty to their past, and they are curious as to what the Catholic tradition might have that is special and unique in the contemporary world.[81]

Coleman points out that the emergence of the communal Catholic in America entails three different changes in the post-Vatican period:

1. A selective and self-conscious style of affiliation with institutional Catholicism which nevertheless keeps social and other ties with the Catholic community;

2. A desire for new religious forms, e.g., the charismatic movement, which provide personalized experiences of community among Catholics;

3. The emergence of Catholics into the wider community in spawning—as the Protestant churches did in the nineteenth century—voluntary, nondenominational associations of social reform such as Bread for the World or the Movement for Responsible Investment.[82]

Gallup and Castelli assert that one thing that has not been appreciated is that this new breed of Catholics, because of their sheer numbers, has forced the American bishops to accept their new definition of Catholicism. The bishops, faced with widespread dissent on such issues as birth control, divorce, and abortion, have had two basic choices: either attempt to discipline the dissenters or accommodate the new American Catholicism. Since the first option would probably create massive disruption and unrest in the Church, the bishops have adopted the second. In other words, on a practical level, they have tacitly accepted "widespread dissent as the cost of continued unchallenged acceptance as members of the Catholic family."[83] This, of course, is another reason for the Vatican's dissatisfaction with the U.S. Church and contributes to the tension with Rome.

VOCATIONS

Before concluding this chapter on the Church a word should be said about the significant drop in the number of priests and religious in the Church since the Second Vatican Council. This has been due to several factors: a large exodus of priests and nuns; fewer aspirants to the priesthood and religious life; and the natural aging process. The number of religious women has dropped approximately a third since 1966. While the number of priests declined only slightly from 59,192 in 1970 to 57,317 in 1985, many more of the 1985 priests are retired (8 percent) than was the case in 1970 (3 percent). The reason statistics do not show a greater decrease in the number of priests is due to the large ordination classes from 1966–69, the large number of priests returning from the missions in Latin America and Africa, and the influx of priests immigrating from Asia. However, two sources of priests—those immigrating from Asia and those returning from the field—have now dried up.

The full impact of the present situation comes home when one considers the number of aspirants to the priesthood and religious life. While there were over eleven thousand novices in women's communities in 1962, there are now only around one thousand. Similarly, while there were almost forty-nine thousand seminarians (religious and diocesan) in 1965, there are now only around twelve thousand. The greatest drop is in religious seminarians, those men in religious communities studying for the priesthood. If one looks only at the priesthood, one finds that there are only one-half the number of priests in 1990 capable of pastoral work as there were in 1980.

Finally, it is important to keep in mind that there is a current decline in the number of young Catholics aged 18 to 24. It is projected that between 1980 and 2000 there will be a 15 percent decline in this age group, which, traditionally, has yielded the greatest number of vocations to the priesthood and religious life.

A study by Dean Hoge on attitudes of Catholic college students toward vocations and lay ministries found that the two main factors discouraging vocations today are celibacy and lack of encouragement of young people. At the same time, the study discovered that there is a very large number of young people who are interested in full-time lay ministry within the Church. In fact, within the total Catholic population the pool of people now interested in full-time lay ministry is about fifty times larger than the pool of people interested in the classical forms of priestly and religious vocations![84]

The average age of those entering religious life and the seminary has changed significantly over the last few decades. A recent study of seminarians revealed that 30 percent were over thirty and 60 percent over twenty-five. This is a significant change from the past when almost all seminarians would have been between twenty and twenty-five. The average age of a priest, brother, or sister candidate for religious life in 1987 was 27. Moreover, over 10 percent of religious novices in 1985 were over 40.

Regarding the cultural backgrounds of candidates for religious life today, Anglos outnumber cultural minorities by three to one. The largest number of these cultural minorities are Hispanic. Within the seminary population Hispanics remain greatly underrepresented; they account for only 7 percent of all seminarians, whereas Hispanics make up 14 percent of the total Catholic population.

Regarding those who enter the seminary today the impression of faculty and administration is that the seminaries are not getting the same proportion of "excellent students" as fifteen years ago.[85] Moreover, studies of seminarians show that seminarians today see the primary task of the Church to be that of encouraging its members to live a Christian life rather than trying to reform the world.[86] Further, concern for social justice and concern for the poor do not rate high in their perspectives on religious ministry. Young priests in 1985 were more institutionally conservative than middle-aged priests.

The drop in the number of priests is one factor contributing to the significant changes taking place today in the whole area of ministry, ordained and nonordained. Nonordained religious and laity are taking over many of the traditional roles of the priest; this will occur even more in the future. To a great extent, priests are increasingly forced into the role of being primarily celebrators of the sacraments. One finding of a Hoge study on attitudes of Catholic adults and college students about the priest shortage and parish life is that the Catholic laity will not accept any substantial reduction of priestly services. The most sensitive area would be any reduction of access to the Eucharist and Last Rites. As Hoge points out, the laity will press for other leadership options and other innovations before acquiescing on this point. Hence, he says, "The ecclesiastical policy option of simply passively allowing priestly services to decline as the shortage worsens carries potential costs in support and loyalty." This is the same issue we saw earlier, that is, that most Catholics see the present priest crisis as a "leadership structure crisis." As Hoge points out, "given a choice of restructured parish leadership or a surge of new priests to bring back the situation of two decades ago, the majority would choose the former."[87] All this is important to keep in mind when doing Church planning.

ANALYSIS

History

The Church in the United States has been affected by several historical events. First, there was the Revolution with its ideals of equality and independence. It was this event that occasioned the first attempt at the Americanization of the U.S. Church under the leadership of John Carroll. Then came the waves of immigrants in the nineteenth century. These immigrants rapidly outnumbered the original core of Catholics in the early years of the nation. These immigrants brought with them their European clergy and European form of Catholicism. However, from the struggle to assimilate these new citizens into the United States there emerged a second attempt at the Americanization of the U.S. Church under the leadership of John Ireland. The condemnation of Americanism in 1899, together with the condemnation of Modernism, less than a decade later, effectively brought an end to any further attempts at Americanization for over half a century. These Roman actions also silenced any original theological thought in this country for several decades as the U.S. Church became completely romanized.

With the coming of age, politically and religiously, of the U.S. Church through the election of John Kennedy and the Second Vatican Council, another attempt at Americanization surfaced. What has given further impetus to this now vigorous movement have been the recent pastoral letters of the U.S. bishops on disarmament and the economy. These letters are significant because of their content and the attempt of the bishops to enter fully into the national policy debate. However, even more significant has been the process of dialogue and consultation that has accompanied the writing of the letters. This process presages a more participative way of being Church in the United States.

The recent measures of Rome with regard to the U.S. Church have raised suspicions, fears, and anxieties within the American Church regarding the future. These measures have included actions taken against certain American theologians and religious, the pontifical investigation of American seminaries, and the study of religious life.

Finally, the new wave of immigrants into the United States over the last couple of decades from Central and Latin America, as well as Asia—many of whom are Catholic—has made the U.S. Church realize just how middle class it has become. The Church has had significant problems in knowing how to serve these new sisters and brothers.

Structures

Socially, the U.S. Church is culturally diverse but becoming more and more enculturated into modern culture. Meanwhile, its ecclesial structure has remained quite Roman and hierarchical, a structure that is creating tensions with a membership much more attuned to equality, due process, and participation in decision making. As a result, what one finds among many Catholics is a selective and self-conscious style of affiliation with institutional Catholicism. Also, laity in increasing numbers are entering ministerial and leadership positions within the Church and thus, at least potentially, deeply affecting the structures of the Church.

Values

American Catholics are accepting and tolerant, pragmatic and concerned with this world, and able, without much difficulty, to reconcile faith and reason. While American Catholics view religion as an individual choice and do not publicly proselytize, they do have a strong sense of community and are concerned with social justice and an equitable sharing of the goods of this world. The older ethos of the immigrant Church is no longer as prevalent as it was; however, it still casts its shadow over the U.S. Church and creates tensions at times in the areas of authority, the rights of the individual conscience, perspectives on the priesthood, and the place of women in the Church. This older ethos is most obvious in the actions of some of the hierarchy, but it is also prevalent in more conservative elements of the laity.

Having become primarily middle class, Catholics have generally accepted mainstream middle-class values. Politically, most are middle of the road and right of center; however, overall, Catholics are more liberal than Protestants in such areas as sex, morality, family life, and religion. Catholics have shown themselves to be very committed to peace. Indeed, the potential for more and more Catholics to become involved in attempting to effect socioeconomic change out of a commitment to peace and justice seems to be significant. A difficulty that must be dealt with, however, is that, like most other American citizens, most Catholics see religion as something individual. They primarily look for intimacy and support in their local communities, and prefer that politics be kept out of the pulpit. That religion, and so also the Church, has a social responsibility and a role to play in the public sector of politics and economics must be better communicated to Catholics.

Catholics today do not automatically accept the values the Church preaches. Individual Catholics make up their own minds about what they believe. They listen to priests and bishops only to the extent that they believe the priests and bishops know what they are talking about.

The laity seem to place a great value on Church participation. This participation extends considerably beyond Sunday Mass attendance and includes involvement in various ministry roles and leadership as well as attending various Church functions. Women value being treated better within the Church.

The Future

As one looks to the future of the Church in the United States, it is clear that a continuous restructuring of the Church will be needed. This follows from the present vocation picture and the present involvement of the laity in ministerial and leadership roles. More tasks, both ministerial and administrative, will be handed over to the laity. At least some instruction of the laity and clergy will be called for in this process. The role changes that will take place, especially for the priest, will not always be easy. The laity, given their greater responsibilities, will demand more say in the life of the Church on local, diocesan, and national levels. If the bishops can extend their participative process beyond their teaching role, the laity will welcome the opportunity to take part. Meanwhile, the whole Church must face the challenge that because it has become middle class, it may not be able to serve well those who do not fit this mold. This "middle classness" of the U.S. Church also affects its ability to understand well the call to a fundamental option for the poor.

Tensions within the Church will grow as the Church, through its bishops, struggles to find its proper political role. There will be a growing mistrust between the laity and the bishops unless the bishops can articulate more clearly their rationale for speaking out on public issues. They must also convince their membership that they know what they are talking about and that they are not acting in a partisan way nor trying to tell the people how to vote. Similarly, the individualism that is so prevalent in American society must be addressed if the members of the Church are to be moved to greater action on behalf of justice. Also, the conservatism of the young clergy needs to be addressed. Catholic social teaching will have to be taught much better than in the past to both laity and seminarians. Catholics need to realize that they are the most important swing vote in American society and therefore carry significant political power. They can be a major force for justice and peace, if they use their votes.

Catholics will also be important for the broader society in the United States. They have been and can continue to be an influence for tolerance within society, for support of the cause of women, and for bringing a greater communal sense to U.S. society. Hopefully, they will also be an instrument of structural change for the sake of peace and justice.

Finally, as one looks to the future, there will be more tension between the American Church and Rome. At this stage it is difficult to tell what will happen. The United States hierarchy may extend to all aspects of the life of the Church the participative mode used in the writing of their recent pastoral letters. It is desirable that the American Church be allowed to live out its American heritage. This heritage includes those biblical values of equality, liberty, respect for the person, and self-determination that have been so central to the greatness of the United States. It is also to be hoped that the American Church will be willing to share its riches with the broader, global Church and human community. The U.S. Church must also be open to receive the riches that the rest of the world, including Rome, have to share with it.

Ultimately, if the Church is to face these myriad issues with clarity and purpose and some hope for success, it must fashion a national pastoral plan that will give direction to its activities. Otherwise, the Church will dissipate its energies and resources in trying to go in too many directions at once.

CONCLUSION TO PART 1

As we come to the end of this rapid survey and analysis of the present situation in the United States and the U.S. Church, certain core issues begin to emerge. These core issues are realities that underlie all else that is taking place; they must be addressed before there can be any significant transformation of structures within our society. They are also issues that the Church must address, since they are all ultimately religious issues.

First, there is the sense of chosenness that runs through Americans' understanding of themselves as a people. In the beginning this sense of chosenness led the white Anglo-Saxon to look down on the black and Native American. This in turn resulted in the racism, discrimination, and prejudice that cuts through American society toward anyone who has a different colored skin, speaks a different language, and has different customs or beliefs. Together with this sense of chosenness there is often found among Americans the sense of manifest destiny to impose their way of life, structures, and values on the rest of the world. Much of American foreign policy is colored by a feeling of superiority and arrogance that flows from this sense of chosenness and manifest destiny.

Second, there has been the association of salvation with worldly success and the accumulation of wealth. This perception of reality has allowed the wealthy and powerful to set the rules in society and led many to look down on the poor and to blame them for their plight. Furthermore, it has resulted in a lack of real concern for the poor, even the poor in our midst, and for a proper distribution of the goods of this earth. Finally, this perception of reality has given justification to a rapaciousness and concern for economic prosperity that allows the United States to justify almost any action in the name of national security. The "National Security State" and the "Secret Government" have been logical results of the American sense of chosenness combined with the concern for economic prosperity. The same concern for economic prosperity has also led to an unwillingness to deal in a significant way with the serious environmental issues that face the country.

The third issue is individualism and its impact on all aspects of American life. As this individualism has become an ever stronger influence, it has led to a loss of a sense of public virtue and of the common good among many Americans. It has become difficult for Americans to see themselves as a people held together by a common vision, common hopes, and common goals. This same individualism has also resulted in the lack of a national vision that would fully integrate the United States into the global reality in which we live and which would help the United States to deal in a just way with the issues that confront the country and the globe. Furthermore, individualism has affected the view of religion and its role within society that is held by most Americans. How individuals relate to their local Church community has also been influenced by individualism.

It is these issues that will give focus to the remainder of this book as I turn to the mission of the Church in the United States and the strategies to achieve this mission.

I said elsewhere that one of my presuppositions is that the Church must be involved in the transformation of society; I have also spoken of the need for the transformation of society's structures. However, the three issues that have emerged from this analysis of U.S. society and the U.S. Catholic Church deal with attitudes and perspectives on life. How does transformation of society and its structures relate to attitudes and perspectives on life? The relationship lies in the fact that certain attitudes and perspectives lead to particular structures. Hence, these attitudes and perspectives must be dealt with before there can be a change in the structures of society. The three core issues that have emerged in this part of the book are those issues that have instigated and continue to legitimize the present political, economic, and social structures of our society. Hence, these issues must be dealt with if there is to be any hope of transforming structures.

Aside from these three core issues, a question has also emerged regarding the nature and mission of the Church in general. This question has arisen for us as Catholics in the United States from the history of our attempts to bring together our American experience and values with our understanding of what it means to be Church. We need to deal with this issue before we can talk more specifically about the Church's mission in the United States.

PART 2

GOSPEL REFLECTION
ON THE UNITED STATES

5

THEOLOGICAL REFLECTION: ANOTHER TOOL FOR CHURCH PLANNING

In this second part of the book my purpose is to begin a theological reflection on the present situation of the United States. In view of the analysis in the first part of the book, I will be looking at what the Gospel affirms about the United States, what the Gospel calls into question about the United States, and to what the Gospel calls the United States as a country today.

My ultimate goal in this book is to address the question of the mission of the Church in the United States. The primary purpose of these reflections is to discover those specific areas in the life of the United States where there is need for growth in the light of the Gospel. It is these issues that will then focus my reflections on the Church's mission.

Before proceeding to a theological reflection on the situation in the United States today, a few words on the method of theological reflection may be helpful. The first part of this work involved social analysis, a task that makes sense of reality by putting it into a broader picture and drawing connections. Social analysis examines causes, probes consequences, delineates linkages, and identifies actors. This part of the book, theological reflection, is an effort to understand more broadly and deeply the analyzed reality in the light of living faith, the Scriptures, Church teaching, and the resources of tradition.

Theological reflection, as used here, involves two movements.[1] The first sets forth those aspects of the Christian faith tradition that relate to the core issues emerging from social analysis. Sometimes this faith tradition is referred to as the Christian community's "Story." Here "Story" is used as a metaphor for what one would normally refer to as Scripture and Tradition. Thomas Groome explains what is involved:

As our people have made their pilgrimage through history, God has been active in their lives (as God is active in the lives of all peoples).

105

They, in turn, have attempted to respond to God's actions and invitations. From this covenanted relationship there have emerged particular roles and expected lifestyles, written scriptures, interpretations, pious practices, sacraments, symbols, rituals, feast days, communal structures, artifacts, "holy" places, and so on. All of these embody, express, or re-create some part of the history of that covenant. The term "Story" is intended as a metaphor for all such expressions of our faith tradition as they are all part of our Christian Story. From that Story, by God's grace, we draw our life of Christian faith, and by making it accessible again, we experience God's saving deeds on our behalf.[2]

Also to be spelled out in this first movement of theological reflection is the "Vision" or lived response to which Christians are invited by the faith tradition. Again, the word "Vision" is used as a metaphor; it refers to the lived response to which the Christian Story invites us and to the promise that God makes in that Story. To put this in another way, we can say that God's promise and goal or vision for creation is the Reign of God. This vision in turn invites a lived response from us that is faithful to the Reign of God. As we respond, we help to make that Reign a present reality.

Story and Vision are not two separate realities but two aspects of the same reality. As Groome states, "The Story is the Story of the Kingdom; the Vision is the Vision of the Kingdom. The Vision is our response to God's promise in the Story, and the Story is the unfolding of the Vision."[3]

The second movement in theological reflection involves a hermeneutical or interpretative dialectic between the Story and the Vision, on the one hand, and the topic under study, on the other hand. This dialectic proceeds through several steps. First, the community Story is a source of critique for the issue under study. One looks here to see how the Story affirms what is happening, what it calls into question in this activity, and what is called for in order to live the tradition more faithfully.

However, the direction of the dialectic moves not only from the Story to present activity but also from present activity to the Story; the Story itself is to be critically reflected upon rather than passively accepted. The version of the Story that any group of Christians owns and shares can have elements of distortion, since it is passed down to them in the context of history. Hence, "each historical context, with its particular social/cultural ethos and ideologies, influences our interpretation and can give rise to distortions and certainly to 'incompleteness.' "[4] It is important, then, to consider how present experience affirms what is true in the Story and to search for insights and truth not previously found in the Story. It is also important to see if present experience points to aspects of the Story that we must refuse to accept or to go beyond.

Finally, as part of this dialectical process, it is important to ask, "How is our present action creative or noncreative of the Vision (the Reign of

God), and how will we act in the future?" The emphasis here is on action for the sake of making the Reign of God a reality. It is important to keep in mind that while the Reign of God is a measure of the present, the Vision is also an open future that is being shaped by present activity. Hence, we can only know the Vision, the Reign of God, as we shape it. Our present understanding of the Vision, then, can never be put forth as the blueprint for the final form of the Reign of God.[5]

In the following chapters the above process provides the context for reflection. In the following two chapters I will set forth the elements of the Story and Vision that relate to the core issues that emerged from the social analysis in Part One. The section concludes with a reflection on the conditions in the United States in light of these themes.

6

BIBLICAL PERSPECTIVES ON LIFE

Before looking at specific theological themes, I would like to present a biblical perspective or reflection on life. The perspective presented here received its inspiration from Walter Brueggemann's fine book *The Bible Makes Sense.*[1] When I first read this book several years ago, it helped me verbalize my own developing understanding of a biblical perspective on life. I present this perspective here because I am aware of how basic it has become in my own thinking on life and how it has significantly shaped my thinking on the mission of the Church in the United States. I also present it as a background against which to read the reflections on more specific theological themes in the following chapter.[2]

Those who belong to the Judeo-Christian tradition are above all "people of the Bible." The Bible is the very source of their tradition and the constitution to which they constantly return in order to understand themselves and reform themselves.

Such "people of the Bible" attempt to understand the perspective on life offered by the Bible and to conform their life-world to the life-world which is central to the Bible. It is important to understand that the Bible does not give specific answers to all questions people may have today. Rather, the Bible presents a way of life, a way of looking at life and dealing with it, and a model for living life.

I will, first, give a general description of this biblical model and contrast it with other possible models for viewing life. Doing this, I hope, will highlight the uniqueness of the biblical model. Second, I will attempt to explain the consequences of accepting the biblical perspective on life.

THE BIBLICAL MODEL

Each person, by living in certain contexts and listening to certain voices, has adopted, often unconsciously, one or more models for living. In other words, each person has embraced one or more perspectives for viewing life that control how they act and relate to others. The voices listened to include the voices of parents and teachers, siblings and peers, as well as the voices of the media, especially television. They probably also include the voices of tradition as well as the voices of possible dreams. All these voices and many others have, in different ways, gripped our lives and shaped our experiences. In the process these voices have come to shape our consciousness and urged us to a particular notion of life. In this way these voices, to a greater or lesser extent, have defined our identity and destiny.

The model or perspective for viewing life that is central to the Bible is what Walter Brueggemann calls a "covenantal-historical model." In this biblical perspective on life, life is above all seen as shaped by covenants, by enduring commitments of God to the people, and of the people to God and to one another.

Second, the biblical perspective on life always sees life as part of a historical process. In this perspective the primary sources of meaning are the historical memories that the community has of its decisive interaction in history with its covenant partner, God. In other words, the interactions between God and God's people in history—which run the gamut from love to hate—are seen as the primary source of meaning and knowledge about God, self, others, and life. How one does or does not act is primarily determined by the history of the people as the people of God and by their hopes for the future, which are also rooted in the past. Good moral decisions cannot be made based solely on what is good for the present, by what will work or not work.

To sum up, life in the biblical perspective consists of living in history in covenant relationship with God and one another. Moreover, it is specifically through reflection upon the vast deposit of memories of the interactions in history of the covenant partners, God and God's people, that one finds the meaning of life.

The uniqueness of this biblical model stands out when it is contrasted with three other perspectives on life that shape the lives of people today. Although no one ever fully or intentionally embodies any of them, they do exercise a great influence on many people and, in varying ways, define cultural values and expectations.

First, there is the modern-industrial-scientific model that has been a decisive influence in shaping many public institutions. In this life perspective knowledge is power. Hence, life consists in acquiring enough knowledge to control and predict the world and thereby secure one's life against every danger and threat. In this perspective, everyone and everything is valued for their usefulness and high value is placed on competence and achieving, on success and getting ahead. People have value for what they do or, even worse, for what they have. Those who earn little and are not competent, such as the poor and the underprivileged, do not even exist for all practical purposes. This view, then, puts a premium on what is knowable, manageable, and predictable. It does not appreciate grace, because everything is earned. It is not open to mystery, because everything must be explained. It has no place for transcendence, because everything must be managed. This perspective prevails in public institutions and dominates the job market that pays primary attention to competence and performance for the sake of profit.

In contrast to this modern-scientific-industrial model, the biblical perspective on life affirms that human existence does not consist primarily in the capacity to know and control and manage. Rather, the biblical perspective asserts that real life consists in risking commitments to God and to others and living out those commitments—without knowing where they will lead—with deep trust in God's mysterious empowering grace. How to live out these commitments is learned from memories of the past about the interactions between God and God's people. One is urged on by compelling visions of the future that are also rooted in this past.

The biblical perspective also asserts that the individual person has value because each has been created in the image and likeness of God. One's value does not come from what the person can do or has or has done. Hence, every human person possesses an inalienable dignity that stamps human existence prior to any division into races or nations and prior to human labor and human achievement. Through the covenant, God has entered into a personal relationship with each person, offering love to each.

The existentialist model asserts that meaning exists only in and derives from the decisions made by the individual in the present moment. In other words, the individual human decision-maker is the sole agent of meaning. In this perspective meanings cannot be appropriated from others, nor is there any possibility of transcendent meaning in experience. No meanings can be given to or be prior to the individual in the present moment.

Obviously, this model for life tends to deny the importance of community since it locates meaning only in terms of the solitary decision-maker. This perspective on life also devalues the historical process as a source of meaning since meaning is located only in the "now" of the present decision. Memories and hopes have no significance for the identity or destiny of the individual. This perspective on life is very appealing to the young who have difficulty understanding the importance of the past and accepting the wisdom of the community. This perspective is also closely related to the individualism discussed in chapters three and four.

In contrast, the biblical perspective on life asserts that meanings are never private but always communal. Meanings are never to be found in an isolated "now" but always as part of an ongoing historical process. This biblical perspective insists that God is a serious partner in people's lives and that life consists of a dialogue with God. While God is merciful, God insists on loyalty and holds people accountable. Moreover, in the biblical model, people live as members of a community in which deep ties exist among the members. These ties result from all having experienced a common history and from all being partners of a covenant that God has made with all the people. No decision can be made as though other people do not exist. Others do exist and all that one does or does not do affects them as well as oneself. Finally, in the biblical perspective, life must always be seen in a historical perspective. Decisions must be determined by the community's history and by its hopes for the future.

Third, the transcendentalist model maintains that life is too complicated to endure and too messy to be the source of meaning. The real meanings are to be found in another sphere of reality that is simple, clear, unspoiled, and uncomplicated. This model appears in notions of love and marriage that envision a "little house in love-land" where there is no telephone and reality cannot break in. In its religious form this model finds expression in pious language and religious services behind stained-glass windows that attempt to block the cries of hunger and the groans of injustice. It also manifests itself in a type of mystical meditation that seeks to shut out historical experience and to find meaning in eternal mysteries rather than in the realities of everyday life. Hence, those who hold to this view tend to shy away from getting involved in life, its struggles, and its hurts. For them, issues of social justice are not all that important. This perspective is a form of escapism in which no responsibility is taken for the historical process.

In contrast to this model the biblical perspective asserts that we must be deeply involved in life and take responsibility for the historical process. The biblical perspective denies that meaning can be immune from the incongruities and discontinuities of history. Rather, decisive meanings are located in and derived precisely from the hurts and surprises of historical experience, and these historical hurts and surprises form the basis for reflection and contemplation. The practice of religion cannot be a form of escapism from life and the injustice, the pain, and the confusion that often exist. The biblical perspective demands involvement in life in all its messiness and pain as well as its joys.

No one ever fully or intentionally embodies any of these three models in a pure form. However, these ways of viewing life do exist in the world and exercise great influence on many people. Presenting these clear alternatives helps us understand better what is involved in the biblical perspective.

CONSEQUENCES OF THE BIBLICAL PERSPECTIVE

The consequences of accepting the biblical perspective on life are three:
• one receives in the Bible a precise memory of the past from which to draw meaning and direction for today;
• one receives a special expectation for the future from which to draw hope;
• one receives a new vocation.

The historical memory we receive is very specific. It is a memory of historical liberation, as found in the Exodus, and of empowerment, as seen in what God accomplished for Israel through Moses, the Judges, and David. It is also a memory of passionate caring-suffering, as seen in the crucifixion of Jesus, and the surprise of new life, as experienced in the resurrection. When asked to identify ourselves, we can answer, with the community, by reciting those concrete events that have happened in the community's past: We are a people who have been liberated and empowered and given new life through the passionate caring-suffering of one who loves us.

There are many things we can learn from this historical memory that give direction for life today. Most important is a knowledge of the God in whose image all were created and whom all are to imitate. As we peruse this history, we discern that God is not a remote agent concerned only about self. Rather, the God of the Bible is above all a God who is with the people and for the people. God's goodness lies not in some transcendent and remote majesty but in God's constant readiness to be with and for the people simply because God wills to. This God is a God who is for others.

This quality of God as one who is with and for the people comes out especially in the theme of the covenant. This theme is central in the Bible because God is revealed there primarily as a covenant-making and covenant-keeping God. In the Hebrew Scriptures there are four dimensions of God as the covenant-maker, four dimensions to the commitments that God makes.

First, from the Exodus event, God is seen as one who creates a people and gives them freedom. God does this by becoming actively involved in their lives when they cry out in desperation. As God says in Exodus 3: "I have seen the affliction of my people ... and have heard their cry ... I know their sufferings ... I have come down to deliver them."

However, God's powerful intervention on behalf of Israel is not for the sake of people who are honorable or worthy or impressive. It is for a rabble and ignoble lot that God acts and to whom God makes a commitment. God does it because God wills to.

Second, the Lord is one who comes and is present with power.

God acts powerfully on behalf of Israel when Israel is helpless and has no power of its own. God fights for those who cannot defend themselves, that is, the poor, the weak, and the oppressed. The message of the Exodus event is that in the midst of conflicts where all seems lost, deliverance is possible because of God's commitment to those who trust. God is constantly with the people and present with power.

A third characteristic of God is God's abiding presence in the midst of the people. This is apparent especially in the traditions about the temple and its cult that show God taking up permanent presence in the temple. God is not a passive object in the temple to be adored but One who is always acting and taking initiative. God is always doing on behalf of the people to make their lives better. So God not only abides with the people but is engaged for the people, doing what they most need but cannot do, that is, securing their own existence.

The fourth characteristic of God is that where God is, life is changed and hope is possible. As God says in Isaiah: "Fear not, I am with you; be not dismayed, I am your God. I will strengthen you, and help you, and uphold you" (41:10).

The history of God with the people and for the people comes to full expression in Jesus who is Emmanuel, "God with us." In the ministry of Jesus we see most decidedly who this God is: a God who is above all concerned for the poor and takes the side of the poor and brings power to people whose power is faint and low; one who brings food to people who are hungry; one who brings healing where disease seems to rule; a God who brings life where death was all that could be anticipated. From the ministry of Jesus it becomes clear that being with and for another means to share in the life of the other and to be vulnerable to the situation of another. Being with and for another means to be subjected to the conditions and risks of another, even to the point of suffering and death.

This God who is with and for the people promises to be present to the end of time. Moreover, nothing and no one can separate the people from this God who has entered into covenant with them. The very presence of this God brings transformation, making all things new.

This view of God, taken from the communal historical memory, forces us to question our own self-perception. If all have been created "in God's image" and are "to be perfect as God is perfect," then the central task of each life is covenant-making and covenant-keeping. The central human vocation is to be with one's brothers and sisters and for one's brothers and sisters, to be actively engaged in their midst, empowering them to deal with life. This must be an abiding presence and not just now and again. We must also be willing to be vulnerable to the situation of others, to be willing to suffer with them and die for them and have our own person called into question. This engagement above all must be with and for the poor, the weak, and the oppressed.

Another consequence of accepting the biblical faith is that from the Bible we also receive a special expectation for the future from which we can draw hope. What that future will be we find from reflection on God's past actions with the people. Because God is faithful, God's people can trust God to act in the future in ways characteristic of God's past actions. At least three shapes for God's future acts arise from God's history with the people: God as Freedom-Giver; God as Exile-Ender; God as Life-Bringer.

The most powerful and decisive action of God in Israel's past was the Exodus event. When Israel was enslaved God gave the people freedom even when it seemed impossible. From the time of the Exodus Israel understood its life differently. The Exodus became the prism through which other experiences were understood. The crossing of the Jordan was later presented as a new Exodus and the salvation brought by Jesus can only be understood against this background. The Exodus, then, was God's most decisive action and symbolic of God's most characteristic way of acting. God is essentially the Freedom-Giver.

Having been made in God's image and given the responsibility to make God present in the world today, those who believe are also called to be freedom-givers like God. They are called to be practitioners of freedom in their daily lives. Today Exodus is about the great liberation movements going on in the world. Exodus is about deliverance from political and economic oppression, from unjust working conditions, from inhuman housing situations, from discrimination based on race, color, sex. Exodus is about the liberation of a child from fear or of an older person from loneliness and bitterness. Liberation is about working for change in the oppressive structures in Church and society. The Exodus, then, is the shape of God's promised future for the people.

Aside from being Freedom-Giver, God is also the Exile-Ender and Home-Bringer. In 587 B.C.E. Israel was led into Exile. In this context the people felt displaced, alienated, forgotten, and bitter. However, in the Exile the Bible affirms that because God did not will that the people be displaced, God acted to bring them home. The faith of Israel, then, is that Exile is not a permanent condition. God wills that people be settled safely in a world where they are at home politically and economically as well as psychologically and spiritually.

At the present time there is a pervasive sense of displacement among many people who have felt the homelessness and alienation of the modern world dominated by industrialism, urbanization, and impersonalism. Moreover, homelessness also refers to refugees in many parts of the world and those uprooted by urban projects. Homelessness further describes those who no longer seem to belong; those who are alienated not only from their own group or family but from a sense of meaning in their own lives. It is this homelessness that needs to be dealt with. Transformation of those public institutions that are part of the alienating process is mandatory. Also needed is caring intervention in peoples' lives which ends estrangement and gives people a sense of belonging. God's actions in the past give hope that God will not be satisfied until all people are at home in God's Kingdom.

Finally, God is Life-Bringer. Israel intended to confess above all in its creation stories that God has the power and the will to turn chaos to creation, to deal with the forces of death, and to bring life. However, it is especially in the resurrection of Jesus from the dead that God the Life-Bringer is manifested. In the risen Jesus the Church has come to know that the power of death does not have to conquer. Rather, there is One who is stronger and who gives life, a life that is eternal, a life that is a life with God. We can trust that life will continue to be given to those who believe in Jesus and struggle to bring freedom and an end to estrangement.

The future that opens up through biblical faith is clear from God's actions in the past. We can trust that it will come because of God's past faithfulness to the promises made. It is also important to trust that our own struggles as God's instruments to bring about this future will succeed. Finally, it is crucial to see that the future envisioned here is not a withdrawal from history, but a renewal of humanness in history, so that new humanness may emerge, especially among the powerless, the homeless, and the poor.

A third consequence of accepting the biblical perspective on life is that we receive a new vocation, a vocation to live life completely in a way consonant with the covenant relationship with God. In other words, we are called to conversion, the double process of turning from the way things were and embracing the way God has promised they will be. With conversion a decisive change takes place in our lives. This change is not about joining another organization along with others, nor adding another loyalty alongside all the others. Rather, this change involves a sharp reorientation of every loyalty already laying claim to our allegiance.

Conversion, as it is understood in the Bible, is an act of entering into covenant with a new covenant partner, God. This new covenant involves commitment to a new set of demands, entering a different history, embracing a different memory, and living with different promises. As a result, life is discerned in new ways and we live in a very different way.

Conversion demands more than a mere change of external appearances. What is involved is a conversion of the heart, that organ of decision making through which one's whole life-orientation is determined. While such conversion is a human task it is possible only if it is empowered by God. In other words, the Bible recognizes that a person can convert only if God gives that person a new heart to replace the stony one (Ez 36:22–32).

Conversion, however, is not a private event, confined to a spiritual or private agenda. When we enter into a covenant with God we also enter into a covenant with God's people. Covenant with God is always a covenant in a community of people who have made similar commitments and received parallel promises from the Lord. Conversion calls for a decision that has social and political implications. Conversion demands becoming involved in community and attempting to reorient even public institutions so that they might serve the purposes of the Lord.

The resurrection of Jesus made this community possible in its fullest sense, because it was the resurrection that made it possible for all to receive the Spirit that makes them totally one with Jesus and hence totally one with one another.

Conversion also involves entering into solidarity with the weak, the poor, the powerless. This is difficult because we would rather practice charity *toward* "them" than solidarity *with* "them." However, Jesus saved us, not by practicing charity toward us but by becoming one of us, by entering into solidarity with us and suffering with us so as to empower us to be able to take responsibility for ourselves.

In the same way all believers are now called to become vulnerable and to enter into solidarity with the weak, the poor, and the powerless as Jesus did in his public life. Such solidarity has as its purpose to help them gain economic and political freedom so that they can care for and have responsibility for themselves. In attempting to bring about reconciliation, however, individual acts of compassion are of little significance unless they are coupled with a radical address to the public institutions that shape common life.

Finally, the call to conversion involves concern for God's good earth. It means treating with care and responsibility the environment, the resources the earth has to offer. All creation is a gift and men and women are to be faithful stewards in caring for it. As Genesis points out, men and women are to be fruitful, to care for the earth, and to have "dominion" over it. This means, as the Book of Wisdom says, that they are "to govern the world in holiness and justice and to render judgment in integrity of heart"(9:3).

This, then, is the vocation to which all have been called by their covenant partner. Life is not for self-indulgence, nor for desperate coping, nor for frantic, empty surviving. Rather, it is life lived after the manner of this very God who empties himself to obedience in the life of Jesus. Human vocation consists of that emptying activity after the manner of God in Jesus. However, it is not emptying as a simple spiritual discipline. It is rather emptying for the sake of healing, caring, and bringing newness and life. Since God has become vulnerable in caring ways for people, we are now called to become vulnerable in caring ways for our brothers and sisters. Vocation is not simply what we do with our lives; it is the very shape of that life. The call of God is to embrace passion and suffering, to care for the weak—that which God does all through biblical history.

Biblical faith, then, provides an alternative identity, an alternative way of relating to the world. It offers a radical and uncompromising challenge to ordinary ways of self-understanding. It is an invitation to join in the continuing pilgrimage of those who live in history, caring in ways that matter, secured by the covenanting God who is always present with power in history. This way of understanding life lets us be open to hurts but also to healing surprises of new life which emerge in the life of the community.

The crucifixion of Jesus, like the compassion of God in the Old Testament, provides a model for the solidarity that should be practiced with the poor and the powerless. The resurrection of Jesus, like every life-giving act of God in the Old Testament, provides a model for all the surprises of new life that happen among people—those surprises that come when people think that things are settled and closed and impossible to escape from. Moreover, this way of understanding, provided by biblical faith, lets all embrace their own experience as important and the life of their brother and sister as part of their own.

Most of all, however, biblical faith is about a God who is committed to people, who promises to be with them in every hurting and rejoicing place in life. While other perspectives on life promise other things, the biblical faith perspective promises that the Lord of glory, the One hidden and yet known, is present with people in all the hurting and healing of historical existence. This demands that all be present to their brothers and sisters in the same way. Ultimately, that is the soul of social justice, which is clear from Matthew 25 when the just ask:

"Lord, when did we see you hungry and feed you or see you thirsty and give you drink? When did we welcome you away from home or clothe you in your nakedness? When did we visit you when you were ill or in prison?" The king will answer them: "I assure you, as often as you did it for one of my least brothers, you did it for me." (vv. 37–40)

7

OUR LIVING FAITH

Against the background of the previous chapter on the biblical model of life, the purpose of this chapter is to take up in more depth selected biblical and theological themes. These themes were suggested by the core issues that emerged from the analysis in the first part of the book.

ELECTION

The idea of Israel as the special people of God can be found in early texts in the Hebrew Scriptures (for example, Ex 19:5; Jdg 5:11). The traditions of the Pentateuch, outside of the book of Deuteronomy, trace the call of Israel to the call of Abraham:

> The LORD said to Abram: "Go forth from the land of your kinsfolk and from your father's house to a land that I will show you. I will make of you a great nation, and I will bless you; I will make your name great, so that you will be a blessing. I will bless those who bless you and curse those who curse you. All the communities of the earth shall find blessing in you." (Gn 12:1–3)

However, the classical vocabulary for speaking of Israel's election by God appears for the first time in the book of Deuteronomy (7th century B.C.E.).

> For you are a people sacred to the LORD, your God; he has chosen you from all the nations on the face of the earth to be a people peculiarly his own. It was not because you are the largest of all nations that the LORD set his heart on you and chose you, for you are really the smallest of all nations. It was because the LORD loved you and because of his fidelity to the oath he had sworn to your fathers, that he brought you out with his strong hand from the place of slavery. . . . (Dt 7:6–8)

Notice that it is clear that Israel's election was not due to any merits on Israel's part (see also Dt 9:4). Rather, Israel's election was due solely to God's love and the oath that God had made to Israel's ancestors. It is important to understand that Israel's election did not follow from its obedience or depend upon its obedience. Rather, obedience is to be Israel's response to its election (see Dt 27:9f.). However, the fulfillment of the promises that God makes to this chosen people will depend upon Israel's obedience.[1]

As the prophets make clear, Israel's consciousness of election could be distorted in popular belief into national pride and unfounded assurance in God's protection (Mic 3:11). In his temple sermon Jeremiah strongly condemned such a distortion. In this passage he condemns the people of Jerusalem for their almost magical trust that, because of the presence of the temple in their city, they were safe from all enemies. As he tells them:

"Only if you thoroughly reform your ways and your deeds; if each of you deals justly with his neighbor; if you no longer oppress the resident alien, the orphan, and the widow; if you no longer shed innocent blood in this place, or follow strange gods to your own harm, will I remain with you in this place, in the land which I gave your fathers long ago and forever." (Jer 7:5–7)

Election therefore carried no guarantees of salvation and protection for a sinful people.

Election also carried with it the idea of mission. The people were not chosen for their own sakes but for others. Genesis 12:1–3 states that Abraham and his descendants were chosen to be a source of blessings to all the other nations (see also Gn 26:4; 28:14). However one wishes to explain the "Servant Songs" in the book of Isaiah, it is clear that Israel in some way is to be identified with the servant (see Is 41:8; 43:10; 44:1; 45:4, and so forth). In these songs the servant is specifically said to have been called to establish justice, to be a light for the nations, to open the eyes of the blind, to bring prisoners out of confinement, to bring God's salvation to the ends of the earth (see Is 42:4, 6f; 49:6). It is also clear that the servant is to bring deliverance through suffering, spending his life for the sake of others and giving his life as an offering for sin (Is 50:5f; 53:3–11).

The counterpart of election is not reprobation but simply nonelection for the purposes for which Israel was chosen. Israel's election did not mean that God was not concerned with the other nations. The prophet Amos clearly brings out Yahweh's concern for other nations (Amos 9:7). Moreover, as Genesis 12:1–3 proves, Israel's election is to be understood in the context of God's relations to every nation.

That Israel's election did not automatically guarantee God's presence and protection was brought home to Israel through the destruction of Jerusalem in 587 B.C.E. and the Exile. As a result of these incidents the prophets came to understand that the old election was finished. It was not God but the people who broke the relationship through their sinfulness. However, Jeremiah and Ezekiel, especially, look forward to a new election based on a new covenant (Jer 31:31–34; Ez 36:24–28; see also Second Isaiah's many references to Israel as the "chosen," for example, 43:10; 43:20; 44:1; 45:4).

The early Church saw these promises of a new covenant fulfilled in Jesus, and those who believed in him were understood to be the new elect. In the synoptic Gospels the "elect"are always mentioned in connection with the final catastrophe and judgment (Mt 22:14; 24:22f; Mk 13:20f; Lk 18:7); the term here would appear to refer to those who survive the tribulations at the end of time and remain faithful (see also Rom 8:28–39). In other passages (Col 3:12; 2 Tm 2:10; Tt 1:1; Rev 17:14) the term "chosen" appears to have become a conventional title for Christians (see also 2 Jn 1, 13). Election in the New Testament, then, is a continuation and enlargement of the election of Israel. The emphasis is on the divine initiative in the process of salvation. In Romans 9:14–33 Paul asserts the freedom of God to show mercy to whom God wishes. Election in the New Testament, as in the Old Testament, imposes responsibilities upon the elect; it is clear in the New Testament that the elect have a mission, that is, to make disciples of all the nations and to baptize them (Mt 28:18–20).

It is clear that election by God is a gratuitous act and is not dependent upon the merits of the one chosen. Being chosen carries with it responsibilities but gives no guarantee of salvation to the chosen unless they respond in obedience to God's will. Being chosen also carries with it a mission to reach out to others and to bring them God's blessings even if that means giving up one's own life.

PEOPLE OF GOD

Because God had chosen Israel and delivered the people from slavery and then made a covenant with them, Israel came to understand itself as the people of God (Ex 6:6–8; Lev 26:9–12; Dt 7:6–8). Israel was both God's creation and God's special possession. It is important to understand that in Hebrew thinking the people formed a whole: it was to the people as such that God was understood to have made promises and it was the people who were saved. The individual Israelite was saved only insofar as he or she was a member of the people and involved with the people. There was no idea of an individual being saved apart from the people.

This special relationship of being the people of God obliged Israel in a special way to be loyal to God. The Ten Commandments, as the statutes of the covenant, were intended to express the core of this loyalty. Israel was told very specifically that if it was faithful, God would be faithful to the promises of the covenant of Sinai regarding the land and prosperity (Ex 19:3–6; Dt 6:1–3; 6:17–19). If Israel was not faithful to the covenant, God promised to punish them severely, even to the point of extermination

(Josh 23:14–16). The reality was that Israel was unfaithful to the covenant. In fact Ezekiel saw the whole history of Israel as a history of sin (see Ezekiel 16 and 20). Because of its infidelity Israel lost everything. The northern kingdom (2 Kgs 17:7–18) and then the southern kingdom (2 Kgs 21:11–15) were destroyed, and the people were led off into exile. In the Exile Israel came to understand that because of its sinfulness it was responsible for the broken covenant. However, Israel continued to believe in its special relationship to God because of the even older and unconditional covenant that God had made with Abraham (Gn 17:3–8). Moreover, through the prophets, Israel came to understand that God would make a new covenant with them much like the earlier Sinai covenant. At that time, God would also give Israel a new heart and a new spirit that would enable it to stay true to the covenant this time (Jer 32:36–41; Ez 36:24–27).

For the early Christian community it was this covenant, promised through the prophets, that God established through Christ's death and resurrection. God established this new covenant specifically because of the promises to Abraham (see Galatians 3). Hence, the community of believers in Christ came to see itself as the legitimate successor of Israel as the people of God (Acts 3:25). 1 Peter 2:9–10 brings out this understanding very well:

You, however, are a "chosen race, a royal priesthood, a holy nation, a people he claims for his own to proclaim the glorious works" of the One who called you from darkness into his marvelous light. Once you were no people, but now you are God's people; once there was no mercy for you, but now you have found mercy. (See also 2 Cor 6:16 and Heb 8:10.)

As with the Old Testament people of God, being God's people carries a responsibility of fidelity to God. The Second Vatican Council picked up on this image of the people of God to refer to the community of those who believe in Christ (LG, Chapter 2). The Council makes the point that it has pleased God to make people holy and save them, not merely as individuals without any mutual bonds, "but by making them into a single people, a people which acknowledge Him in truth and serve Him in holiness" (LG 9). Again we see the important point that people are saved not as individuals but as members of a people. Individuals live in a network of historical and social relationships by which they are bound to each other and which have a function in the mediation of salvation.

The Council points out that the members of the new people of God are those who believe in Christ and are united in the Spirit with Christ (see Gal 3:7f and Jn 3:5–6) who is the head of this people. The heritage of this people is the dignity and freedom of the children of God through the power of the Spirit. Its law is the command to love as Christ has loved us. Its goal is to establish the Reign of God that was begun by Christ but will not reach its fullness until the end. This people is to be a lasting and sure seed of unity, hope, and salvation for the whole human race. Established by Christ as a fellowship of life, charity, and truth, it is also used by Him as an instrument for the redemption of all, and is sent forth into the whole world as the light of the world and the salt of the earth (cf. Mt 5:13–16) (LG 9).

All the members of this people of God share in Christ's prophetic office and have a responsibility to be living witnesses to Christ, especially by a life of faith and charity. They are to proclaim Christ by struggling against the forces of evil, as they manifest themselves in the world, and by the spoken word (LG 12).

Christ's mission is to make the subjection of all things to himself a reality so that he can offer all of them to the Father. It is through this new people of God that Christ now works to subject all things to himself. Hence, this people of God must work to subject all things to Christ.

The people of God, then, must learn the deepest meaning and value of all creation and how to relate it to the praise of God. They must assist one another to live holier lives even in their daily occupations so as to subject themselves better to Christ. By human labor, technical skill, and civic culture they must perfect all created goods for the benefit of every person. They must work to see that created goods are fittingly distributed among people and that such goods in their own way lead to general progress in human and Christian liberty. Furthermore, they must remedy any institutions and conditions of the world that are customarily an inducement to sin. They are to see that all things are conformed to the norms of justice and favor the practice of virtue rather than hinder it. Finally, they must imbue culture and human activity with moral values (LG 36).

The image of the people of God accents the continuity between Israel and the Christian community as well as the human nature of this society. The image of the Body of Christ, on the other hand, brings out the specific difference between the Old Testament people of God and the New Testament people of God. The image of the Body of Christ expresses the new reality that Christ has brought about for the people of God through his death, resurrection, and sending of the Spirit, that is, the intimate union that now exists between Christ and the people of God.

It was, of course, St. Paul who developed this image of the Body of Christ. To understand this image it is important to keep in mind that in speaking of the Body of Christ, Paul is referring to the personal body of the dead and risen Christ. Hence, the Body of Christ, to which all are united, refers to the personal but resurrected body of Christ. Also, for Paul "body" refers to the whole individual person. In other words, "body" does not refer just to the physical body as something distinct from the soul. Rather, the word "body" designates the whole individual person, body and soul.

The classical text for understanding Paul's idea of the Body of Christ is 1 Corinthians 12:12–27. In this passage Paul clearly understands the union between Christ and all Christians to be a corporal union. This is much more than a corporate union, which would only be a moral union. Moreover, because of their intimate union with Christ, Christians are also one with each other. What effects this union? It is, says St. Paul, the possession of the Spirit of Christ: "We have all been baptized in one Spirit to form one body." The same Spirit that is in the human Christ and which brought about his resurrection and exaltation is also in each Christian who believes in Jesus. What preserves this union is the Eucharist. As Paul says in 1 Corinthians 10:16–17: "Is not the cup of blessing we bless a sharing in the blood of Christ? And is not the bread we break a sharing in the body of Christ? Because the loaf of bread is one, we, many though we are, are one body, for we all partake of the one loaf."

As Paul points out in 1 Corinthians 12, in a human body different members have different functions; however, all members depend upon each other. If each Christian forms one physical individual with Christ, then, "if one member suffers, all the members suffer with it; if one member is honored, all the members share its joy" (v. 26). In other words, the actions of each affect all the other members of the Body of Christ, not just in some moral way but in some real, almost physical, way. This notion is easy to understand today when we consider how all peoples around the globe are interrelated with one another.

All that is expressed in the image of the Body of Christ regarding the intimate union of Christ and Christians is also expressed in John's Gospel through the allegory of the vine and the branches (15:1–8). The union of the Christian with Christ is like the union of a branch with the vine. As the branch totally depends upon and receives its life from the vine, so Christians are so closely joined to Christ that they completely depend upon Christ for life. The basis of this union is Christ's love. Keeping the commandments, which are summed up in the commandment of love (15:9–10, 12), is the prerequisite for remaining in this love and this sharing in the life of Christ.

In sum, we can see that among all the nations of the earth there is ultimately only one people of God, which is made up of people from every race scattered throughout the world (LG 13). Hence, no individual, no people, no race, no nation can ever act only for its own interests or even put its interests above those of everyone else. There is something greater than the individual that gives the individual meaning and significance and that calls the individual constantly out of herself/himself. It is the common good, the Reign of God, the People of God, the Body of Christ.

SALVATION

Salvation involves the idea of deliverance from a dangerous situation that threatens harm. In reading passages from the Hebrew Scriptures regarding the nature of salvation, a few things need to be kept in mind. The ancient Israelites had no idea of a spiritual reality separate from material reality and they had no awareness of an afterlife. The only good life for the ancient Israelite was seen in terms of the concrete existence that one knows by experience. Salvation, then, was seen in terms of concrete experiences and situations such as victory in battle, good crops, healing in sickness, liberation from captivity, ransom from slavery, freedom from debt, or freedom from oppression by overlords and landlords. More than this was not looked for. These material blessings are not merely symbols of spiritual blessings, they are the effect of spiritual blessings. The situation changes, though, when there is an awareness of an afterlife and a perception of a spiritual reality separate from material reality. In this context the possession of material blessings cannot be associated with salvation in such a simplistic fashion.

In the Hebrew Scriptures God saved primarily through human means, especially by raising up people to be saviors and empowering them to save, such as the judges and the kings. At the same time it is emphasized that it was Yahweh who was responsible (Jdg 7; Is 63:8f; Hosea 13:4–8). The basis for Yahweh's constant reaching out to save Israel was the covenant relationship that existed between Yahweh and Israel.

The first and greatest act of salvation by Yahweh was the Exodus, the deliverance of the people from slavery in Egypt (Ex 14:10–31; 15:1–2). The subsequent saving acts of Yahweh on behalf of the people included guidance through the desert, the occupation of the Promised Land, deliverance from enemies through the judges, and the establishment of the monarchy and deliverance from the Philistines. With the period of the judges and the monarchy we find more and more stress in the Scriptures on Israel's lack of fidelity to Yahweh in spite of Yahweh's constant saving activity and blessing. This lack of fidelity led the prophets to understand that the further salvation of Israel would be through a judgment that would reduce the nation to a mere remnant. The judgment came in the destruction of the northern kingdom of Israel in 721 B.C.E. and the destruction of the southern kingdom of Judah in 587 B.C.E. This latter destruction was followed by the exile of the leaders of the people to Babylon.

In the period of the Exile (587–535 B.C.E.) and afterward, the idea of salvation in Israel deepened and expanded. Salvation came to be viewed as a restoration of Israel to its own land. Therefore, salvation was viewed under the image of God bringing home the remnant (Is 43:5–6; Jer 23:6–8; 30:10). However, it soon became clear that a simple restoration of historic Israel would not suffice: a restoration that amounted to a new creation of Israel was necessary. A new Exodus, a new Zion, a new Israel, a new heaven and earth, a new covenant were required (see Is 40–55; Jer 30–31). Moreover, being a blood member of Israel was not enough for salvation. It became mandatory for each individual to be committed to Yahweh and to live a virtuous life (Ez 18). The newly granted salvation was to be realized in a kingdom of peace in which God would reign as king (Is 52:7). The idea of salvation now approached the idea of liberation from all evil, collective and personal, and the acquisition of complete security. However, salvation in the Old Testament never quite reached the idea of salvation from sin and the granting of spiritual good. Salvation was always seen primarily from a material, militant, and political perspective.

To the extent that salvation was seen as affecting nations other than Israel, salvation was sometimes presented as Israel's rule over defeated nations. In this connection it is important to understand that even the political supremacy of Israel was not a purely secular form of salvation. In Israel's perspective Israel was the people of God and so God would be revealed to the nations only through Israel. In the thinking of the ancient world, the people whose god is the most powerful obtains supremacy over other nations. For the Israelites, to the extent that salvation was to be extended to other nations, it could only be through Israel's supremacy over other nations. Another development needed to take place before they could understand that salvation could come to other peoples without the people of God overcoming them and imposing upon them their cultural/religious perspectives and values. This development was the idea that Yahweh was the God of all peoples. This happened only in the late sixth century B.C.E. with the understanding that Yahweh was not just the only God of Israel, but the only God in the world (Is 45:18–25).

It is only in the New Testament that it is clearly stated that God desires the salvation of all people (the classical text is 1 Tim 2:1–6; see also Mk 10:45; Rom 11:32). Theologians later came to understand this to mean that God gives everyone the grace sufficient to attain salvation, if the individual but responds to that grace.

In the New Testament the word "salvation" as a religious term is almost never applied to purely earthly conditions. Even where salvation is thought of as a healing from illness, help in a storm, or deliverance from mortal danger, it points to a deeper reality because of its connection with faith. Any healing is a sign of the salvation bestowed by Christ; also, the salvation Jesus brings is a salvation from sin, a forgiveness of sins (Acts 5:31; 1 Tim 1:15; Lk 1:77; Mt 1:21). For such salvation from sin faith is demanded (Lk 7:50), a faith through which one accepts the Gospel preached and the salvation it proclaims (Acts 16:30f; Rom 10:10; 1 Cor 1:21; Eph 2:8).

The New Testament emphasizes that salvation is a work of divine initiative (1 Th 5:9; 2 Th 2:13; 2 Tim 1:9) and God's mercy. Moreover, salvation is not something that is achieved in a once-and-for-all action. Rather, salvation is a process. One experiences here on earth only the beginning of a salvation that is ultimately achieved only in the eschatological event (1 Cor 3:1f; 5:5; Heb 6:9f; 9:28; 1 Pt 1:5; 2:2; 2 Tim 2:10; Rom 13:11). Present salvation is the situation that has been created by the redemptive death and resurrection of Jesus: liberation from sin and the law (Rom 6–8; Eph 2:1–10; 1 Tim 1:15); forgiveness of sins (Acts 10:43); divine sonship (Rom 8:14–17); justification by grace (Rom 3:24). Future salvation in the eschaton consists in deliverance on the Day of the Lord (1 Cor 3:13–15; 5:5); deliverance from the anger of God (Rom 5:9); sitting down at table with the patriarchs (Mt 8:11f) in eternal life in the world to come (Mk 10:30). The Christian's earthly existence is lived in tension between these two aspects of salvation (Heb 9:28; Rom 8:24f; 13:11; Phil 3:20). What is demanded now is continuing growth. The fullness of salvation will happen only in the final days and be dependent upon continuing fidelity to God. The final realization is not different in kind from present salvation, but only in degree.

The development in the New Testament of the notion of salvation that no longer applied to purely earthly conditions and its association with deliverance on a spiritual plane had a significant ramification. The idea of salvation as deliverance from concrete historical situations, as found in the Old Testament, is lost sight of. With the emphasis on the "already but not yet" aspect of salvation in the New Testament, salvation is also understood in its fullest sense as being on a spiritual plane, outside of history. Salvation therefore has little to do with history and the present and is what one hopes for at the end of time: freedom, deliverance from all that oppresses and holds one down in this life. However, by understanding salvation as taking place primarily at the end of time and on a nebulous spiritual plane, much has been lost regarding the present, concrete, physical aspects of salvation. Liberation theology has made an important contribution toward a more balanced perspective by recalling these concrete aspects of salvation.

Liberation theology arose in Latin America as a response to the large-scale human suffering there, a poverty and oppression that are due to identifiable cultural, social, and political factors. These factors have led to a situation that dehumanizes masses of people by depriving them of freedom. Theologian Roger Haight writes,

> To be human is to be free. Human existence is the ability to stand back from matter and nature, to transcend it even in ourselves, the ability to consider, judge and make decisions, to create new things, to take responsibility, to change, to make oneself and the world different, and, if possible, better.[2]

Such freedom is denied today to masses of people. In Latin America such massive poverty and oppression is a scandal to the Christian faith since it exists on a continent that has been dominated by Christianity and the Church for four centuries. This situation also exists in many parts of Africa and Asia.

According to the biblical tradition God is concerned for human existence. God's plan is not that huge masses of the human race exist in such poverty and oppression. Rather, God offers salvation from such an existence. The question, however, is in what does this salvation consist? For liberation theology it does not suffice simply to say that salvation consists in the completion and fulfillment of human existence at the end of time. The biblical witness, especially as found in the Hebrew Scriptures, points to the reality that God is concerned with a salvation that is real in this world, in time. Moreover, the issue that liberation theology responds to is a state of lack of meaning in this life, here and now, for masses of people. Hence, the notion of salvation must have a meaning that can be put in historical terms.

For liberation theology salvation is not just a goal of history but a process of humanization within history, a movement toward an ever greater degree of human freedom. This process of humanization is, then, a process of liberation, a process of becoming free and responsible. Who is to effect this process of humanization and hence salvation within history?—human beings under the grace and Spirit of God. Individuals do this through praxis, which is specifically a practice or behavior or struggle to increase freedom in society. As Roger Haight comments, "salvation is affirmed and is real and is experienced as such when one is actually engaged in work for increased social justice and freedom."[3]

In the Christian tradition, God's ultimate act of salvation was in Jesus Christ. The salvation mediated through Jesus is found above all in his way of life, his service to fellow human beings in need. His life was not simply an affirmation of the Reign of God but a creation of the Reign of God. Haight contends that "were it generalized or extended out into the social sphere of public history, the result would be a just social order, constituted by just social relationships, where the lives of the suffering and oppressed would be attended to through the institutions that human beings create."[4]

Salvation, then, is attained not through the accumulation of wealth and goods and a sinking into the self, nor through an "act of faith," but rather through an "action of faith." This action of faith is specifically living a life after the pattern of Jesus and reaching out in service to fellow human beings in need. Through the power of the Spirit salvation is about creating the Reign of God here on earth. This is done by joining in the struggle to transform society by changing sinful social structures and establishing a just social order in which people can exercise their freedom. Salvation is about helping people to find freedom from oppression and needless suffering and death. Salvation is above all service to those in need, whoever they may be, because the Lord desires the salvation of all. The model for such service is the epitome of the suffering servant of Isaiah, Jesus Christ, who gave his life to make freedom possible in this world.

Finally, it is important to keep in mind that salvation, the Reign of God, will never be fully attained and made totally present in this world. The Reign of God in its fullness will exist only at the end of time. Therefore, there will never be sinless social structures and a totally just social order; however, this reality must never stop us from constantly seeking to make the Reign of God a reality in this world. For our efforts on behalf of the Reign of God here will affect the shape it will take in eternity.

HUMAN DIGNITY AND HUMAN RIGHTS

As *Lumen Gentium* says, "At the summit of creation stands the creation of man and woman, made in God's image (Gn 1:26–27). As such every human being possesses an inalienable dignity that stamps human existence prior to any division into races or nations and prior to human labor and human achievement (Gn 4–11)" (LG 32). Human beings, then, are sacred because they are the clearest reflection of God on earth, having been made in the image and likeness of God. This is said of no other creature of God. What confirms this dignity is God's willingness to make human beings the stewards of God's creation, to enter into a covenant with them, and to make them "God's people." This dignity of humanity was confirmed in the highest fashion when the Son of God became human and willingly gave his life for all other humans so that they might be saved.

According to the biblical and Christian perspective, human dignity can be realized and protected only in community.[5] By nature every person is social and so achieves dignity in community with others and not individually. In fact, unless a person relates to others, the individual person can neither live nor develop his or her potential (GS 12). The U.S. bishops add that, "how we organize our society—in economics and politics, in law and policy—directly affects human dignity and the capacity of individuals to grow in community. The obligation to 'love our neighbor' has an individual dimension, but it also requires a broader social commitment to the common good."[6] All human beings are to be ends served by institutions, of whatever kind, and not pawns to be used.

Because of the basic dignity of human beings, all have a right to participate in making the decisions that affect their lives, whether these be ecclesial, political, social, or economic (EJ 77). Such participation is an essential expression of the social nature of human beings.

Flowing from the dignity of humanity are basic human rights bestowed by God on each person. These rights include civil and political rights as well as social and economic rights. Following John XXIII's description of these rights in his 1963 encyclical letter *Peace on Earth*, the American bishops explain these rights in the following passage:

> These rights include the civil and political rights to freedom of speech, worship, and assembly. Several human rights also concern human welfare and are of a specifically economic nature. First among these are the rights to life, food, clothing, shelter, rest, medical care, and basic education. These are indispensable to the protection of human dignity. In order to ensure these necessities, all persons have a right to earn a living, which for most people in our economy is through remunerative employment. All persons also have a right to security in the event of sickness, unemployment, and old age. Participation in the life of the community calls for the protection of this same right to employment, as well as the right to healthful working conditions, to wages, and other benefits sufficient to provide individuals and their families with a standard of property ownership. (EJ 80)

These rights, essential to human dignity and to the integral development of both individuals and society, thus have a moral dimension.

To understand the importance of the bishops' teaching regarding rights it has to be kept in mind that in Catholic tradition two types of rights have been spoken of: civil-political rights and socioeconomic rights. Civil-political rights are known as negative rights and are understood as immunities against abusive interference from others, especially from government. In the U.S. Bill of Rights, they set the limits for the government in its dealings with the individual, the family, or voluntary associations.

Socioeconomic rights, on the other hand, are known as positive rights and provide people with empowerments that call for positive action by individuals and society at large. What the bishops spell out in their letter is an "economic bill of rights" comparable to the present civil-political Bill of Rights in the Constitution. It is important to realize, however, that these individual rights, both civil-political and socioeconomic, are always experienced within the context of the promotion of the common good:

> The biblical emphasis on covenant and community also shows that human dignity can only be realized and protected in solidarity with others. In Catholic social thought, therefore, respect for human rights and a strong sense of both personal and community responsibility are linked, not opposed. (EJ 79)

Society as a whole, acting through both public and private institutions, has the moral responsibility to enhance human dignity and protect human rights. This follows from the responsibility of society as a whole to build up the common good. In addition, however, government has an essential responsibility "to guarantee the minimum conditions that make this rich social activity possible, namely, human rights and justice" (EJ 122). This does not mean that the government has the primary or exclusive role to play in this regard; however, it does have a positive moral responsibility to protect human rights and to see that minimum conditions of human dignity are available for all.

OPTION FOR THE POOR

The poor receive a significant amount of attention in the Bible. So that we may understand the contemporary call to a "preferential option for the poor," we must ascertain how the Bible deals with the theme of the poor.

Within Israel there was no distinction between the wealthy and the poor before the period of the settlement in the land (toward the end of the second millennium B.C.E.) because there was a more egalitarian sharing of goods. It was only with the growth of individual ownership, after the people settled in the land, that a wealthy class developed. The disparity between the rich and poor became a significant problem in the period of the monarchy.

Throughout the history of Israel we find a variety of theological understandings regarding poverty and wealth. This variety of understandings was closely related to the socioeconomic situation of Israel at various stages in its history. In some of the earlier material poverty and disaster were viewed as signs of God's negative response to infidelity (see Dt 28 especially). This perception of poverty followed from the interpretation of prosperity as God's blessing and reward for fidelity (as in Ps 112)[7]; it even developed into a work ethic that saw poverty as the result of idleness and laziness (Prov 20:13; 28:19). However, it was also recognized that wealth and righteousness and poverty and evil did not necessarily go together (Prov 28). The book of Job makes it very clear that the correlation between prosperity and righteousness is too simple.

The prophets are very clear in asserting that there is no necessary connection between righteousness and prosperity. They condemn all wealth that has been gained at the expense of the poor (Amos 2:6–7; 5:10–12; 8:4–6; Is 3:13–24; Mic 2:1-2). As the prophets came to understand that injustice shown to the poor was one of the main reasons why Israel would be destroyed (Ez 22:29f), they portrayed the future as a time of equity and prosperity for all. The ideal ruler would be one who safeguarded the rights of the poor (Is 11:3–5). Isaiah's hope of a remnant that would survive the destruction to come was understood by Zephaniah to be a remnant of the lowly and the poor (3:12–13). In this way "the poor" acquired a spiritual meaning. Poverty was opposed to pride, to an attitude of self-sufficiency, and was seen as synonymous with faith, with abandonment and trust in the Lord. Israelite piety came to believe that God was especially concerned with the poor and correcting the plight of the poor who were understood to be special "clients" of God (Pss 10; 25; 34; 37).

Jesus was not unusually poor by contemporary standards. Yet from the beginning he turned his attention to a well-defined section of the population that would best be described as the poor or lower classes. They are referred to by a variety of terms: the poor, blind, lame, crippled, lepers, hungry, miserable (those who weep), sinners, prostitutes, tax collectors, possessed people, persecuted, downtrodden, captives, all who labor and are overburdened, and so forth.[8] What motivated Jesus to turn to these people? It was, we are told, out of compassion (Mt 9:36; 14:14; 20:34; Mk 1:41; 8:2; Lk 7:13). The Greek word translated as "compassion" is derived from a noun that means intestines, bowels, entrails, or heart. Hence, compassion implies a deeply felt reaction and emotion.

Jesus expected that the Reign of God would bring about a reversal of the present circumstances (Lk 6:22–26) and so correct all that was perverted, especially the condition of the poor. Hence, he directed his mission to them (Mt 11:4–5; Lk 7:22). The Gospel of Luke gives special attention to the issue of the poor and presents a Jesus who was poor and was especially concerned for the poor (1:46–55; 4:16–22; 16:19–31; 12:13–21). Jesus is not shown romanticizing the goodness of the poor nor idealizing poverty, nor regarding wealth as inherently evil. However, he warns against the dangers of wealth (Mt 6:24–34; Lk 12:15–21). Jesus did not demand that the wealthy totally renounce all their goods. However, he wanted those who did not renounce their goods to know what they were doing, and he reminded them of the need to depend totally upon God (Mt 19:16–30; Lk 12:33–34). Certainly the most powerful expression of the concern for the poor in the Gospels is the parable of the Last Judgment found in Mt 25:31–46 where the people were judged on how they had responded to the hungry, the needy, and the naked. Care for the needy was a basic theme of early Christian preaching (Eph 4:28; 1 Tim 6:17–19; Jas 1:27; 2:14–17; 1 Jn 3:17; 1 Clem 38:2; Did 4:8).

This is the background for understanding the "preferential option for the poor." As the U.S. bishops say in their letter on the economy, "Though in the Gospels and in the New Testament as a whole the offer of salvation is extended to all peoples, Jesus takes the side of those most in need, physically and spiritually" (EJ 52). This option for the poor, after the example of Jesus, poses several challenges to the contemporary Church:

> It imposes a prophetic mandate to speak for those who have no one to speak for them, to be a defender of the defenseless, who in biblical terms are the poor. It also demands a compassionate vision that enables the Church to see things from the side of the poor and powerless and to assess lifestyle, policies, and social institutions in terms of their impact on the poor. It summons the Church also to be an instrument in assisting people to experience the liberating power of God in their own lives so that they may respond to the Gospel in freedom and in dignity. Finally, and most radically, it calls for an emptying of self, both individually and corporately, that allows the Church to experience the power of God in the midst of poverty and powerlessness. (EJ 52)

The prime purpose of this special commitment to the poor, the bishops say, is to enable them to become active participants in the life of society. In this way all persons will be enabled to share in and contribute to the common good. "The 'option for the poor,' therefore, is not an adversarial slogan that pits one group or class against another. Rather it states that the deprivation and powerlessness of the poor wounds the whole community. The extent of their suffering is a measure of how far we are from being a true community of persons. These wounds will be healed only by greater solidarity with the poor and among the poor themselves" (EJ 88). As the bishops remind us, "The way society responds to the needs of the poor through its public policies is the litmus test of its justice or injustice" (EJ 123, 38).

JUSTICE

Biblical Background

When looking for the biblical roots of the contemporary notion of justice, it is important to realize that there was no abstract notion of justice in Israelite thought. This is not to say that the contemporary notion of justice does not have biblical roots. Biblical roots do exist but they are to be found in many different concerns of Israel.

I will present here only those more important elements of the biblical background for the notion of justice that have not been dealt with in the previous material. A good, concise overview of this background is to be found in chapter 2 of the U.S. bishops' pastoral letter, *Economic Justice for All*.

First, God is the creator of all that exists in heaven and on earth. Human beings, who have been created in the image and likeness of God, are to share in God's creative activity by being fruitful and multiplying and using the earth's resources in a responsible fashion (Gn 1:26–28; 2:15).

Having saved the Israelites from slavery, God made a covenant with them and promised to watch over them (Ex 19:1–6; Jos 24 and 23; Dt 4:31). In response the people were to live their lives according to God's law. This law, especially as seen in the Ten Commandments (Dt 5:6–21; Ex 20:1–17), protects human life and property, demands respect for parents, and the spouses and children of one's neighbors. The law of Israel also manifests a special care for the poor and vulnerable who are presented primarily as the widow, the orphans, and the strangers in the land (Ex 22:20–27). With regard to the land, the people were reminded that the land belongs to Yahweh and they were but aliens who had become Yahweh's tenants (Lev 25:23). Hence, the land was for all Israel (see Dt 24:19–22). Robert Gnuse points out that Israel believed that human need was more important than property: "The laws of Israel called for the release and redistribution of property for the sake of human need. The commandment not to steal meant that no individual had the right to deprive another person of possessions necessary for meaningful existence."[9] The Sabbath year and Jubilee legislation (Ex 23:10–11; Lev 25) represent later attempts to create economic justice and provide economic balance and harmony in Israel.[10]

The prophets in a special way admonished the people for their lack of care and concern for the poor (see, for example, Is 10:1–4; Amos 2:6–8). Before the people's offerings will be received and their prayers heard, they must cease doing evil and learn to do good (Is 1:16).

At the center of Jesus' proclamation of the Reign of God was the summons to love God and one's neighbor (Mk 12:28–34). The parable of the Good Samaritan in Luke (10:25–37) is a beautiful illustration of the compassion for the hurting that is to be part of the Christian life. Jesus warned against laying up treasures on earth. Instead he encouraged all to seek the Reign of God (Mt 6:19–33). The picture of the Last Judgment in Matthew (25:31–46) shows that the judgment will be based on how one has responded to those in need.

Being a disciple of Jesus means imitating the pattern of Jesus' life, a life of service to others (Mk 10:35–45). Disciples are called to lose their lives for the sake of the Gospel (Mk 8:34–37) and to be willing to lay down their lives for others after the example of Jesus (Jn 15:12–17).

As a result of Jesus' own concern for the poor, the early community in Jerusalem is shown in Acts as holding all things in common and dividing everything based on each one's need (Acts 2:42–47; 4:32–35).

Theological Notion of Justice

The notion of the virtue of justice, as it has been developed by the theologians, is concerned with rights and the duties that correspond to those rights. A right is a person's moral claim upon other persons or society in general to the means of reaching an end that is theirs as rational and free persons and an end that they are responsible for reaching.

Because we live in a world affected by sin, we do not experience a society built on perfect love. As a result there are inevitable conflicts between individuals, groups, and nations that do not love one another and that need to be harmonized. The study of justice is intended to assist in this process. There is no conflict between justice and love; rather, justice is both a manifestation of love and a condition for love to grow (EJ 39).

Normally, theologians speak of three different types of justice corresponding to the three different types of relationships existing within society.[11] First, there is commutative justice that governs the relationship of individuals to individuals. It is blind to personal differences and is characterized by an emphasis on arithmetic equality. Hence, it "calls for fundamental fairness in all agreements and exchanges between individuals or private social groups. It demands respect for the equal human dignity of all persons in economic transactions, contracts, or promises" (EJ 69).

Distributive justice governs the relationship of society to individuals regarding the proper distribution of goods and services. Distributive justice is not blind. Rather, it must take account of persons. Hence, it involves a proportional and not an arithmetic equality. In other words, in distributing various burdens, society must take into account the abilities of individuals to contribute. In distributing goods several norms apply, but the basic criterion is human need.

Social justice governs the relationship of individuals to society. It is also characterized by a proportional equality and by the need to take account of persons and their differences. It governs the contribution that each makes to the good of the whole, the common good. The individual member of society is morally obligated to work for the common good. "Social Justice

implies that persons have an obligation to be active and productive participants in the life of society and that society has a duty to enable them to
participate in this way" (EJ 71).

Methodological Shifts

Against the above background I now wish to look at some of the more
important issues of distributive justice and social justice that are found in
recent Church documents. However, it is important to realize that since
Vatican II there has been a significant shift in the approach of Church
documents and Catholic theology to social issues.[12]

This methodological shift has its origin in various sources, the first of
which were the documents from Vatican II. Very important were the *Declaration on Human Freedom*, with its emphasis on religious freedom, and
the inductive process used by the *Pastoral Constitution on the Church in the
Modern World*. There was also a growing sensitivity in Church documents,
especially since Pope Pius XII, to such issues as the dignity, freedom, and
responsibility of the individual; the equal dignity of all human beings; and
the right of all persons to participate in those processes and decisions that
affect them. Third, there has been a growing historical consciousness within
the Church.

These forces have resulted in two major shifts. First, there has been a
move away from speaking of a "Catholic Social Doctrine" to speaking of
"Catholic Social Teaching." This shift reflects a move away from a universal
papal plan or ideology of social reconstruction that was deductively derived
from natural law and proposed authoritatively by the Church magisterium,
applicable to all parts of the world. The complexity of social problems and
the historical and cultural differences among peoples make it impossible
for one universal plan to be applicable to all parts of the world. Rather,
there is a recognition that each community must begin with the signs of
the times and an analysis of its contemporary situation. It must then reflect
on this situation in the light of the Gospel and the teachings of the Church.

The most important shift has been away from a deductive, natural-law
approach in dealing with social ethics questions to an inductive approach
of social analysis and theological reflection. Behind the older, natural-law
approach there was a dual-layer approach to reality. Here below was the
natural realm, the area of the world, which was primarily directed by reason
and natural law. Above was the realm of the supernatural, which was primarily the area of the Church and which was governed by grace and the
Gospel. In this approach grace, the Gospel, and Jesus were not directly
related to an understanding of moral life in this world. At best one found
a few scriptural quotations to support positions already proven by natural
law. The result of this approach was not only to separate the realm of the
Gospel and the realm of daily life but also to separate the Church and the
world.

With Vatican II has come an understanding that there are not two realms of reality but only one. Hence, both reason and the Gospel, grace and Jesus are to have a direct relation to and an effect on the daily life of Christians in the world. This realization, together with a greater historical consciousness, is what has led to a more inductive approach to dealing with social ethics issues.

Charles Curran has pointed out that Catholic theology and ethics have historically not given enough importance to the reality of sin as affecting and infecting all human life and structures. Sin was primarily seen as a particular act. Sin as a power present in and affecting the world was not emphasized. He is concerned that the emphasis on the presence of the Gospel and redemption in the newer approach will lead to an even greater temptation at times to forget the impact of human sinfulness. We need a continuing remembrance that the fullness of the Reign of God will only come at the end of time; perfection will not be reached here on earth. Individuals and human structures will always be affected by human limitations and human sinfulness and so will always be in the need of reform. The Reign of God, then, is not to be identified with any particular culture, political system, economic system or social system, nor with any cause, philosophy, or ideology.

The State

In the Roman Catholic tradition the state is understood to be a natural society. Human beings are by nature both social and political. They are called by nature to join in a political society to work for the common good which ultimately redounds to the good of the individual. There are some things that individuals by themselves are unable to achieve but which are necessary for their good and fulfillment. By coming together in a political society they are able to accomplish these things. Hence, the goal of the state is the common good. The *Pastoral Constitution on the Church in the Modern World* defines the common good as "the sum of those conditions of social life which allow social groups and their individual members relatively thorough and ready access to their own fulfillment" (GS 26).

To understand the role of the state one must also comprehend the distinction between society and the state. Society is constituted by the total network of social, political, economic, cultural, and religious relationships that are necessary for full human development. The state is the civil authority by which the purposes of society are procured and preserved. Hence, the common good is properly the care of society as a whole; the immediate concern of the state is with the more limited idea of public order. Public order is the order of justice, the order of public peace, and the order of public morality, which are necessary for the procurement of the common good.

The principle that governs to what degree the state should intervene in the life of its citizens is determined by two principles. First is the principle of subsidiarity. This principle states that nothing is to be done at a higher level that can be done as well or better at a lower level. Concerning government, it states that "in order to protect basic justice, government should undertake only those initiatives which exceed the capacity of individuals or private groups acting independently" (EJ 124).

However, the principle of subsidiarity needs to be balanced by what has come to be known as the principle of socialization that emerged in the encyclicals of Pope John XXIII (MM 59-67). The pope pointed out that one of the principal characteristics of our modern age is an increase in social relationships. This will at times call for greater government intervention and for national and international movements. However, even if the increased complexity of modern economics and political life requires more intervention by the state, this intervention should be done without prejudice to the principle of subsidiarity.

As the U.S. bishops point out, "Society as a whole and in all its diversity is responsible for building up the common good. But it is government's role to guarantee the minimum conditions that make this rich social activity possible, namely, human rights and justice" (EJ 122).

Distributive Justice and Private Property

Closely related to a consideration of the role of the state is the issue of distributive justice. As was pointed out above, in distributing various burdens, society must take into account the abilities of individuals to contribute, for example, their wealth, education, background, and so forth. In distributing goods the basic criterion is human need: "Every human being has a right to that basic level of human goods which is necessary for a minimally decent human existence. What is just from the viewpoint of distributive justice is not the same for all but is proportionate to the needs and abilities of the persons involved."[13] Hence, "distributive justice requires that the allocation of income, wealth, and power in society be evaluated in light of its effects on persons whose basic material needs are unmet" (EJ 70).

As the U.S. bishops point out:

Catholic social teaching does not maintain that a flat, arithmetical equality of income and wealth is a demand of justice, but it does challenge economic arrangements that leave large numbers of people impoverished. Further, it sees extreme inequality as a threat to the solidarity of the human community, for great disparities lead to deep social divisions and conflict. (EJ 74)

The issue of distributive justice is very important today because of the vast inequality in the distribution of the goods of the earth that exists in the present world. The basic requirement of distributive justice is clear — a person has the right to that minimum which is necessary for living a decent human life and society has a responsibility to provide it. However, the application of the principle can be quite complex as many issues must be considered. Is one discussing internal goods, such as freedom, or external goods, such as food, clothing, shelter, education, health? If we mean the equitable distribution of external goods, much will depend on the nature and amount of goods available at a given time in a given society. There is also the issue of the relative needs of those within a society where the needs of some may be greater than those of others. Also, nations that have more than the minimum necessary for a decent human life for all its members must consider their obligations to other nations that do not have such an abundance. The wealthier nations may even need to reconsider what they view as the minimum necessary for living a decent human life in view of the needs of other nations.

Closely related to the issue of distributive justice is the question of the ultimate goal of the goods of creation and the question of private property. The basic understanding of the Judeo-Christian tradition has always been that the goods of creation exist to serve the needs of all. Pope Paul VI in his 1967 encyclical letter *On the Development of Peoples* insists "All other rights whatsoever, including those of property and free commerce, are to be subordinated to this principle" (PP 22-24). Everyone, then, has a right to a share of earthly goods sufficient for oneself and one's family to live a decent human life.

The right to private property, however one understands the basis of this right (see EJ 114), must always be modified by and subordinated to the common destiny of the goods of creation. The right to private property is not absolute and unconditioned. We are only stewards of those goods of creation that we have. One has the right to keep what is necessary for one's sustenance, but there is also the obligation to give superfluous goods to those who do not have what is necessary to live a decent human life. These principles do not apply only to individuals and their private property. As the bishops explain:

> Business and finance have the duty to be faithful trustees of the resources at their disposal. No one can ever own capital resources absolutely or control their use without regard for others and society as a whole. This applies first of all to land and natural resources. Short-term profits reaped at the cost of depletion of natural resources or the pollution of the environment violate this trust. Resources created by human industry are also held in trust. Owners and managers have not created this capital on their own. They have benefited from the work of many others and from the local communities that support their endeavors. They are accountable to these workers and communities when making decisions. (EJ 112–13)

The right to private property today must be looked at especially in the context of the preferential option for the poor. No individual can amass the goods of creation at the expense of the truly human needs of a neighbor. "No one is justified in keeping for his exclusive use what he does not need, when others lack necessities" (PP 23). What applies to individuals also applies to nations (EJ 34).

A concern for distributive justice is what led the U.S. bishops to their central concern for "participation" in their letter *Economic Justice for All*: "Basic justice demands the establishment of minimum levels of participation in the life of the human community for all persons" (EJ 77). In this context they remind us that those excluded are not found only within our own country; the situation is even more severe beyond our borders in the least-developed countries:

> Whole nations are prevented from fully participating in the international economic order because they lack the power to change their disadvantaged position. Many people within the less developed countries are excluded from sharing in the meager resources available in their homelands by unjust elites and unjust governments. (EJ 77)

They later state that justice demands that social institutions be ordered in a way that guarantees all persons the ability to participate actively in the economic, political and cultural life of society (EJ 78).

Relations between Nations

Two themes will be considered here: the moral principles governing the relations of the industrialized countries with the developing countries, and the principles governing war, especially nuclear war. I will primarily summarize recent Church teachings on these issues and will not repeat what has been said in other contexts regarding relations between nations.

As Pope John Paul II pointed out in his encyclical, *On Social Concern* (SRS 20–22), tension between the two opposing blocs of the East and West in the Northern hemisphere has dominated the world since the close of the Second World War. That tension is an important cause of the retardation or stagnation of the South. In this context the developing nations simply "become parts of a machine, cogs on a gigantic wheel." The cold war between the East and the West and an exaggerated concern for security impede a united cooperation by all for the common good of the human race (SRS 22).

The U.S. bishops point toward another significant problem—"One of the most vexing problems for developing a just international order is that of reconciling the transnational corporation's profit orientation with the common good that they, along with governments and their multilateral agencies, are supposed to serve" (EJ 256).

Pope John Paul II further asserts that the true nature of the evil which faces the world today with respect to the development of peoples concerns moral evil. This moral evil is "the fruit of many sins which lead to 'structures of sin' " (SRS 37). Social sin refers to the social institutions and structures that crush people, oppress them, cause suffering, and push many to untimely and unnecessary death. These structures are more than the effects of sin. They can be called sin because they are the products of human beings. These

> structures of sin are rooted in personal sin, and thus always linked to the concrete acts of individuals who introduce these structures, consolidate them and make them difficult to remove. Thus they grow stronger, spread, and become the source of other sins, and so influence people's behavior. (SRS 36)

Among the actions and attitudes giving rise to such structures of sin are especially the "all-consuming desire for profit" and the thirst for power "at any price." Not only do individuals fall victim to this double attitude of sin; nations and blocs do so also.

The desire for profit and thirst for power and the structures of sin that they have caused are conquered only by a diametrically opposed attitude. This attitude is "a commitment to the good of one's neighbor with the readiness, in the Gospel sense, to 'lose oneself' for the sake of the other instead of exploiting him, and to 'serve him' instead of oppressing him for one's own advantage" (SRS 38). Such solidarity helps one to see the "other"—whether a person, a people, or a nation—not just as some kind of instrument to be used and discarded, but as a neighbor, a helper who is to be a sharer in the world's goods on a par with oneself. The demands of Christian love and human solidarity challenge all economic actors "to choose community over chaos" (EJ 258).

The more developed countries, then, have a serious responsibility to help the developing countries (GS 86, PP 48, EJ 265–66). "Those who are more influential, because they have a greater share of goods and common services, should feel responsible for the weaker and be ready to share with them all they possess" (SRS 39). The pope adds: "Stronger and richer nations must have a sense of moral responsibility for the other nations, so that a real international system may be established which will rest on the foundation of the equality of all peoples and on the necessary respect for their legitimate differences" (SRS 39). Flowing from this is what Pope Paul VI spoke of as the "duty of solidarity" (PP 48):

> Political leaders, and citizens of rich countries considered as individuals, especially if they are Christians, have the moral obligation, according to the degree of each one's responsibility, to take into consideration, in personal decisions and decisions of government, this

relationship of universality, this interdependence which exists between their conduct and the poverty and underdevelopment of so many millions of people. (SRS 9)

In the process of development and giving aid, there is always to be complete respect for the identity of each people, with its own historical and cultural characteristics. Industrial countries need to respect the cultures of developing countries and aid is to be offered without the intent to dominate (MM 170–72). The pope affirms, "Not even the need for development can be used as an excuse for imposing on others one's own way of life or own religious belief" (SRS 32). People are always to be allowed the freedom to exercise their right to determine their own future, including sovereignty over natural resources and over production, distribution, and consumption of goods and services.

This perspective constitutes a call for a fundamental reform in the international economic order. Here, as elsewhere, the preferential option for the poor is to be the central priority for policy change (EJ 259–60). Pope John Paul II suggests that these reforms should include

> the "reform of the international trade system," which is mortgaged to protectionism and increasing bilateralism; the "reform of the world monetary and financial system," today recognized as inadequate; the "question of technological exchanges" and their proper use; the "need" for a "review of the structure of the existing international organizations," in the framework of an international juridical order. (SRS 43, see EJ 261–87)

The U.S. bishops suggest that the world's food problem has a special urgency (EJ 281f).

Solidarity among peoples and nations is the path to peace:

> For world peace is inconceivable unless the world's leaders come to recognize that interdependence in itself demands the abandonment of the politics of blocs, the sacrifice of all forms of economic, military or political imperialism, and the transformation of mutual distrust into collaboration. This is precisely the act proper to solidarity among individuals and nations. (SRS 39)

Pope Paul VI suggested that "development is the new name for peace" (PP 87). If so, then war and military preparations are the major enemy of the integral development of peoples and the second major moral issue affecting relations between nations.

War and the Arms Race

As Vatican II pointed out in the *Pastoral Constitution on the Church in the Modern World* (GS 80), a fresh appraisal of war is needed today because of the effects of new scientific weapons. Especially since the Second World War, the teaching of the Church on war has developed significantly. For the United States that development is seen especially in the 1983 Pastoral Letter of the bishops, *The Challenge of Peace: God's Promise and Our Response*. This letter is rooted in the *Pastoral Constitution on the Church in the Modern World*. Certain basic issues are clear from these documents.

First, the only legitimate reason for war today is the defense of one's own nation or that of another against unjust attack—once every means of peaceful settlement has been exhausted (GS 79, CP 71–78). Offensive war of any kind is not morally justifiable.

Even for a defensive war to be just, certain criteria must be met (CP 85–99). There must be a just cause; "war is permissible only to confront a real and certain danger, i.e., to protect innocent life, to preserve conditions necessary for decent human existence, and to secure basic human rights" (CP 86). War must be declared by competent authorities, by those who have responsibility for public order, not by private groups or individuals.

There is also the principle of comparative justice: in other words, do the rights and values involved justify killing? Comparative justice stresses that no state should act on the basis that it has "absolute justice" on its side. There is the need for right intention; in other words, war can be legitimately intended only for the reasons proposed as a just cause. For resort to war to be justified, all peaceful alternatives must have been exhausted and there must be a probability of success. Finally, there is a need for proportionality, meaning that the damage to be inflicted and the costs incurred by war must be proportionate to the good expected by taking up arms.

Even when the above conditions have been met, the conduct of war (strategy, tactics, and individual actions) must be subjected to continuous scrutiny in the light of the principles of proportionality and discrimination (CP 101–10). According to the principle of proportionality, response to aggression must not exceed the nature of the aggression. Proportionality demands that there be a proportion between the military advantages to be achieved by using a particular means and all the harm reasonably expected to follow. According to the principle of discrimination, just response to aggression must be discriminate—it must be directed against unjust aggressors and not against innocent people caught up in a war not of their making.

In the light of the above principles the U.S. bishops addressed certain issues regarding the use of nuclear weapons (CP 146–61). They point out that under no circumstances may nuclear weapons or other instruments of mass slaughter be used for the purpose of destroying population centers or other predominantly civilian targets. Moreover, retaliatory action, whether nuclear or conventional, that would indiscriminately take many wholly innocent lives is also condemned. The bishops assert, "We do not perceive any situation in which the deliberate initiation of nuclear warfare, on however restricted a scale, can be morally justified. Non-nuclear attacks by another state must be resisted by other than nuclear means" (CP 150). What lies behind this judgment is the bishops' extreme skepticism about the prospects for controlling a nuclear exchange, however limited the first use might be. Moreover, because a nuclear response to either conventional or nuclear attack can cause destruction that goes far beyond "legitimate defense," such use of nuclear weapons would not be justified. The first imperative is to prevent any use of nuclear weapons.

It is not surprising, then, that the arms race has been unequivocally condemned by the Church. The *Pastoral Constitution on the Church in the Modern World* has some very strong words to this effect: "The arms race is an utterly treacherous trap for humanity, and one which ensnares the poor to an intolerable degree." They further assert, "While extravagant sums are being spent for the furnishing of ever new weapons, an adequate remedy cannot be provided for the multiple miseries afflicting the whole modern world" (GS 81). Negotiations toward disarmament must be pursued in every reasonable form possible.

The responsibility for disarmament rests on everyone and not just government officials.

> For government officials who must at one and the same time guarantee the good of their own people and promote the universal good are very greatly dependent on public opinion and feeling. It does them no good to work for peace as long as feelings of hostility, contempt and distrust, as well as racial hatred and unbending ideologies, continue to divide men and place them in opposing camps. Consequently there is above all a pressing need for a renewed education of attitudes and for new inspiration in public opinion. (GS 82)

In a discussion regarding war and the use of nuclear weapons, the most difficult issue is the threat of using nuclear weapons in a policy of deterrence. In their letter the bishops arrive at a strictly conditioned moral acceptance of nuclear deterrence. At the same time they point out that they cannot consider such a policy adequate as a long-term basis for peace.[14] They assert that no use of nuclear weapons that would violate principles of discrimination or proportionality may be intended in a strategy of deterrence. Moreover, nuclear deterrence is not an adequate strategy as a long-term basis for peace; it can only be a transitional strategy justifiable in conjunction with resolute determination to pursue arms control and disarmament. Nuclear deterrence should be used as a step on the way toward progressive disarmament. If nuclear deterrence is the goal, "sufficiency" to deter is an adequate strategy. Therefore, the quest for nuclear superiority must be rejected.

Ultimately all must strive for peace. However, as Pope Paul VI pointed out,

Peace cannot be limited to a mere absence of war, the result of an ever precarious balance of forces. No, peace is something built up day after day, in the pursuit of an order intended by God, which implies a more perfect form of justice among men and women. (PP 76)

8

REFLECTIONS ON THE UNITED STATES

The purpose of this chapter is to offer a critical reflection on the present situation in the United States in light of the biblical perspective on life and the various "themes" presented in the two previous chapters. More specifically, this chapter offers some reflections on what the Gospel[1] affirms about the United States, what the Gospel calls into question about the United States, and what the Gospel calls the United States to as a country today.

It is not my purpose to offer specific solutions to contemporary problems in the light of the Gospel. That is not the role of the theologian. Nor are Gospel values the only thing that must be considered in making practical decisions. Many practical and technical considerations must also come into play, especially when one moves into the arena of public policy. However, while Gospel values may not be a sufficient guide for policy formation, they are a necessary guide.

The ultimate goal of this book is to address the question of the mission of the Church in the United States. The primary purpose of these reflections is to discover those specific areas in the life of the United States that need growth in the light of the Gospel. These issues will then give direction to my consideration of the mission of the Church in the United States.

The three issues discovered in my analysis in the first part of the book — the sense of chosenness, the association of wealth with salvation, and individualism — provide a focus for these present reflections. These issues underlie much of what is happening in the United States today and so appear to be the best starting points for this discussion.

In proposing to consider the situation in the United States in light of the Gospel, one is immediately faced with a significant methodological issue. The basic problem is this: How does one transfer meaning from one historical, cultural context to another? Put in another way: How can one legitimately apply to contemporary issues Scriptures that were written two to three thousand years ago? The Scriptures, as well as Church teachings from the past, were written in particular historical, cultural contexts and were addressed to specific issues of their day. The Scriptures, in their original language and in the response they give, reflect the times and the cultures they come from and have been shaped by the contemporary issues they were attempting to respond to. We live in a very different historical and cultural context. Moreover, we are facing issues today that the biblical authors never imagined. How can we apply these Scriptures to contemporary problems?

Our faith tells us that the Scriptures do have meaning for us today and are, in some sense, normative for life today. However, what exactly is it in the Scriptures that is normative for us today if the Scriptures were not written to deal with our issues? My position is that what is normative in the texts is to be found in their perspectives on God, on life, and how one is to interact with God and others. What is normative are the values, insights, and goals of life embedded in the biblical texts. The biblical texts reflect applications of these values, insights, and perspectives to issues being addressed in the biblical authors' times. We need to go back and try to understand the Scriptures, as well as Church traditions, in the light of the historical, cultural contexts they were written in as well as the issues that the authors were attempting to address. We then try to grasp the insights, values, and perspectives reflected in the text to gain direction for today.

The next question concerns how we can come to specific conclusions regarding contemporary issues in the light of the insights, values, and perspectives found in the Scriptures and Church teachings. The answer is, through human reason and the use of human sciences and human experience. In other words, we find God's will and plan for human action mediated through our understanding of the human. As Charles Curran says, "The divine plan in no way short-circuits the human reasoning process, but precisely in and through human reason reflecting on existence we arrive at what God wants us to do."[2]

The above principles apply to all aspects of Christian life, including the particulars of the social, political, and economic world in which we live. However, even with the focus that these three core issues (chosenness, association of wealth with salvation, and individualism) provide, we could still go in many different directions trying to apply the Word of God to our contemporary reality. We must ask if we can focus our reflections even more. Is there any one specific mediating principle or focus that we ought to use to evaluate the situation in the United States in the light of the Gospel? Charles Curran suggests that distributive justice[3] might offer the mediating principle for the United States that liberation has played in Latin American theology.[4]

There are some very good reasons for accepting distributive justice as a mediating principle for reflecting on the reality in the United States. First, the particular social questions being raised today in this country do fit under the category of distributive justice. As my analysis has shown, the basic issues on both the global and national levels are those dealing with the proper distribution of the goods of this world. Even the foreign policy of the United States, insofar as it is determined by economics, is an issue of distributive justice. Moreover, the issues of communication and culture ultimately come down to the proper distribution of technology and power in the world today.

Also, as Curran points out, distributive justice properly emphasizes the biblical idea that God destined the goods of creation for all human beings. A rugged individualism and a deficient concept of freedom often characterize our understanding of the ownership of goods. The use of distributive justice as a mediating principle avoids these dangers of an individualistic concept of justice. Also, the concept of distributive justice remains sufficiently generic to allow for disagreements about particular ramifications and applications.

In the following examination, the principle of distributive justice provides a primary focus for my reflections, though not an exclusive one.

WHAT THE GOSPEL AFFIRMS

First, what does the Gospel affirm about the United States as we look at ourselves today? In other words, what in the history of the United States and what in its values and structures reflect Gospel values, perspectives, and ideals? The following discussion makes no claim to being complete; other people may think of other things that could be said, and some may not agree with what I see as reflecting the Gospel. Also, I do not claim that everything that I mention here completely mirrors the Gospel. In many areas of our life as a country we have fallen very short of the Gospel ideal, at least in practice. However, many of our ideals and goals and our continuing struggles to make many of these issues real, do reflect the Gospel.

Definitely in conformity with the Gospel vision regarding human dignity and justice were the goals of our Revolution and the ideals found in the Declaration of Independence and the Preamble to the Constitution. These goals and ideals include justice, freedom, equality of peoples, the inalienable right to life, liberty and the pursuit of happiness, and self-determination. The civil and political rights spelled out in the Bill of Rights are also in keeping with the dignity of the individual that emerges from the Scriptures. The democratic system with its emphasis on government by the people, of the people, and for the people echoes the Gospel values and ideals connected with human dignity and self-determination. The belief in the dignity, the sacredness of the individual person, and the continuing struggle for individual rights and individual autonomy in our society reflect these same Gospel values as do the humane procedures of law and due process.

To the extent that our doors have truly been open to immigrants and refugees throughout our history, we have lived the Gospel in providing a home for these people. The Gospel is further reflected in the continuing struggle for true equality and respect for all persons no matter their religion, color, or sex. This struggle is seen at its best in the emancipation of the slaves, the granting of the vote to women, the elimination of legal impediments to equality, and the continuing struggle to wipe out discrimination in all areas of life.

Attempts to effect more economic justice and distribute more equitably the goods of the nation also reflect the values associated with distributive justice. Examples are the various social welfare programs that have been developed over the last sixty years, as flawed as they may be at times. The Social Security system and the public insurance programs such as Medicare and Medicaid especially stand out. These truly attempt to respect the socio-economic rights of people. The eventual acceptance of labor unions and their integration into the economic life of the nation together with minimum wage laws also reflect Gospel values.

Our willingness to share the riches of our country with others is also praiseworthy, for example, American readiness to offer disaster relief to countries around the world at times of natural catastrophes. There have also been genuine aid programs to other nations; the Marshall Plan, after the Second World War, continues to exemplify the type of generosity we are capable of as a people.

While recognizing the many limitations of contemporary industrial capitalism, one has to admit that industrial capitalism in the West has produced a better material life for a larger number of people than any other system in history. We have not buried our talents but have set out to be fruitful and multiply, to fill the earth. We have opened up the resources of our country and developed them. We have called upon the talents of our people and developed those talents through a massive public education program. Moreover, we have used the results of our technological expertise and discoveries for the betterment of life and often shared this expertise with other nations. I do not intend to ignore the many negative consequences of this development or to say that the institution of industrial capitalism as such is in keeping with the Gospel. However, one has to see that the human creativity and energy that have gone into such productivity and growth are in keeping with Gospel values.

WHAT THE GOSPEL CALLS INTO QUESTION

Many aspects of our life as a people, however, do not reflect Gospel values and ideals and are strongly challenged by the Gospel. In this section the issue of distributive justice will focus my reflections. The main objects of my reflection will be the three items that emerged from my analysis in Part One.

Sense of Chosenness

The sense of chosenness figures predominantly in the way Americans look at themselves. This sense of chosenness includes our understanding of ourselves as a people chosen by God and brought across the sea to the promised land where we have been greatly blessed. Traditionally we have also understood that our election has imposed upon us a responsibility toward others.

From the beginning this sense of chosenness led the white Anglo-Saxon to look down on the black and Native American. This results in the racism, discrimination, and prejudice that cut through all American society toward anyone who has a different colored skin, speaks a different language, and has different customs or beliefs. Together with this sense of chosenness there is often found among Americans the sense of a manifest destiny to impose their way of life, structures, and values on the rest of the world. Much of American foreign policy is colored by a feeling of superiority and arrogance that flows from this sense of chosenness and manifest destiny.

It is important to understand that there is nothing intrinsically wrong in our attempt to understand ourselves as a people in the light of the biblical images of election, covenant, and exodus. These images have often been used by people down through the ages. They are popular because they strike something very basic in peoples' hopes and desires, that is, the hope of being blessed by God and delivered from oppression. However, if we are going to use this imagery, we should allow our use of it to be critiqued in terms of its biblical background.

The Bible always understands election to be a gift, a gratuitous act of God based on God's mysterious love and not on anything that the people had or had done. Moreover, election does not carry with it any special privileges to wealth or status nor does it guarantee salvation. Hence, the Gospel calls into question any arrogant self-righteousness and pride before the rest of the world as though whatever the United States does is acceptable because it has been "chosen." Rather, election demands obedience to God's will. All the United States does is subject to the same rules of morality as is any other nation.

Election for Israel included a mission toward others. As Genesis 12:1–3 points out, Israel's mission was to be a source of blessings for all the other nations. By the period of the Exile Israel had come to understand these blessings to include being a light to the nations, establishing justice, and freeing the oppressed. The Gospel, then, calls into question any sense of a people being called only for themselves and so given the right to look after themselves and to discriminate against those who are not part of the chosen.

When we look at specifics, we find the ramifications of a misguided sense of chosenness both internally, in the discrimination that runs through so much of our society, and externally, in our dealings with other nations. What do we find the Gospel questioning in these areas of our life?

Internally much of the discrimination in our country translates into economic and job policies by federal and local governments and private businesses. The norms for evaluating what is taking place are those of human dignity and distributive justice. As has already been pointed out, the dignity of the human person is prior to color, race, sex, religion, or human achievement and is a result of all having been created in the image of God. Out of this basic human dignity flows the right of all people to participate in decisions that affect their lives. Respect for the uniqueness of people and their culture is also demanded. Moreover, every person has certain rights, including the right to life, food, clothing, shelter, rest, medical care, and basic education.

The goods of this earth belong to all, and every person has a right to the basic level of goods necessary for a minimally decent human existence. Hence, allocation of wealth, income, and power in society must be evaluated in light of its effects on those whose basic material needs are unmet. No one is justified in keeping for one's exclusive use what is not needed when others lack necessities. Society as a whole, acting through its public and private institutions, has a moral responsibility to enhance human dignity and protect human rights.

Considering these norms the following policies and programs in the United States could be called into question:

• Any form of sexism.

• Any form of job discrimination and those economic structures that make minorities, especially blacks, to be the last hired and first fired.

• Lack of equal opportunity programs or their nonenforcement in government or in industry.

• Policies of structural unemployment and permanent marginalization of parts of society.

• Discrimination based upon where one lives, when it comes to getting insurance and loans (i.e., "redlining").

• Welfare programs that in any way discriminate because of color, race, or sex or affront the dignity of the individual and the right of individuals to participate in decisions affecting their lives.

• Immigration programs and policies that affront the dignity of the individual and the unity of the family and that refuse legitimate sanctuary.

• Policies establishing English as the official language, which remove the ability of many to participate fully in society.

• Policies and programs that keep inner-city schools, mostly attended by minorities, in such appalling conditions.

• Cutbacks in welfare programs for the poor while continuing government transfers to those who already have what they need to live life with dignity (e.g., some aspects of social security and some farm subsidies).

• Cutbacks in welfare programs while constructing far more arms than needed for a legitimate deterrence strategy.

• Tax programs that put an inordinate burden on the poor and do not provide the income needed for legitimate assistance to the poor.

Several areas of U.S. foreign policy and foreign aid programs must be questioned, because they flow from a warped sense of chosenness. The norms that cover this area include the principles of human dignity, participation, and human rights, especially socioeconomic rights. International decisions, institutions, and policies must be shaped by more than economic values. All nations have a right to participate in international decisions in a way that preserves their freedom and dignity. Giving aid must always be done with total respect for the dignity of each people and their culture. Aid should never be given with the intention to dominate. Nations that have more than the minimum necessary for decent human life must consider their obligations to those nations that do not have the minimum. Wealthier nations are even to reconsider the level of their own standard of life because of those who have so little.

One must also look to an international common good to which society as a whole has a responsibility. There is an obligation on the countries in the Northern Hemisphere to transform and overcome the tension between the East and the West for the sake of the poor in the Southern Hemisphere. Meeting the basic needs of millions of deprived and hungry in the world is, then, to be the number one objective of international policy. Finally, transnationals, as other institutions, are called to serve the common good.

Considering these norms the following are called into question:

• Any deliberate acts to continue the present tension between the East and West or to aggravate it or not to seek solutions to it. Such actions are acts of discrimination against the poor. The expenditure of billions of dollars in the arms race, above all, affects what is contributed to the relief of the millions of poor and hungry.

• A refusal to be involved in discussions regarding the transformation of the international economic system in which the developing countries have a full voice.

• Any policies and programs that make meeting the basic needs of people depend upon their conformity to the desires of the United States.

• Selective assistance to developing countries based on an assessment of East-West problems at the expense of basic human needs.

• Support of nations that maintain apartheid or similar discriminatory and oppressive policies.

• Attempts to use foreign aid programs as a way of forcing countries into dependence upon the United States.

• Refusing to aid countries who are not allies or with whose policies the United States objects even when significant natural disasters hit; forcing countries into submission by the refusal of assistance.

• Giving aid primarily for the purchase of arms or for the benefit of United States companies.

• Lack of respect for native cultures and self-determination when aid or development assistance is given.

• Monetary and fiscal policies that make the plight of the poor on an international level even worse, especially any manipulations of the dollar to this effect.

• Actions of transnationals that are against the international common good. This would include actions that significantly affect individual countries where these countries are not given the opportunity for significant input into such decisions (e.g., plant closings and corporate pullouts).

• A consumerism that brings us to consume 25 percent of the goods produced on this earth though we are only 5 percent of the world's population.

• Attempts at controlling or manipulating others by using the media.

Individualism

The philosophy of individualism that entered the American scene in the eighteenth century had a significant impact on the founders of the United States. From the very beginning there was a significant tension between the philosophy of individualism and the biblical tradition. Because both traditions stressed the dignity and sacredness of the individual, the tensions were easily overlooked and the traditions were able to live side by side well into the twentieth century.[5] What allowed the two traditions to coexist in the beginning was a pietist-Protestant form of religion that stressed "every man his own priest," "Scripture alone," and emphasized adult baptism and the importance of the decision of the individual for salvation. Individualism, with its stress on the priority of the individual, fit easily into this context. In its utilitarian aspects individualism felt even more at home with the Puritan stress on hard work and the eventual identification of salvation with worldly success. During this period of coexistence an important aspect of early Puritan thought was lost, namely, the importance of the common good over individual interest. Also lost was the republican idea of public virtue.[6] Individualism overrode these concerns for the common good and the greater community.

I do not intend to condemn the emphasis of individualism on the sacredness of the individual and the benefits this emphasis has generated in our society. However, it is important to see what the older biblical tradition, as seen through the prism of Roman Catholicism, might call into question regarding the tenets of modern individualism.

For individualism the individual antedates society. A society comes into existence only through the voluntary contract of individuals trying to maximize their own self-interest. The state is justified only by its utility to the individual and social concord is based on self-interest alone. There is no need for the state to help educate the individual to moral responsibility since each person is born morally complete.

The biblical tradition would question this priority of the individual and its understanding of the state. As reflected in Roman Catholic tradition, the state is understood to be a natural society, and human beings are by their nature both social and political. Each person is called by nature to join in a political society in order to work for the common good that ultimately redounds to the good of the individual.

This concept of the individual and society is based on a biblical perspective in which the people formed a whole and in which it was the people that was saved. Individuals took their identity and destiny from that of the people. Individuals were seen as living in a network of historical and social relationships by which they were bound to each other and which had a function in the mediation of salvation. Hence, life was seen as being shaped by covenants, in which people made commitments to God and to one another and in the process took on responsibilities and obligations to one another.

The image of the Body of Christ forcefully brings out the intimate connection between all believers. While different members may have different functions, they are all dependent on one another. As a result, if one suffers, all the members suffer. Hence, there is the command to love one another.

Individualism sees the ultimate goals of life to be matters of personal choice. Therefore, it stresses the freedom of individuals to become their own persons and not to have other peoples' values, ideas, or ways of life imposed upon them. In contrast the biblical perspective insists that meanings are not found in an isolated "now" but as part of an ongoing historical process. By becoming part of the community an individual receives memories of the past that provide meaning, and visions of the future that provide hope. Human dignity can be realized and protected only in community. Individuals can neither live nor realize their potential except by relating to others.

According to individualism the individual achieves fulfillment through work, so that one can be self-supporting, and by becoming part of a group of like-minded people where one can find love, acceptance, and happiness. In one's work what is important is economic success so that a person can afford to live as he or she wishes. Little or no concern is given to the wider social and political implications of one's work or to the larger society in which one lives.

In contrast, in the biblical perspective, fulfillment is found in reaching out to others in love, giving oneself to others, and allowing oneself to be vulnerable with others so that they become empowered to achieve life. Solidarity with others is demanded. As Christ became one of us to empower us to help ourselves, so we are called to become one with the poor and hurting. While love of neighbor has an individual dimension, it also requires a broader social commitment to the common good; for the way a society (political, economic, religious) is organized directly affects human dignity and the capacity of the individual to grow in community. Each person has a responsibility to see to the organization of society in a way that supports human dignity and the growth of community.

In individualism justice is a matter of equal opportunities for all to pursue what they understand as happiness. Private property is seen as an absolute right and the role of the state is to help one hold on to what one has. No thought is given to how the goods of creation should be distributed. In contrast, the biblical perspective, as it has evolved, has a strong concern for the issue of distributive justice. Hence, every human being has a right to that level of human goods necessary for a minimally decent human existence. The goods of creation exist to serve the needs of all. A person is obliged to give superfluous goods to those who do not have what is necessary to live a decent human life. This principle applies to the state and other public institutions as well as to individuals.

Individualism effects the loss of common values and a common vision beyond concern for the economy and economic success. Consumerism (seeking happiness through material goods) is a logical corollary. It is easy to see a transference of this individualism to the nation itself. Only the nation's own prosperity and security as a country are important. Foreign investors are not welcome because they eventually might detract from the nation's freedom to do as it wishes. The major issue in foreign policy is what is important for the economic success of the nation. A strong defense is necessary to defend the nation against the intrusions of others. As a consequence there is no national vision to fully integrate the United States into the interdependent global reality in which we live. This can often leave the United States without options for dealing in a just way with the problems of global poverty and oppression.

In contrast the developed biblical perspective does provide the basis for the type of national vision that is needed today. The basis for such a vision is found in the principles of distributive justice and the call to reach out in love and solidarity to those less fortunate.

I am well aware that the organized action of politics and the practical art of statecraft cannot be directly controlled by the Christian values that govern personal and family life. Rather, the imperatives of political and social morality derive from the fivefold obligatory political ends spelled out in the preamble of our Constitution: justice, freedom, security, the general welfare, and civil unity or peace. Further, there is a place for the centrality of self-interest as the motive of national action. However, as John Courtney Murray has pointed out so well,

> The tradition of reason requires, with particular stringency today, that national interest, remaining always valid and omnipresent as a "motive," be given only a relative and proximate status as an "end" of national action. Political action stands always under the imperative to realize, at least in some minimal human measure, the fivefold structure of obligatory political ends. Political action by the nation-state projected in the form of foreign policy today stands with historical clarity ... under the imperative to realize this structure of political ends in the international community, within the limits—narrow but real—of the possible. Today, in fact as in theory, the national interest

must be related to this international realization, which stands higher and more ultimate in political value than itself.[7]

If our international action is to be based on the fivefold structure of obligatory political ends spelled out in the Constitution, these ends must be understood against the biblical background that participated in their birth.

Salvation and Success

The third root issue is the association of salvation with worldly success and the accumulation of wealth. This attitude had its origins in the high value the original Puritans placed on work and their belief that good Christian work would not go unrewarded. As a result of the emphasis put on worldly success in the nineteenth century, such success became identified with moral goodness and evidence of religious salvation. The belief developed that if one worked hard, the American Dream would be realized and salvation would be won. The corollary assumed that the poor were listless, lazy and immoral, and responsible for their own plight; this attitude provided the justification for allowing the wealthy and the powerful to set the rules in society and even for overlooking the situation of the poor.

This attitude has created a lack of real concern for the poor and disregard for a proper distribution of the goods of this earth. Furthermore, a concern for economic prosperity has resulted that allows the United States to justify almost any action in the name of national security.

The impact of this perception of reality can be seen on the level of the individual and society, the level of the corporation, and the level of foreign policy. I will now look at challenges offered by the Gospel on all these levels. I will begin with the level of the individual, for individual attitudes have given birth to the public structures and systems (business and government) and allow such structures to continue.

The Individual. The basic individual attitudes contained in this association of wealth and success with salvation are found in what was called earlier the modern-industrial-scientific model of life. In this perspective life consists in acquiring enough knowledge to control and predict the world and thereby to secure one's life against every danger and threat. Everyone and everything is valued for their usefulness. Great value is placed on competence and achieving, on success and getting ahead. People have value for what they do or for what they have, and those who succeed and are competent are the important ones. Those who earn little and are less competent do not exist for all practical purposes.

The biblical perspective on life challenges these attitudes. The biblical perspective asserts that human existence is not primarily about the capacity to know and control and manage. Rather, the biblical perspective asserts that real life consists in risking commitments to God and to others. A person then lives out those commitments without knowing where they will lead but having deep trust in God's mysterious empowering grace. The individual has value because each one person has been created in the image and likeness of God, not because of what he or she can do or have.

Being successful does not give one the right to impose one's rules or way of life on the less successful. Such interference in the lives of others is against the right to self-determination and the right to participate in decisions that affect one's life.

Similarly, being successful does not give anyone the right to make judgments about the morality of those who have been less successful. The facts show that the real causes of poverty have nothing to do with the morality of the poor but are such issues as low wages, unemployment, lack of proper education and training, job structures, prejudice, arbitrary and callous actions of business and government, and so forth.[8] Even if some poor may share some responsibility for their present situation of poverty, this does not diminish the fact that they are human beings who have rights, civil and political as well as socioeconomic.

Finally, one can never associate wealth and earthly success with salvation. Wealth guarantees nothing when it comes to God. What is important is obedience. In the New Testament obedience is keeping the law of love. Salvation comes to those who reach out in love to God and to other human beings by doing justice.

While salvation will be achieved in its fullness only at the end of time, salvation is also a process within history. It is a process of humanization, of liberation, of becoming free and responsible. Salvation is not just about deliverance from sin on some nebulous spiritual plane, but is about being involved in history and working for social justice and freedom. Salvation is attained not through the accumulation of wealth but by reaching out in service to fellow human beings in need. Salvation is about striving to create the Reign of God here on earth by joining in the struggle to transform social structures into a just social order. Salvation is about helping people find freedom from oppression and needless suffering and death. The model for such service is the epitome of the suffering servant of Isaiah, Jesus Christ, who gave his life to make freedom possible in this world.

The Corporation. The Gospel also calls into question much about the modern corporation, especially the large transnational corporations. These corporations are the outgrowth of capitalism foreseen by Adam Smith. Based on an economy of scale they are the most efficient means to make profit, which is, of course, their driving force. The American association of wealth and success with moral goodness and salvation has led to an easy acceptance of corporations because of the wealth they produce. While there may be some uneasiness in society today over the megaliths formed through various mergers, it is questionable that the basic moral goodness of the corporation would be called into question.

However, as human institutions that deeply affect the lives of people in society, the corporations must come under moral evaluation. While this applies to all corporations, it applies in a special way to the giant transnational corporations. Manuel G. Velasquez provides some help in this matter by establishing moral criteria for evaluating the performance of the American corporate economy.[9] These criteria would also apply to individual corporations.

Velasquez suggests three types of ethical principles or criteria: moral criteria for evaluating what is produced; criteria for evaluating the way in which goods are distributed; criteria for evaluating the process used in the production and distribution of goods. It is important to keep in mind that, according to the continuous tradition of the Church, social institutions in general and corporations in particular are neither intrinsically evil nor intrinsically salvific. Rather, they are merely a form of organization used to produce the earthly necessities of humans.

Concerning production, the basic criterion, suggests Velasquez, is whether the American corporate economy is productive in the sense of being creative (carrying out God's call in Genesis to produce from the earth's resources the goods that can meet human needs) and if it is creating those goods needed to meet real human needs. Velasquez concludes that because of its very size and the division of labor on which it rests, the modern corporation has been remarkably productive of those goods that meet real human needs. At the same time, however, the very size and division of labor that enable the corporation to be so productive are also the bases of its tendency to waste resources (due to monopolistic inefficiencies), to produce socially useless commodities (such as massive advertising and military expenditures), and to punish the worker (such as job designs that result in the worker's experience of alienation and take little account of worker safety, worker autonomy, work variety, and job satisfaction).

In evaluating this aspect of the American economy we must also consider its impact on the economies of developing countries. While the corporations have produced goods that have met real human needs in the United States, at times this has been at great cost to developing countries. This cost to the developing countries has resulted from corporations using the internal resources of those countries for industrial development with the result that these resources could not be used to meet local needs. Developing countries gain little if the best local talent and electrical energy are used for export-oriented industrial production. The principles of distributive justice call into question our right to such goods at such a cost to the economy of the developing country.

Regarding the distribution of goods, the basic criterion would be: To what extent does the corporate economy embody a sense of solidarity among all peoples that brings about a sharing of goods with the poor and the dispossessed? The basis of this criterion is two principles of Catholic social teaching: the privileged place of the poor and needy, and the reality that all people are united in a social solidarity that implies an obligation to share goods. As the U.S. bishops point out in their letter on the economy, the economy of a community is just when it has established minimum levels of participation by all persons in the life of the human community. To the extent that some do not participate in the economic life of the community (because minimal needs are not met or people are not given the means to enable them to be active and productive, such as education and job training), the economy is unjust. The bishops have pointed out that three groups of people have been effectively barred from full participation in the economic community's activities and from sharing its benefits—the unemployed, those whose incomes fall below the government's official "poverty line," and the disadvantaged members of the developing nations.

The third area of concern is how the individual is treated by society's productive processes. Hence, the criterion would evaluate whether the corporate economy embodies a positive respect for the freedom and dignity of the individual. Does the economy respect the basic right of self-determination? Velasquez concludes that the corporate economy does not fare well when measured against the criterion of the right to self-determination:

> In myriad ways, the economy's core institution—the large scale corporation—uses its considerable power to determine the behavior of consumers and to manipulate the political process. Within the corporation, a well-defined class—the managerial class—controls the corporation and puts its assets at the service of profit and growth, even to the detriment of the interests of other corporate constituencies. Workers in particular can be at the mercy of the unilateral decision-making power of the managerial class. . . .[10]

What can be said of the actions of the corporations in the United States can too often be found to an even greater degree in poorer countries where U.S. transnationals may be operating. In this context, the shifting of investments by transnational corporations from the Third World to other first-world countries and into high-tech industries is to be lamented. Given the concerns of corporations and the present-day market, such shifts are understandable from a particular perspective; however, the impact upon the developing countries is horrendous. Such shifts mean that less, if any, investment is being put into the development of the basic infrastructure of the third-world countries (such as roads, schools, hospitals) or into the further development of their resources. Also, fewer jobs are available for a poor and often untrained work force. The demands of an international common good and distributive justice would question whether transnationals can make such decisions without also considering the needs of third-world countries and their people.

It must also be kept in mind that corporations, like individuals, have no absolute right to private property, either raw materials or goods that have been produced. They also come under the demands of distributive justice. The U.S. bishops say:

> Business and finance have the duty to be faithful trustees of the resources at their disposal. No one can ever own capital resources absolutely or control their use without regard for others and society as a whole. This applies first of all to land and natural resources. Short-term profits reaped at the cost of depletion of natural resources or the pollution of the environment violate this trust. Resources created by human industry are also held in trust. Owners and managers have not created this capital on their own. They have benefited from the work of many others and from the local communities that support their endeavors. They are accountable to these workers and communities when making decisions. (EJ 112–13)

In view of these principles one must also challenge the quest for short-term profits that leads to the continuing use of environmentally harmful production technologies by corporations, both in the United States and in third-world countries. The capitalist precept that the choice of production technology is governed solely by private interest in profit maximization or market share is simply not valid, especially when that technology is harmful to society as a whole and to the continuing health of the planet. Corporations have a social responsibility.

Velasquez concludes by pointing out that the failures of distributive justice and the violations of self-determination are truly serious defects in the American economy. However, they are not necessary concomitants of corporate production:

> At bottom, both arise from the way in which ownership and control of corporate assets are distributed in our society, and current patterns of ownership and control are not necessary aspects of the socialized production that the corporation makes possible. They are, instead, social patterns that are amenable to change.[11]

John Paul II has suggested that the means of production in Western economies should be "socialized" by making each worker "a part owner of these means."

Foreign Policy. Much of foreign policy is determined by economic concerns. To the extent that wealth and success are associated with moral goodness and salvation, improper actions by the government are approved by most people or overlooked as part of the process of doing business. Yet the Gospel would denounce many of these actions. On the basis of the principle of self-determination some of those actions that require reevaluation are:

• Interference in the internal affairs of a foreign country, especially if it is kept secret from the foreign government, to achieve the goals of the United States and its business interests;

• U.S. support of repressive dictatorships for the sake of security;

• Attempts by the United States, directly or through the IMF, to dictate internal policies to developing countries as a condition for new loans or for refinancing existing ones.

Based on the responsibility of the wealthy nations—such as the United States—to help the developing nations and to share wealth and knowledge with them, the following actions demand scrutiny:

• Refusal of a country to put more of its GNP into foreign aid programs and development programs so as not to erode further its present lifestyle;

• Any refusal to adjust significantly the debts of the developing countries by the first-world powers in an attempt to avoid having their present way of life altered.

The national security state and the secret government are logical results of the sense of chosenness and concern for economic prosperity in the United States. Aside from the threat to the Constitution that they pose, these developments all too often use immoral means to achieve dubious ends. They infringe on the right of self-determination by the American people and their right to participate, at least through their elected representatives, in decisions that affect their lives.

Finally, the size of the arms buildup in the United States for the sake of deterrence and defense of the country's economic interests cannot be justified in view of the needs of the poor both in the United States and globally. The same can be said of the international arms trade. Especially when it concerns nuclear weapons, such a buildup cannot be justified when the end of deterrence could be achieved with a much smaller nuclear arsenal.

WHAT THE GOSPEL CALLS US TO

What the Gospel calls us to as a nation, as a people, and as individuals seems quite clear. Certainly, the call of the Gospel that emerges most strongly is the call to the preferential option for the poor, a challenge addressed to us as a nation, as an economy, and as individuals. However, in view of our American attitudes and perspectives on life, it is difficult for us to hear the Gospel's command. Before we can hear and respond to this call to an option for the poor, it will be necessary for us to hear the position of the Gospel on even more fundamental issues.

The most fundamental call of the Gospel is the call to recognize the basic dignity and equality of every human being no matter their color, race, religion, sex, nationality, economic status or human achievement. There is also the Gospel imperatives to recognize the solidarity of the human race and to understand that we are all one with one another and dependent upon one another. Along with this call to discern the solidarity of the human race is a call to work for the common good. Today this common good cannot be looked at only from a local or national perspective. Because the world has become so interdependent, we must answer a summons to a global common good. There is also the charge of the Gospel to imitate the compassion of Jesus for the poor and outcast (EJ 52). Finally, we must heed the Gospel's call to recognize that the goods of creation exist to serve the needs of all peoples. There is no absolute and unconditioned right to private property. We are only stewards of the goods of creation that we have.

Once we have begun to hear, to understand, and to respond to these more fundamental calls of the Gospel, hopefully we will be able to hear and respond to a preferential option for the poor. This challenge involves, minimally, speaking for those who have no one to speak for them, defending the defenseless, seeing things from the side of the poor and powerless, and assessing lifestyle, policies, and social institutions in terms of their impact on the poor.

There are several other Gospel commands we need to hear. Primary among these is the call to overcome and transform the "structures of sin," those social, political, and economic structures that oppress and destroy people. Those structures that especially need to be transformed are those created from an all-consuming desire for profit and thirst for power (EJ 36-37).

Another call of the Gospel is to recognize the socioeconomic rights of all and even the establishment of an economic bill of rights (EJ 80).[12]

The Gospel also demands that we respect to an even greater degree than we have the right of all people to participate in those decisions that affect their lives. This right pertains to all levels of life in society from foreign policy to local politics. It also includes having a say in the life of the business enterprise one works for and the union one belongs to (EJ 78, 297).

The Gospel also insists upon an ever-deepening sense of distributive justice in the global society in which we live today. It issues an imperative that the wealthy share with the poor; this call applies to nations as well as to individuals. Such a sharing of goods demands a reconsideration of the present level of our lifestyle and a controlling of consumerism.

The Gospel further calls us to find a way to bring together the drive and need for legitimate profit within the business firm and the firm's responsibility to respect the common good, dignity, and rights of all people and the good of the environment. This respect for others concerns both those the firm serves and those who work for it. Respect for the environment means using and handing on to developing countries only those production technologies that are environmentally sound.

There is also a strong call in the Gospel to remedy the distortion of priorities brought on by massive spending in the United States on defense. We must recognize the horrible impact of this spending on the poor and vulnerable members of our own nation as well as other nations. There is a call for the great powers to continue the struggle to find a way toward permanent peace and respect for one another and to turn their energies and resources toward the goal of real development in the world. The Gospel especially summons the great powers to share with the developing countries at least some of the resources saved through any cutbacks in arms production.

As we set about transforming structures, the Gospel reminds us that reaching out to others must be in the form of service—service that invites us to empty ourselves, to walk gently, to listen, and to learn from those we wish to serve. We must be open especially to listening to and learning from the poor, those in our midst and those around the world. Out of their experiences the poor may have insights into the meaning of the Gospel that are not evident to others but are nonetheless true. Some would say that the poor, because of their condition and experiences, have a hermeneutically privileged position from which to hear the Gospel.[13] This does not mean that whatever the poor say can be accepted uncritically as an expression of the Gospel. However, when helped to articulate their questions and insights into the Gospel, they may well have a privileged position from which to hear the Gospel message.

We need then to allow the cries of the poor for help, their insights into the meaning of the Gospel, their aspirations, and attempts at new life speak to us and allow our ways and our perceptions of reality to be questioned. We need to realize that the poor can hear and see things in the Gospel that we can no longer hear.

Finally, the poor must be the primary architects of their own future. Our role is to share with them our wealth of knowledge, technology, and goods, and to support and enable them to find their own way, the way they see is best for them. We may not agree with their conclusions, but we have no right to impose our values and our way of life on anyone. We must be open and allow ourselves to be led and evangelized by them. As St. Vincent de Paul always reminded the members of his family, "The poor are your masters."

PART 3

PLANNING: THE NEED
FOR A NATIONAL MISSION

9

THE CHURCH AND ITS MISSION

In the light of the social analysis and theological reflections in the first two parts of the book, my purpose in this third and final part is to address the question of the mission of the Church in the United States. In this chapter I deal with the mission of the Church in general and some related issues. In the final chapter I take up the specific question of the Church's mission in the United States. It is not my intention to present a complete ecclesiology; my concern is only with the mission of the Church.

THE CHURCH AND THE REIGN OF GOD

According to the *Dogmatic Constitution on the Church* from Vatican II, the Church is above all a "mystery" (LG 1), "a reality inbued with the hidden presence of God."[1] The Church can also be called a "sacrament" since it is a "sign of intimate union with God, and of the unity of all humankind . . . and also an instrument for the achievement of such union and unity" (LG 1). The Church is the visible embodiment of the Trinity, since it has been called by the Father for union with Christ through the power of the Holy Spirit. Christ inaugurated the Church by proclaiming the coming of the Kingdom of God which was revealed in his word, works, and presence (LG 2-5).

As a visible society the Church is an assembly of people called together by God for a particular mission, namely, "to proclaim and to establish among all peoples the kingdom of Christ and of God" (LG 5). While the Church is not to be identified with the Kingdom of God, the Church on earth is to be the initial budding forth of that kingdom. Having been called together for a specific mission, the Church, as a visible society, must be organized in view of that mission. In other words, the mission of the Church takes priority over, or gives direction to, the community life of the Church.[2]

The mission of the Church is focused on the Kingdom of God. The Kingdom of God is the reign or rule of God, and the Reign/Kingdom happens whenever and wherever the will of God is fulfilled. God rules where God's will is at work.[3]

The concept of the Reign of God goes back to the early days of Israel when it referred to God's protective kingship over the chosen people. This Reign of God was understood to be in history and yet would achieve its fullness beyond history. The Reign of God was seen as being over not only Israel but all people and creation. With the Reign would come a whole new moral order of peace, justice, and mercy (cf. Is 61:1; Lk 4:18). In later Judaism the apocalyptic literature saw the Reign as the heavenly Jerusalem and paradise as the home of the elect. The emphasis was on God's action, and attention was focused primarily on the signs and portents of the coming Reign.

Jesus was sent into the world to announce the Reign of God and to make it a reality. When Jesus began to preach he proclaimed that the Reign was near at hand (Mk 1:15), and he called for conversion, repentance, and watchfulness. Entrance into the Reign is determined by one's response to those in need (Mt 25:31-46) and the Reign is especially for sinners and outcasts, the poor and despised (Lk 6:20). The early Church emphasized that while the Reign of God had broken into history in the words and actions of Jesus, the Reign in its fullness would come only at the end of time. The mission of the Church is to continue the mission of Christ and so announce and enable this Reign to come to its full fruition.

The Second Vatican Council in its *Pastoral Constitution on the Church in the Modern World* describes the Reign as "the consummation of the earth and humanity" and "a new dwelling place and a new earth where justice will abide, and whose blessedness will answer and surpass all the longings for peace which spring up in the human heart" (GS 39). While this Reign is present on this earth, it is present only in mystery and will be brought to its fullness when the Lord returns. The signs of God's growing rule are the nurturing on earth of the values of "human dignity, brotherhood and freedom, and indeed all the good fruits of our nature and enterprise." While ultimately the Reign is a gift of God it is important that we do all we can to make it a reality now. However, earthly progress is not to be identified with the growth of God's kingdom; "nevertheless, to the extent that the former can contribute to the better ordering of human society, it is of vital concern to the kingdom of God" (GS 39).

The mission of the Church, then, is to proclaim and enable the Reign of God to become a reality. More specifically, the mission of the Church is to bring all things into one in Christ, to bring all under the rule of Christ so that at the end of time Christ can present all to God who will then rule over all for eternity. From another perspective it can be said that the mission of the Church is to seek freedom for all people from everything that keeps them from totally surrendering themselves to God. It is also to empower them to give the worship of total love and praise to God. The mission of the Church is, then, to bring liberation and to foster empowerment.

The liberation envisioned here is above all liberation from sin. However, sin and its effects exist not only in the human being but also in humanly created structures and systems that oppress and destroy. The liberation that the Church seeks involves more than the salvation and redemption of the individual from personal sin. Rather, the Church seeks to liberate peoples from all structures, systems, and institutions that oppress and destroy and hinder them from achieving full human dignity. The mission of the Church, then, is ultimately twofold. It is to liberate people from personal sin as well as from all those human structures and systems (social, political, and economic) that hold them back from achieving full human dignity and exercising their full personalities. The Church also has the mission of empowering people so that they can stand before God, in, with, and through Christ, and give God the worship of total love and praise.

EVANGELIZATION

How is the Church to effect this liberation and empowerment? Through the proclamation of the Word, through evangelization. Evangelization is the one task of the Church and all else is to be seen in light of it. As Pope Paul VI pointed out in *On the Evangelization of Peoples*, "Evangelizing is in fact the grace and vocation proper to the Church, her deepest identity. She exists in order to evangelize. . . ." (EN 14). The Church "prolongs and continues" Jesus in the world and "it is above all his mission and his condition of being an evangelizer that she is called upon to continue" (EN 15).

In terms of the traditional categories of prophet, king, and priest, the primary function of the Church is to be prophet. The kingly and priestly roles of the Church must be seen as extensions of its prophetic role.

Evangelization means bringing the Good News into all strata of human life, thereby transforming humanity from within and making it new. The purpose of evangelization is to convert, "solely through the divine power of the Message she proclaims, both the personal and collective consciences of people, the activities in which they engage, and the lives and concrete milieux which are theirs" (EN 18). What the Church intends in preaching the Gospel is "affecting and as it were upsetting, through the power of the Gospel, humanity's criteria of judgment, determining values, points of interest, lines of thought, sources of inspiration and models of life, which are in contrast with the Word of God and the plan of salvation" (EN 19). In other words, what is important is to evangelize cultures at their very roots.

Evangelization must take account of the unceasing interplay between the Gospel and the concrete life of human beings, both personal and social. That is why evangelization includes a message about the rights and duties of all human beings, about family life and life in society, and international life, peace, justice, and development. The Church has the duty to proclaim the liberation of those millions of human beings condemned to remain on the margins of life because of famine, poverty, illiteracy, injustices in international relations, and cultural neocolonialism. The Church has "the duty of assisting the birth of this liberation, of giving witness to it, of ensuring that it is complete. This is not foreign to evangelization" (EN 30).

The task of evangelizing belongs to everyone in the Church since the entire people of God make up the Church, not just the hierarchy (EN 59). The first means of evangelization is the witness of an authentically Christian life (EN 41); this duty pertains to individuals as well as to the Church as a whole. In other words,

> the Church must also be a sign of what God "is" actually doing in history and of what the human community "should" be doing in response to God's saving action. . . . The Church must be a community marked by faith, hope, love, freedom, and truthfulness, not only in its official proclamations but in its lifestyle as well.[4]

Though the Church is not to be identified with the Reign of God, it cannot be a sacrament of the Reign unless the Reign exists somehow within the community. The Church, then, must continually reform itself in the light of the Gospel and this reform must include its own structures and institutions. The only thing that is absolute is the Reign of God. Everything else is for the sake of the Reign and is relative to it (see EN 8).

Certainly the most important means of evangelization, the source and apex of the Christian life, is the celebration of the Eucharist and the other sacraments. Christian liturgy is the fully empowered proclamation of the death and resurrection of the Lord, those deeds that above all have begun to make the Reign of God a reality. This proclamation, especially as it is found in the Eucharist, is of such power that it brings about the actual presence of the Lord's death and resurrection. It is above all through this fully empowered and presence-creating proclamation of the saving deeds of Jesus that the Lord of the resurrection comes among us and frees us from all that hold us back from totally surrendering ourselves to God and empowers us to give the worship of total love and praise of God.

Other means of evangelization include the various kinds of preaching, especially homilies, catechetical instruction, and popular piety. Paul VI points out, "Our century is characterized by the mass media or means of social communication, and the first proclamation, catechesis or the further deepening of faith cannot do without these means" (EN 45). However, even with the potential of the mass media for enabling the Good News to reach millions of people, personal contact and person-to-person transmission of the Gospel remain very important: "In the long run, is there any other way of handing on the Gospel than by transmitting to another person one's personal experience of faith?" (EN 46).

THE CHURCH AND THE WORLD

The *Pastoral Constitution on the Church in the Modern World* points out that the Church is a community which "realizes that it is truly and intimately linked with humankind and its history" and so is in solidarity with the whole of humanity (GS 1). In other words, the Church exists not alongside the world but within the world, not in domination over the world but as the servant of the world. According to *Gaudium et Spes*, "Inspired by no earthly ambition, the Church seeks but a solitary goal: to carry forward the work of Christ himself under the lead of the befriending Spirit. And Christ entered this world to give witness to the truth, to rescue and not to sit in judgment, to serve and not to be served" (GS 3).

These passages reflect a significant development in the thinking of the Church and its relationship to the world. For centuries the Church had distinguished itself from "the world" and presented itself as a "perfect society" against that other perfect but inferior society that is the secular state. In other words, the Church had seen itself in an adversarial position with regard to the world, but that perspective has now changed.

What stands behind this change of perspective by the Church is a better historical sense and the concomitant realization that it exists in the world and takes life through people and cultures that have been shaped by the demands of history and locale. As Pope Paul VI pointed out, the "universal Church is in practice incarnate in the individual Churches made up of such or such an actual part of humanity, speaking such and such a language, heirs of a cultural patrimony, of a vision of the world, of an historical past, of a particular human substratum" (EN 62). Existing in the midst of such historically determined societies the role of the Church is to evangelize peoples and cultures from within—it is to be a leaven in the midst of the world. The Church does this by proclaiming the values of the Gospel, supporting those aspects of society that are in keeping with the Gospel, and challenging those that are not.

One of the great dangers that the Church always faces, insofar as it is human and in the world, is the temptation to become identified with a given culture and/or a particular economic/political system. While the Church always expresses itself through the language and cultural symbols of the people it is addressing—symbols that can be deeply related to the social, economic, and political systems of a people—the Church is never to become so identified with a particular language and culture that this particular language and culture are presented as the norm against which all else is judged. Once this happens the Church's perspective becomes narrow and closed and, above all, the Church loses its ability to stand back and critique the culture and the economic/political system in which it lives. In such a situation, the proclamation of the Word can very easily end up being a defense of a system that enslaves and oppresses. Hence, though the Church is, of necessity, in the world, it is not to be of the world in the sense of letting itself become identified with a particular culture and/or economic/political system (GS 42). How is the institutional Church to avoid such identification? A very important means is the one presented from the time of Christ, that is, to be poor and to identify with the poor. A Church that is poor and identifies with the poor is free in the face of the system. Having nothing, it has nothing to lose and nothing to defend. Only when the Church identifies itself with the poor and the oppressed can it accomplish its prophetic function of proclaiming the Word.

THE UNIVERSAL AND PARTICULAR CHURCH

We have been speaking of the mission of the Church in general, the common mission of the Church throughout the world. However, the Church always takes concrete form as a visible community in a particular place and at a particular time in history. In talking about the mission of the Church, we need to reflect on the nature of the particular or local church and its relationship to the Universal Church.

In the centuries before the Second Vatican Council, for a variety of historical reasons, the word "church" in Catholic speech, for all practical purposes, had come to refer to the worldwide assembly of the Church that was centralized in the Vatican under the supreme authority of the pope. Each diocese was considered to be an administrative division of this worldwide Church and each parish, in turn, an administrative subdivision of the diocese. As a result local churches on the diocesan and parish levels were considered to be "imperfect societies" and incapable of being fully "church" by themselves.

However, the Second Vatican Council returned to the original New Testament usage in which the word "church" is used to refer to individual local churches as well as to the worldwide assembly of Christians. The local church is not simply a subdivision of the universal Church but a genuine church in itself. This is clear when Paul speaks of "the church of God which is in Corinth" (1 Cor 1:2; 2 Cor 1:1). Nor is the Church universal simply the sum total of local churches. Rather, the universal Church is the fullness of the body of Christ who is its head (Eph 1:22–23; Col 1:18–20) and it is through the Church that the mystery of salvation is revealed (Eph 3:10). However, the precise relationship between the local and universal Church is not made clear in the New Testament.

In returning to the New Testament usage of the word "church," Vatican II intends to recognize the local or particular church as a genuine Church. However, it does not develop a complete theology of the local church.

Two important statements regarding the local church are found in the *Decree on the Bishops' Pastoral Office in the Church* and in the *Dogmatic Constitution on the Church*. The first of these documents defines the particular church as that portion of God's people which is entrusted to a bishop to be shepherded by him with the cooperation of the presbytery. Adhering thus to its pastor and gathered by him in the Holy Spirit through the Gospel and the Eucharist, this portion constitutes a particular church in which the one, holy, catholic, and apostolic church of Christ is truly present and operative. (CD 11)

While this definition appears to identify the local church with the diocese, the *Dogmatic Constitution on the Church* provides a broader concept.

This Church of Christ is truly present in all legitimate local congregations of the faithful which, united with their pastors, are themselves called churches in the New Testament. ... In them the faithful are gathered together by the preaching of the Gospel of Christ, and the mystery of the Lord's supper is celebrated, "that by the flesh and blood of the Lord's body the whole brotherhood may be joined together. ..." In these communities, though frequently small and poor, or living far from any other, Christ is present. By virtue of Him the one, holy, catholic, and apostolic Church gathers together. (LG 26)

What is clear is that for Vatican II the essential constitutive elements of a particular church as Church are the Gospel, the Eucharist, and the presence of the apostolic succession in the person of the bishop.

The question remains of how to understand the relationship between the universal and particular church. Leonardo Boff suggests that to solve this question we need to turn to the New Testament, which speaks of the church as one but multiple:

The one, universal church, for Paul, for instance, consists in the mystery of salvation of God, realized by the Son, in the power of the Holy Spirit acting within history and reaching all human beings. This mystery is one because God is one. It is universal because it touches each and every human being. The universality of the church resides in the universality of God's salvific offer. But this universal salvific mystery is manifested in space and time, and in being revealed it takes on the particularities of age and places. Thus there arises a particular church. This particular church is the universal church, manifested—concretized, historicized.[5]

Hence, "the one and universal Church does not manifest herself, nor has she any concrete existence, properly speaking, except in the local churches."[6] Boff adds,

The particular church is the universal church concretized; and in being concretized, taking flesh; and in taking flesh, assuming the limits of place, time, culture, and human beings. . . . The particular church is the church wholly, but not the whole church. *It is the church wholly* because in each particular church is contained the whole mystery of salvation. But *it is not the whole church* because no particular church exhausts by itself the whole wealth of the mystery of salvation.[7]

Hence, while there is a common mission for the worldwide assembly of the Church, this mission always takes life and form in a particular church, in a particular place and at a particular time in history, in a particular culture and language, with its own needs and problems. Each particular church then needs to reflect upon what it means to be Church in its specific context. This is why it is legitimate to speak specifically of the mission of the Church in the United States, in Latin America, and so forth. As Pope Paul VI has pointed out,

> The individual Churches, intimately built up not only of people but also of aspirations, of riches and limitations, of ways of praying, of loving, of looking at life and the world which distinguish this or that human gathering, have the task of assimilating the essence of the Gospel message and of transposing it, without the slightest betrayal of its essential truth, into the language that these particular people understand, then of proclaiming it in this language. (EN 63)

This transposition is to be done in liturgical expression, catechesis, theological formulation, secondary ecclesial structures, and ministries.

In this process each particular church must be open to receiving input, ideas, and inspiration from other particular churches, since no particular church encompasses the entire mystery of salvation. Each particular church must be open to the universal Church—to the salvific mystery manifested in other particular churches—as it attempts to determine its own mission (EN 64).

SOCIAL MISSION OF THE CHURCH

It is indisputable that the Church has a definite social mission. The 1971 Synod of Bishops made this clear in their now famous statement:

> Action on behalf of justice and participation in the transformation of the world fully appear to us as a constitutive dimension of the preaching of the Gospel, or, in other words, of the Church's mission for the redemption of the human race and its liberation from every oppressive situation. (JW 6)

The social mission of the Church, understood as "action on behalf of justice and participation in the transformation of the world," is a constitutive dimension of the Church's mission. As Pope Paul VI pointed out a few years later,

> Between evangelization and human advancement—development and liberation—there are in fact profound links. These include links of an anthropological order, because the man who is to be evangelized is not an abstract being but is subject to social and economic questions. They also include links in the theological order, since one cannot dissociate the plan of creation from the plan of Redemption. The latter plan touches the very concrete situations of injustice to be combated and of justice to be restored. They include links of the eminently evangelical order, which is that of charity: how in fact can one proclaim the new commandment without promoting in justice and in peace the true, authentic advancement of man? (EN 31)

The Second Synod of Bishops in *Justice in the World* points out the close connection between justice and love of neighbor: "Christian love of neighbor and justice cannot be separated. For love implies an absolute demand for justice, namely, a recognition of the dignity and rights of one's neighbor. Justice attains its inner fullness only in love" (JW 34). The great challenge for the Church today is learning how to carry out this social mission.

Charles Curran has pointed out that there are limits on the social mission of the Church.[8] Above all it is important to realize that the social mission is only a part of the Church's total mission. There are many other aspects such as preaching the Gospel and celebrating the sacraments. While the social mission is not opposed to these other aspects, the mission of the Church cannot be reduced to only its social dimension, as important as it is. However, I would argue that, at certain periods in history, because of the circumstances of the times, it would seem that the social mission of the Church can and must give focus to the other dimensions of the Church's life. Given the immensity of the social issues facing the world, it appears that this is the situation today. As much as is possible, all aspects of the life of the Church must take their direction and inspiration today from the social dimension of the Church.

In carrying out its social mission the Church must always keep in mind that many individuals and groups apart from the Church are also working to transform society. Catholics and other Christians must avoid a narrow triumphalism of claiming to be the only ones working for justice. At the same time, however, the Church "has a proper and specific responsibility which is identified with her mission of giving witness before the world of the need for love and justice contained in the Gospel message, a witness to be carried out in Church institutions themselves and in the lives of Christians" (JW 36). Further, individual Roman Catholics are not only Church members; also they belong to many other groups that are working for the betterment of society. Finally, Christians have no monopoly on social ethical wisdom or insight.

It is also very important for the Church to be sensitive to how it attempts to bring change into society. There is no place for what has been labeled "integralism," an approach that came out of Vatican I's unfinished agenda. According to this view, those Catholics who seek a complete or integral Catholicism in the political realm demand the perfect coalescence of Christian morality with the legal realm of the state and, thus, the suppression of all error. This perspective allowed no place for a concept of the separation of church and state or for error. Moreover, since the Catholic Church was considered by its members to be the source of all truth, its doctrine alone was to dominate in political affairs and in the formation of civil law.

Although this theory was not sustained by Vatican II's *Declaration on Religious Liberty*, it still colors much Catholic thought in our time. Integralism will always be a temptation for any group convinced of the rightness of its positions. It can only be checked by the attitude embodied in Vatican II's *Declaration on Religious Liberty*, an attitude that sees the use of force — psychological or physical — as immoral, as an abuse against conscience. What is called for is persuasion by rational arguments as the only way to obtain political consensus in the public forum.

INTERVENTION IN POLITICS AND ECONOMICS

The Church's right and responsibility to address social, political, and economic issues of the day emerges from the social mission of the Church. As has already been noted, the person to be evangelized is not an abstract being but is subject to social, political, and economic structures and systems. Too often these systems oppress and destroy and impede the attainment of human rights and human dignity. As Pope John Paul II has pointed out, these "structures of sin" are rooted in personal sin and are always linked to concrete acts of individuals who introduce these structures, consolidate them, and make them difficult to remove. Once in place these structures grow stronger, spread, and become the source of other sins as they influence people's behaviors (SRS 36). It is clear that in carrying out its mission the Church must address these structures of sin wherever they exist. Ultimately, to deny God's presence and action in the political and economic orders is to deny God's rule over all creation.

In view of the Church's right and responsibility to address social, political, and economic issues, we may ask how and to what extent the institutional Church[9] should intervene in these issues. It should be kept in mind that the Church enters public or social ministry to protect and promote the transcendent dignity of the individual. In fact the Church always looks at social, political, and economic issues through the prism of the dignity of the person.[10]

The *Pastoral Constitution on the Church in the Modern World* from the Second Vatican Council presents in paragraphs 40–42 three principles that define the role of the Church in the world:

(1) the ministry of the Church is religious in origin and purpose; the Church has no specifically political charism;

(2) the religious ministry has as its primary objective serving the reign of God—the Church is, in a unique way, the "instrument" of the reign of God in history;

(3) as the Church pursues its religious ministry it should contribute to four objectives which have direct social and political consequences: protecting human dignity, promoting human rights, cultivating the unity of the human family and contributing a sense of meaning to every aspect of human activity.[11]

Since the Church has no specifically political charism, then the proper competence of the Church is to address the moral and religious significance of political questions. While the Gospel may suggest perspectives on political and economic questions, it does not provide concrete programs or policies. Thus, the Church's involvement in these issues is always indirect. What might this involvement include?

The Church can and must express very clear denunciations of specific abuses and injustices, especially when they are significant and widespread and silence by the Church could be taken as assent.[12] However, the role of the Church cannot be confined to such a limited prophetic role. The Church must also speak out on public issues that involve human rights, social justice, and the life of the Church in society. How far should the Church go in such statements, especially when it is speaking on a national or regional level? Should it limit itself to stating general moral principles, or should it apply such principles to specific policy and program issues? John Coleman proposes that Church teaching on social issues should aim mainly at what are called "middle axioms."[13] Such a principle or directive would be more concrete than a universal ethical principle, but less specific than a program that includes legislation and political strategy. Such axioms are "directives, inviting toward decision and action."[14] Coleman believes that Pope Paul VI had something like this in mind when he stated in his apostolic letter *Octogesima Adveniens*,

If it [the Church] does not intervene to authenticate a given structure or to propose a ready-made model, it does not thereby limit itself to recalling general principles. It develops through reflection applied to the changing situations of this world, under the driving force of the Gospel as the source of renewal when its message is accepted in its totality and with all its demands. It also develops with the sensitivity proper to the Church which is characterized by a disinterested will to serve and by attention to the poorest. (OA 42)

Bryan Hehir proposes, however, in discussing how specific statements of bishops' conferences should be, that the conferences should be able to apply theological or moral principles to concrete situations.[15] He bases his argument on the same passage from *Octogesima Adveniens* quoted above, and on two other arguments. First, there is the need to incarnate moral principles in the fabric of a social problem to demonstrate their significance and illuminative power. Otherwise, "there is a risk in stating principles so abstractly that all acknowledge them, then proceed to widely divergent conclusions while claiming support of the principle."[16] Second, he argues that the intrinsic merits and persuasive quality of episcopal statements are enhanced if the bishops show a willingness to engage the specific dimensions of the problems.

However, it is also clear that when the institutional Church makes judgments and recommendations on specific concrete issues, such prudential judgments do not carry the same moral authority as statements of universal moral principles and formal church teaching (see EJ 134–35; CP 8–12). Such prudential judgments are based on specific circumstances that can change or can be interpreted differently by people of good will.

Besides forceful social teaching, Coleman argues, "the Church can go beyond directives and principles to sketch ideal visions and imaginative hopes of a healthy communal society in what Paul VI refers to as the rebirth of utopias."[17] Such imaginative projection of utopias are in keeping with the Church's hope for an eschatological transformation of the structures of society. As Pope Paul VI says,

> The appeal to a utopia is often a convenient excuse for those who wish to escape from concrete tasks in order to take refuge in an imaginary world. To live in a hypothetical future is a facile alibi for rejecting immediate responsibilities. But it must clearly be recognized that this kind of criticism of existing society often provokes the forward-looking imagination both to perceive in the present the disregarded possibility hidden within it, and to direct itself towards a fresh future; it thus sustains social dynamism by the confidence that it gives to the inventive powers of the human mind and heart. (OA 37)

My own view would be that the Church should be involved both in stating "middle axioms" and sketching ideal visions (Coleman) as well as in applying principles to concrete situations (Hehir). There is a place for both approaches. Some circumstances will clearly call for applying principles to concrete situations, especially when silence on the part of the Church would appear to convey approval or acceptance of a situation. However, I tend to believe that, as a norm, the Church should aim for middle axioms in its teaching and preaching.

The Church should also have a concern for education for justice that includes not only explicit programs for justice but also is part of catechesis, liturgy, and media. The Church should encourage discussions of major political and economic issues through forums, congresses, consultations, newspapers, and media. In this way the Church will deepen the public debate on important issues and see that Gospel principles are included as an important part of debates about policies and programs.[18]

Finally, it is important that in carrying out its social mission the Church should not attempt to impose norms of personal morality on the formation of public policy. John Courtney Murray comments that "the morality proper to the life and action of society and the state is not univocally the morality of personal life, or even of family life."[19] As Charles Curran points out, "Morality in the Catholic tradition is determined by the ends and the relevant orders of political and individual reality. The end and order of political and social reality are different from the end and order of individual and personal morality."[20] The ends of the two orders are not coextensive. While the end of society itself is the common good or welfare of all, the end of the limited constitutional state, which is only part of society, is the public order.

According to the *Declaration on Religious Freedom*, from the Second Vatican Council, this public order has a threefold content (DH 7).[21] First, there is an order of justice, in which the rights of all citizens are effectively safeguarded. Second, there is an order of peace, which enables human beings to live together harmoniously in society. Third, there is an order of public morality understood to be the minimum of public morality necessary for people to live together in society.

Also, according to the *Declaration on Religious Freedom* (DH 7) the fundamental criterion for law is that the freedom of human beings is to be respected as far as possible and curtailed only when and insofar as necessary. Since the end of the state is the public order then public order—constituted by the three orders of justice, peace, and morality—becomes the criterion justifying the need for law. Because the preservation of these three orders is so necessary, the coercive force of government may be enlisted to protect and vindicate them. As John Murray observes,

It follows, then, that the morality proper to the life and action of society and the state is not univocally the morality of personal life, or even of familial life. Therefore the effort to bring the organized action of politics and the practical art of statecraft directly under the control of the Christian values that govern personal and familial life is inherently fallacious. It makes wreckage not only of public policy but also of morality itself.[22]

10

WHERE IS THE U.S. CHURCH GOING?

This final chapter attempts to pull together the various threads and reflections that have run through this book into a final consideration of the mission of the Church in the United States. As I pointed out in the beginning, it is not my intention to say what the mission of the Church in the United States must be. Rather, my purpose has been to present the types of issues I believe must be considered in any reflection on the mission of the Church in the United States and, in the light of these issues, to present one possible direction for that Church. Ultimately, the Church's mission in the United States must emerge, not from the reflections of one particular individual, but from the corporate reflection of the Church.

AN INSTRUMENT OF LIBERATION

When reflecting on the mission of our Church, it is important to keep in mind the very significant role this country plays on the global level. The United States is a central actor in the relations between the East and the West and an important actor in the interplay between the countries of the Northern hemisphere and the countries of the Southern hemisphere. On the global level, the greatest scandal today is the massive poverty and oppression among so many peoples, especially those who live in the Southern hemisphere. It is a poverty and oppression that is more striking because of the wealth and waste of most of the countries of the Northern hemisphere. This disparity between the North and the South is due, in different ways, to two realities: the colonization policies of the past, and the continuing oppression of the South by the North for the sake of the North's economic stability and progress. The United States has inherited to a significant degree the wealth that came from the colonization policies of the past and shares some of the responsibility for the present oppression of the South. Hence, the United States has a responsibility to end this disparity between the North and the South.

There is a twofold call of the Gospel that emerges most clearly from reflection on the situation of the United States today. There is a call to a preferential option for the poor and a call to transform the social, political, and economic systems and structures that are responsible for the oppression of the South.

The Church's Mission

I would propose the following regarding the mission of the Church in the United States. As an instrument of the Reign of God in history, the Church in the United States is to be an instrument in seeking the liberation of the poor on a global level through a twofold process of empowerment of the poor and the transformation of the systems that oppress. The "poor on a global level" are especially the poor and oppressed in the underdeveloped countries of Latin America, Africa, and Asia. "Liberation" means primarily political and economic liberation, that is, liberation from the systems, the structures of sin, that oppress. Insofar as possible, this mission of the Church should provide the focus for all aspects of the life of the Church in the United States, both internally and externally.

Rationale

The reasons for concluding that the Church's mission in the United States is to be an instrument in seeking the liberation of the poor on a global level can be summarized in the following way. First, the United States must accept some responsibility for the present oppression of the poor in the Third World because of the impact of its foreign policy and some of the policies and actions of its transnational corporations. The members of the Church in the United States, as citizens of a superpower responsible for oppression in the world, have a responsibility to work for the liberation of these poor. This flows from the call of the Gospel, papal pronouncements, and the letters of the U.S. bishops to adopt a preferential option for the poor and to seek justice. Second, election by God is not for oneself; it is always for others. As Genesis 12:1–3 makes clear, Abraham and hence Israel were called by God to be a source of God's blessings and salvation to all other nations. In the same way, if we believe that we have been specially chosen by God as a country, then that election is also a call to be a source of God's blessings, salvation for others. Being an instrument of God's salvation for others means being an instrument of liberation. Third, if all who believe in Christ form one body in Christ and if what affects one member of the body affects the whole body, then the suffering and pain of the oppressed must be the suffering and pain of all who believe in Christ. One cannot ignore a festering sore in one part of the body for it will eventually destroy the whole body. This latter point is not just a theological argument. Given the interdependence of all nations today, no nation can escape the ramifications and consequences of what is taking place in other nations. Fourth, it is clear from the history of God's people that the God of the Hebrew and Christian Scriptures is a God who is always with and for the people with power, bringing them historical liberation from slavery and giving them new life through a passionate caring/suffering. Like this God, all who believe are also called to be freedom-givers and to effect deliverance from economic and political oppression where it exists. To turn one's back on the oppressed and deny one's responsibility to help them is to reject one's God.

The Poor in Our Midst

Insisting that the mission of the Church in the United States is to be an instrument in seeking the liberation of the poor on a global level is not to suggest that the poor in our midst be forgotten. Certainly the Church in the United States must work for the liberation of the poor in the United States. However, it is important to understand that the oppression of the poor in our midst arose from the same structures of sin that enslave and oppress on a global level; the ultimate liberation of the poor in our midst is closely connected to the liberation of the poor on a global level.

Means: Empowerment of the Poor

The Church is to seek the liberation of the poor through a process of empowerment of the poor and transformation of oppressive systems. It is always to be remembered that the poor are to be the architects of their own future. It is not the role of the United States or any other nation to impose its vision or social, political, and economic systems on other peoples and nations. Other peoples have the right to design their own systems. The United States and other advanced nations are to support the poor and empower them through a sharing of their wealth of knowledge and material resources and by entering into solidarity with them. However, the United States has no right to impose its own systems upon others. The mission of the Church in the United States will be to keep this important role of the country before its people.

Means: Transformation of Systems

The Church in the United States must also work toward the transformation of the systems that oppress. I are referring here to social, political, and economic systems in the United States as well as to international structures and systems that the United States contributes to or shares responsibility for. Adaptation of the systems or technical adjustments to them will not suffice. What is needed is the elimination of structures that oppress and their replacement with structures that empower people to help themselves to achieve the fullness of their human dignity. In other words, capital and modern technology must be put to the service of basic human needs and fundamental human rights, rather than primarily to the development of profit.

Immediate Objectives

Against this background it would seem, then, that the most immediate objective of the Church in the United States is to call all people in the United States, but especially Catholics, to a preferential option for the poor. This objective should be at the core of the Church's internal ministry, including the celebration of the sacraments. Until people adopt a preferential option for the poor they are not going to strive for the liberation of the poor. This call to an option for the poor will be a call to a profound change of heart and attitude by both Catholics and others in the United States. The first step in motivating people to respond to this call will be to help them to recognize and accept the basic dignity and equality of every human being, the solidarity of the human race, and the need of all to work for the common good. It will also be important to help people to recognize that the goods of creation exist to serve the needs of all people and that we must imitate the compassion of Jesus for the poor and the outcasts of society. Second, the call to a preferential option for the poor will have to include a proclamation of the Gospel vision of peace and justice and love and show the possibility of living life in a new way.

Long-Range Objective

The call to a preferential option for the poor and solidarity with them must be the most direct focus of the mission of the Church in the United States in the years ahead. However, the U.S. Church will also have to work toward the objective of transforming social, political, and economic systems. In fact, this work toward the transformation of the systems should constitute the long-range objective of the Church in its struggle to liberate the poor. Because the Church does not have the required expertise (nor is it the role of the Church to propose new social, political, and economic systems), its role in the process of transformation must be indirect. Therefore, the Church must critique, in the light of the Gospel, the systems in the United States and those international systems that are responsible for oppression. Even more important, however, the Church must attempt to transform the mindframe and attitudes that give birth to the systems and keep them in place. These attitudes and mindframes are primarily those associated with individualism, the U.S. sense of chosenness, and the identification of salvation with material success.

DIFFICULTIES

1. There is one major difficulty that may prevent the Church in the United States from becoming an effective instrument of transformation and

a credible witness to a call to a preferential option for the poor. This difficulty is that the Church in the United States is predominantly a Church of the middle class. While this Church came into existence as the Church of poor immigrants, it became a Church of the middle class as those same immigrants became part of the American middle class. This is not to deny that there are many poor who are members of the Church. However, as the Church in the United States grew older, it adopted the values and the myths of the American middle class with whom it identifies. This reality applies to the great majority of those who make up the Church—priests, bishops, and religious, as well as the laity. Even the poor members of the Church hope to enter the middle class or have fallen from the middle class and aspire to its values and lifestyle. This identification with the middle class affects how the Gospel is preached, how it is received, and the willingness of the members to follow the Gospel when it is heard.

2. As an institution the U.S. Church has significant wealth in land, buildings, and investment portfolios. Therefore, as an institution, the Church is very concerned about the health of the economy, since it depends upon this economy to retain its level of wealth. This context is not conducive to working for transformation or for making an option for the poor. There is no doubt that, by and large, the Church attempts to be socially and morally responsible in the handling of its investments. However, the Church in the United States does not invest as one body; its investments are made through hundreds of groups investing independently, such as individual dioceses, separate provinces of religious communities, and various institutions. The investing power of the Church is quite diffuse, so that each investing body has no more real power for effecting change than other small investors. Also, the various groups are quite dependent upon the income from their various investments to be able to carry on their works. Given this reality, the various church bodies find it difficult to be free in the face of the system; they are often forced to compromise with the system and with the values of the Gospel.

3. Another difficulty is that most individual Catholics in the United States are part of the middle class with its corresponding standard of living. They interpret the call to an option for the poor and to work toward the transformation of the system as a threat to their present standard of living and security. They may find it difficult to be open to the poor and the minorities in their midst and be unwilling to stand in solidarity with the poor.

4. U.S. Catholics have been deeply affected by American individualism.[1] Like other Americans, they often see religion as something that primarily concerns their private life and plays no public role. Moreover, they believe that their personal relationship with God transcends their involvement in any particular Church. What they primarily look for in a Church body is personal intimacy and support. As a result, they do not want their Church to make them feel uneasy about themselves or their society. Further, they lack a significant sense of a common good and common values. In this

context local religious bodies find it difficult to move beyond an individualistic morality that concentrates on family and personal life to a concern with social, political, and economic issues. To some extent this is the fault of the local churches themselves. Traditionally they have not interpreted problems facing people as having structural causes. Solutions to problems have been presented from the pulpit as a process of personal adjustment or the result of individual effort. The structures themselves have not been critiqued or questioned: "We will hold hands with others for 'Hands Across America' or give millions of dollars to 'Live-Aid' or 'Farm-Aid' concerts, but these largely ignore the underlying structures that produce poverty in the first place."[2]

5. The U.S. Church has had a tendency to assimilate the American political experience without critical judgment. Having struggled for decades to be fully accepted as loyal Americans, U.S. Catholics are very hesitant to appear "un-American" now by criticizing too strongly the actions and policies of the United States. This same uncritical acceptance of the American political experience has also affected Catholics in their attitude toward the separation of Church and state.

6. Catholic social teaching has not been part of the education of many Catholics of this generation. To a great extent catechetical formation has reflected the American view of religion as a private affair. Hence, the social teaching of the Church is new to many good Catholics, and it will take a while for them to assimilate it.

7. Like all Americans, American Catholics are opposed to anyone even remotely appearing to tell them how to vote. One may wonder whether American Catholics will even listen to a Church proclaiming an option for the poor and calling for transformation of the political, social, and economic systems if it appears that they are being told how to vote. The selective nature of present-day Catholicism—where Catholics will accept a Church position if it makes sense to them—will further contribute to the difficulty of the Church's getting a hearing on political issues. However, if they begin to understand that the transformation of systems and an option for the poor is in their own best interest, then a hearing is more likely.

8. Finally, the present tension between the U.S. Catholic Church and Rome makes it difficult for the U.S. Church to fully engage in the strong social mission that I have proposed. Because of the way that Rome has dealt with the Church of Latin America and liberation theology, many bishops, priests, and religious leaders will be very slow to proceed in what might appear to be a radical direction. It might be difficult to find the context where there can be the freedom for the level of creativity that will be demanded to achieve this mission on the levels of Church structure and methods of evangelization.

POSITIVE FACTORS

The picture is not a totally negative one. There are also some positive aspects in the life of the U.S. Church that can assist it in carrying out the mission I have proposed.

1. The Catholic worldview is a communal one. As a result, Catholics place a significant emphasis on social justice and love of neighbor as dimensions of their faith. Also, there is a growing emphasis today, in many parishes, on peace and justice issues and the acceptance, at least by Core Catholics, of the need for structural change in the world. A significant number of parishes now have social action programs which aim to make social structures and institutions more just. Most American Catholics, in fact, are liberal on economic themes and therefore support a strong role for government in economic matters and increased spending for social programs.

2. American Catholics are also firm in their commitment to peace. They are a major force in society for arms control, reduced military spending, and a prudent foreign policy.

3. Another encouraging fact has been that through the efforts of the U.S. bishops, the Church has become a public Church. In other words, the U.S. Church has become a catalyst moving the public argument to grapple with questions of moral values, ethical principles, and the human and religious meaning of policy choices.

4. The shift in post–Vatican II social thought from a "moralist" to a "structuralist" analysis of social problems is also encouraging. The moralist approach sees the solution of social problems lying primarily in the reform of the heart of individuals. The structuralist approach recognizes the reality of structural social sin and sees the need for social analysis and structural change. The recent letter of the bishops on the economy reflects this shift in emphasis.

5. Finally, the large number of new immigrants entering the United States, many of whom are poor and Catholic, is awakening the Church to the reality that it is no longer a Church of the poor and finds it difficult to respond to the needs of the poor. The Church's recognition that it must respond more effectively to the needs of the new poor immigrants and adapt itself so that it can minister to them is a good sign that it may be willing to be open to the poor and to stand in solidarity with them.

STRATEGIC PRESUPPOSITIONS

Before proceeding to outline some possible strategies for achieving the proposed mission of the Church in the United States, I want to pause and consider some basic realities. These issues, which any realistic strategies must take into account, are primarily of a sociological nature. They are important because of our concern for the Church in the United States to become an instrument of change and transformation. If the Church in the United States is to be involved in bringing about social change, it is important to understand some of the issues involved. In the following I am especially dependent upon John Coleman's book, *An American Strategic Theology*.[3]

1. As Coleman points out, "In the United States the major motor for reform and social change has never been an economic class but the social movement—partly religious, partly political, and based on a constituency which joins lower-class rights and demands in a coalition which includes several classes."[4] Hence, strategies for change in the United States should not concentrate on only one economic class, such as the poor.

2. As the long history of religious groups in the United States shows, the key instrument of the Church in affecting the social order in the United States has never been a political party or even the corporate Church as such. Rather, the key instrument has always been voluntary associations of Christians who have formed lobby groups to effect social change.[5] These groups have been most effective when organized along ecumenical and interdenominational lines. However, such voluntarism is effective only if it is joined to a broad social analysis and an attempt to articulate a genuine, concrete historical ideal.

3. In this context the bishops are called upon to play a role of "ethico-cultural leadership."[6] Their role is to address themselves "mainly to religious or moral-value questions in a style which carries, indeed, political implications, but avoids, in the main, the direct insertion of the institutional Church into partisan political battles."[7] The recent pastoral letters of the bishops on disarmament and the economy are good examples of this type of leadership.[8] At times, however, they may be called to apply principles and middle axioms directly to concrete situations and so insert themselves directly into partisan political battles.[9] Whatever the situation, the authority and credibility of the Church with relationship to the larger society will depend on Church-wide consensus. In other words, even though the bishops may speak in unison on important issues, their pronouncements will have little societal impact unless they can bring their constituency with them.[10]

4. This last observation brings us to a serious sociological obstacle to concerted Catholic action for justice and peace, that is, the pluralism of the Church in the United States. This pluralism has several sources. First, needs and issues vary in different parts of the country. For example, while the Church in California must minister to a constant stream of new immigrants, primarily of Hispanic and Asian origin, that is not the case for the Church of Iowa. Similarly, highly urban dioceses must deal with various needs and issues that are quite different from the concerns of predominantly rural dioceses.

A second source of pluralism is even more significant, the pluralism arising from a Church membership that includes people with widely different degrees of commitment, socialization into Gospel values, and identification with the Church. This membership is also composed of people coming from diverse social and economic classes, ethnic backgrounds, and political commitments. This internal pluralism will significantly limit the sociological possibility of a unitary, prophetic stance by the Church. It will be very important to develop effective strategies to target strategic regional and demographic subpopulations for campaigns of intense evangelization and calls to action for justice.[11] Moreover,

> much of the significant secular impact from the Church and much of the stirring up of energies within the Church will be the work of small cadres of committed social Catholics. How to identify this minority, minister to its needs, and allow it voice and access to the pluralistic Church at large, becomes a chief strategic problem in organizing a national Church for justice and peace.[12]

5. A question arises when one speaks of the Church as an instrument of transformation of society's structures. Does such a role breach the separation of Church and state as this issue has been developed against the background of the First Amendment to the United States Constitution? As J. Bryan Hehir has pointed out, the First Amendment "asserts that religious organizations should expect neither favoritism nor discrimination in the exercise of their civil or religious responsibilities."[13] There is hardly any indication in law, history, or policy that the intent of the First Amendment was to silence the religious voices of the nation. In addition, the church-state relationship as defined by the First Amendment governs only the juridical relationship of the institution of the Church to the institution of the state. The state, however, must be distinguished from society, of which the state is only a part.[14] The Church is not separate from society but can play a variety of roles within society, including that of a voluntary association.

Finally, in locating the role of the Church in the wider societal framework, it is important to understand the role of voluntary associations in a democratic society. Such associations are structured organizations that attempt to influence the polity and policies of a society. Such associations bring different contributions to the public arena on issues that interest them. As Hehir says, "The Church should bring a systematic capability to raise and address the moral dimensions of public issues and it also brings the capability to engage the members of its constituency in public discussion about these issues."[15]

6. Coleman presents four dilemmas regarding Church-Society relations.[16] These sociological generalizations about the possible impact of the Church on secular society deal with the problem of keeping a balance between the Church's role as a public agency in society and its need to be faithful to its identity as a Church community.

The first dilemma concerns "political relevance without partisanship." The problem for the Church is not whether it will play a political role in society; rather, the problem is finding the appropriate arena, style, and stance where it can play the political role it is most suited for and that is in keeping with its character as Church.[17]

A second dilemma is that of "religious identification and the worldly calling." As Max Weber pointed out, one key variable in the impact of religion on secular society is the ability of the churches to create structural carriers of motivation for political engagement. Mere pietism or socio-emotional groups of revivalism (such as the Cursillo, charismatic, and Marriage Encounter movements) will not suffice. What is needed is the creation of groups in which there is a delicate balance between an intense, disciplined pietism and an intense sense of mission to transform society. There have been no cases of significant and widespread religious impact on modern culture without the simultaneous combination, of a disciplined group life of prayer, discussion, Gospel reading, and an intense sense of mission to transform society.

The third dilemma is that of "social action and wider pastoral care." Most people turn to religion for personal reasons to find answers to personal hurts, tragedies, failures, or for intense religious experiences. They come to religion to find the ultimate meaning of their lives and the strength to carry on their daily tasks. Any concern around social justice issues is secondary. The challenge is to link people's personal issues with larger structural issues.

The fourth dilemma is that of "Church influence and collaboration with wider secular groups." Following Max Weber, Coleman makes the point that the churches alone can never generate social change. In fact, Church reform can only be successful if it is carried forward by important socio-political trends in society. In other words, churches can make positive, unique contributions to society but only in alliance with secular movements articulating alternative visions of the social order. As a result "no American Catholic strategy for social change will be effective unless [it is] in tactical alliance with wider ecumenical and secular movements for change."[18]

7. The laity are the key social action agents of the Church in the world.[19] It is largely through the laity that transforming Christian action can enter the arenas of economics, politics, the erotic, esthetic, and intellectual spheres. It is through the laity that the ethico-cultural leadership and middle axioms proclaimed by the official voices of the Church can best be translated into concrete programs, struggles, and movements for political and social change. In this regard, it is important to remember that the laity have their own proper mission within the Church (LG 31); the laity are not merely delegates of the hierarchy.

8. The Church in the United States has been principally centered on the parish. The assumption is that the parish is the real Church and so lay initiative has been confined to the parish level. There have been almost no renewal movements among the American laity where the lay sector constituted a diocesan or nationally based constituency. As a result lay renewal movements in the United States have shown a repeated pattern of fragmentation, loss of vigor, and deep ambiguity about whether to focus on an agenda directed toward inner renewal of the Church or outer influence on the wider society.[20] It seems that if the U.S. laity are to influence the wider

society, then lay movements, structurally autonomous from the local parish, will be necessary.

9. For there to be a transformation of our society and culture, there will have to be changes on several levels.[21] First, it is essential that there be personal transformations among large numbers of people—not only transformations of consciousness but transformations that involve action on the part of individuals. For this to happen, people need the support of groups that reinforce their own aspirations. In turn, existing groups and organizations will have to develop social movements dedicated to the idea of the transformation of society and culture.

10. A very important insight of Coleman is that "the Church's main contribution in the international arena is the establishment of a vivid sense of belonging to a real community which consists in some genuine way in the entire world."[22] An important task of each national Church is to keep alive this reality of transnational community. As Coleman points out, it is precisely the ability of religion to link the nation to a larger world community that accounts for the importance of religion to national self-identity; the larger world community both relativizes the individual nation-state and stands in judgment on it.[23]

11. Finally, in formulating goals and strategies for action within society, we need criteria to evaluate these goals and strategies from a faith perspective. Thomas Groome suggests three guidelines for making such decisions: consequences, continuity, and community/Church.[24]

The first guideline asks whether the consequences of a decision contribute to making the Reign of God present now and prepare for its final fulfillment. In other words, is the envisioned response creative of the freedom, peace, justice, and wholeness that flow from the vision of God's Reign?

The second guideline is whether the decision is in continuity with the Story[25] of the Christian community before them. Positions cannot be taken that contradict what is essential to the Story. Decisions can be made to go beyond the Story or not to continue practices from the past or to reformulate beliefs. However, the truth of the tradition must be affirmed and new "truths" must be in continuity with it.

Groome speaks of the third guideline as "community/Church," since he envisions decisions taking place in what he calls a "shared praxis group." Such a group comes together to decide upon an action flowing from social analysis and theological reflection. "Community" means the immediate shared praxis group itself; "Church" implies the larger Christian community to which the small group belongs.

In an actual shared praxis group the discernment of that community itself becomes a guideline for decision making. The corporate quest for discernment, guided by the Holy Spirit, has a reliability greater than the discernment of any individual alone or even the sum total of the individuals. Also, no small group of Christians can be a reliable guide for truth in isolation from the rest of the Christian community to which the small group belongs. The small community, or shared praxis group, must be informed by and measure its decisions against the belief and practice of the whole Church. By "Church" here is meant not only the teaching of the official magisterium but also the research of theologians and Scripture scholars and the discernment of the people of God. None of these three sources of teaching in the Church can stand alone; all three are important and must work together and interrelate with each other "in mutual dialogue, support, insight, correction, and affirmation."[26]

POSSIBLE STRATEGIES

In view of the above, several strategies emerge as a means for achieving the mission and objectives of the U.S. Church.

The U.S. Church as a "Public" Church

The Catholic Church in the United States must continue to broaden its role as a "public church" in American society.[27] A public church is one that "accepts social responsibility for the common good and envisions its teaching role as a participation in the wider societal debate."[28] The role of such a public church, according to Hehir, is "less that of providing definitive answers to complex socio-political questions than it is to act as a catalyst moving the public argument to grapple with questions of moral values, ethical principles and the human and religious meaning of policy choices."[29]

Concentrate on "Structural Sin." This public church should concentrate especially on "structural sin" and the need to transform those social, political, and economic systems and structures that oppress and destroy, nationally and globally. While the Church must normally avoid any unseemly partisan politics in its proclamation of the Word, its presentations must be specific enough to be meaningful. At times certain issues will be so central to the life of the nation that they will demand that the Church address them directly, even at the risk of appearing to enmesh itself in partisan politics. The intention of such proclamations will not be to dictate public policy but to shape public opinion in such a way as to influence public policy.

Be Participative. The Church should continue the participative process that has been used in drafting recent pastoral letters. The purpose of such a process is "to test the persuasive quality with which the moral doctrine is conveyed, the quality of the empirical analysis in the letters and the wisdom of the policy recommendations."[30] The Church should broaden this process by including more people at the parish and diocesan level, both as a means of evangelization and in order to have more contact with the concerns and needs of the "person on the street." However, it will be especially important for the Church to continue the discussions on these issues with representatives of the government, industry, and the military. Such discussions can be carried on directly or indirectly through such institutions as Catholic universities and schools of theology. The purpose of these discussions would be to develop a forum where the Church could clearly voice its concerns and raise consciousness among those most directly involved in giving shape to the structures of society. The Church could also learn more about the complexities of the situations on the practical level and have an opportunity to break down undue suspicions, clarify misunderstandings, and develop a cooperative approach to the transformation of systems.

National Pastoral Plan. If the Church is to play its role as a public church effectively, it must do so in light of a national pastoral plan, a plan for action that will, in the first place, give overall direction and focus and provide priorities for the pastoral activities of the NCCB and the USCC. Such a plan would also offer direction and priorities to the pastoral activities of individual dioceses and other ecclesial organizations so that the Church could focus its myriad resources in a common direction. The plan must be developed in dialogue with the members of the Church in the United States and have clear goals and objectives. A clear set of strategies for achieving the goals and objectives must also be developed.

Concern for Justice. The Church as a public church should be concerned with justice on a variety of levels. It must be involved in consciousness raising through a process of education for justice from the primary level of education to the university and on both parish and diocesan levels. This educational process should include comprehensive social analysis and theological reflection. The Church must also advocate for the poor both through direct lobbying efforts and through various organizations within or connected to the Church, such as Network, the Center of Concern, and peace and justice commissions. And the Church must be involved in providing direct services to those in need. As Coleman points out, "The Church cannot speak realistically 'for' the poor unless it speaks continuously 'with' them through its own programs of service."[31] Finally, the middle-class members of the Church must be willing to stand in solidarity with the poor in their quest for justice.

Ecumenical in Approach. In all the above the Catholic Church needs to become more ecumenical in its approach to issues of justice and peace. The more broad based the movement toward justice, the more hope there is that it can achieve its goals. Moreover, the Catholic Church needs to realize that it is not the only group working for justice and that it needs the input and experience of other denominations. In turn, it can contribute much to other groups who are struggling for the same goals. Recently, the Catholic Church has engaged itself in being a public church to a great extent on its own. As has been pointed out, any successful movements for change in United States society have been ecumenical in nature.

Internal Life Reflecting Proclaimed Message. Finally, as a public church, the internal life of the Church must reflect the message it is proclaiming. In the area of economics, "All the moral principles that govern the just operation of any economic endeavor apply to the Church and its agencies and institutions; indeed the Church should be exemplary" (EJ 347). As the U.S. bishops point out, there is a need for renewal in the economic life of the Church itself. Five areas are presented for special reflection: (1) wages and salaries; (2) the rights of employees, especially the right to organize and bargain collectively; (3) investments and properties; (4) works of charity; and (5) working for economic justice (EJ 351–58).

Bryan Hehir notes two significant issues in which the Church's social witness and the character of its internal life are of great concern: academic freedom in the university and theologate and the role of women in the Church.[32] Both areas need to be much more fully addressed lest they become greater scandals that totally undermine the attempts of the Church to work for justice.

It is also important that the paradigm of "justice as participation" that underlies the bishops' pastoral letter on the economy becomes the basis of life in the Church so that it can be a credible voice for such participation on the economic level of society. Dennis McCann has argued that the new experiment in democracy based on the principles of solidarity, participation, and subsidiarity called for by the bishops (EJ, Chapter 4) must become a reality not only in society as a whole but also in the Church.[33] What this means practically for the Church is that all of the people of God must be involved in formulating the Church's agenda in the world. Moreover, local churches must bear the primary responsibility for shaping their own agendas. The responsibility of the universal Church and dioceses, respectively, would be to keep the broader global and regional perspectives before the local churches. McCann also argues that a Catholic Church truly responsive to the presence of the Holy Spirit in its own local communities must provide for the free election of its leaders.

Evangelize the Middle Class

The second major strategy for the Church is to target the audience it is attempting to reach by evangelization. My proposal is that the Church must seek in a special way to evangelize the middle class regarding issues of justice and peace. What the Church would hope for through such evangelization would be the conversion of the middle class to a preferential option for the poor and a sense of solidarity with the poor. The expectation would be that from such an option for the poor the middle class would then seek a transformation of oppressive social, political, and economic structures.

"Middle class" is being used here to refer to those who earn wages or salaries rather than deriving their income primarily from the ownership of productive resources. This includes most professional people and middle managers as well as manual laborers, clerical workers, factory workers, retail clerks, office workers, and those in the various service occupations. There is a great diversity in this group of people not only with regard to income but also with regard to lifestyles, education, and even culture.

Rationale. There are several reasons for the Church targeting the middle class in its evangelization efforts for the sake of justice and peace. First, the middle class forms the majority of the membership of the Church in the United States as they also form the majority of the U.S. population. Hence, if the Church is to operate effectively as a public church, it is the Catholic middle class that the bishops must convince when they address economic and political issues. Otherwise the institutional Church will have little credibility in attempting to impact the national public political debate.

The middle class bears a significant responsibility for preserving and fueling the political, social, and economic systems that oppress. They do so through their consumerism, their lifestyles, their acceptance of the American myths and belief in the American Dream and its possibilities, their individualism, and their attitudes, especially their attitude about private property as an absolute right.

The middle class also forms the largest part of the electorate. To the extent that the system can still be changed through the vote, the middle class must play a significant role.

Above all it is the middle class that is being affected by the profound changes taking place in society today, especially on the economic level. I refer here to the centralization of the economy in fewer and fewer giant corporations, the spread of the transnational corporations, and the growth of the information revolution. Concomitant with these developments is the concentration of ownership of the means of production in the hands of fewer and fewer people, with control of these assets in the hands of a small group of top-level corporate management. These corporate giants and their small group of top-level managers have become the real source of power in the world today and not the individual nation-states.[34] Further, as a result of the technological revolution taking place, information-managing activities are being automated at a rapid rate with the need for fewer information managers. Middle managers displaced in this fashion are to a great extent being pushed into lower-paying service occupations. The same thing is happening to those being displaced as the result of the pullback in manufacturing in the United States.

In this context most of the middle class are experiencing an increasing economic insecurity and sense of powerlessness with regard to political power and control over significant areas of their work life.[35] Moreover, they are finding that they cannot preserve even their present standard of living and have little if any chance of improving their lot.[36] Caught in the midst of these changes, the middle class is highly susceptible to manipulation by various voices who wish to use the middle class and the power of the United States for their own purposes. Usually these voices attempt to manipulate the middle class under the guise of hopes and promises for preserving their present standard of living. The greatest danger is that the middle class might be manipulated to support the continuing oppression of the poor and possibly even view war as a means of preserving their standard of living.

Target the Professional Management Level. In its process of evangelization for justice, it will be important for the Church to target in a special way the professional-management layer of the middle class because of their number and the critical roles they play in maintaining the social, political, and economic systems. Because of their positions, they have access to a modicum of wealth and the prestige that comes from their positions as professionals and middle- and upper-level managers. These factors have kept them from seeing their similarities with other segments of the middle class. However, as wage earners, they need to realize that they are as susceptible to what is happening today as the working class and the poor. Like the working class and the poor, they are unable to influence the decision-making process and are faced with the same threat of job loss that depends upon the decisions of top-level corporate management. They too are powerless, "victims of polluted air, of callous indifference in the location and use of chemical waste dumps, of nuclear saber-rattling and its associated defense expenditures, of defective consumer products, of bureaucratic corporations and governments, and of a host of other systemic problems."[37] They must understand that it is in their own best interests to cooperate with other members of the middle class and the poor in seeking to transform oppressive social, political, and economic systems.

Reappraise American Myths. As part of the process of evangelization, Americans must be invited to reappraise American myths in the light of the Gospel. This is not just an invitation to return to the original ideals and values of our founders as these present themselves in the Declaration of Independence, the Constitution, and our civil religion; it is a call to evaluate these ideals and values in light of the Gospel. We need to know what in these ideals and values and our living out of them in our history as a nation is in keeping with the Gospel and what must be rejected. This evaluation should lead to an evangelization of our culture like that called for by Pope Paul VI (EN 19–20). Such a reappraisal must take place especially with regard to the themes of chosenness, individualism, and the iden-tification of salvation with wealth and success.

Modes of Evangelization. There are countless ways in which the Church can carry out its role of evangelizing the middle class. Some of these were already mentioned in discussing the Church's role as a public church. More specific modes of evangelization might include the following. First, statements may be given by individual bishops and diocesan or regional synods addressing local and regional issues of justice. Second, sermons should attempt to show how the Gospel relates to local and global issues of justice. Here, as with statements by individual bishops and synods, such sermons need to be specific enough to be meaningful and give some orientation for action or judgment but general enough to keep the insti-tutional Church above partisan politics. Another means of evangelization is to use an entire liturgy to highlight issues such as global hunger, unem-ployment, the North-South development issue, the need for disarmament, and so forth. The emphasis here would be not so much on specific solutions as on consciousness-raising.[38] Collecting money to further specific social justice programs that people can identify with will be also important. Generic giving runs the risk of salving the conscience without raising con-sciousness.[39]

Solidarity with the Poor. By insisting on the need for the Church to target the middle class in its process of evangelization, I do not intend to imply that the Church should ignore its poor members. In fact, it must be from solidarity with the poor that the Church addresses its middle-class members so that they may be drawn into a stance of solidarity. The purpose of the evangelization of the middle class is not to call them to do things for the poor but to call them to stand in solidarity with them and together with them seek the transformation of society.

Strive for Redistribution of Power

If the Church is to realize its goal of transforming the structures that oppress in order to liberate the poor, there needs to be a shift away from a concern for a redistribution of income to a concern for a redistribution of power. In other words, it needs to be recognized that the real source of injustice today lies in the concentration of ownership of productive assets in the hands of a few. As a result, great masses of people are excluded from the decision-making processes that determine the control and direc-tion of the productive process.[40] As the United States bishops point out in their letter, *Economic Justice for All,*

The nation's founders took daring steps to create structures of par-ticipation, mutual accountability, and widely distributed power to ensure the political rights and freedoms of all. We believe that similar steps are needed today to expand economic participation, broaden the sharing of economic power, and make economic decisions more accountable to the common good. (EJ 297)

Base Communities

A very important, if not central, strategy for affecting the transformation of the social, political, and economic systems will be the establishment of base communities.[41] These base communities are small groups where lay people can come together under lay leadership to develop their Christian identity through a communal reflection on the Gospel and together to seek ways to translate the principles and visions found in Church social teaching into concrete programs, recommendations, and movements for political and social change. They will accomplish this latter goal through a process of social analysis, theological reflection, and pastoral planning. These groups should not be parish oriented but organized independently of parish structures. Such groups should not be exclusively Catholic but ecumenical in nature.

The rationale for the above proposal flows from several of the strategic presuppositions pointed out above. The laity, who have their own proper mission in the Church, must be the key action agents of the Christian community in its mission of transforming the structures of society (LG 33, see also 36). Every significant impact which Christianity has made on the social order in modern times has been built upon the pious lay conventicle. In addition, parish-centered lay renewal movements in the United States have repeatedly fragmented and lost their vigor and clarity regarding their agenda. There is thus a need for lay movements that are structurally autonomous from the local parish. Finally the voluntary associations of Christians that have been successful in bringing about social change have been ecumenical in their makeup.

These base communities should be organized not only among the poor but also among the middle class. Though the middle class does share responsibility for the oppression that exists globally and nationally, they, like the poor, are also oppressed by the political and economic systems, and more and more find themselves powerless. In the process of coming to terms with their own oppression and powerlessness and struggling to understand and transform the systems that oppress them, the middle class might also be led to understand their own role as oppressor in the world and their need to become instruments of change. Also, it is hoped that in struggling with the specific structures that oppress them, they will come to understand the wisdom and necessity of respecting the poor as the architects of their own future and the need to join forces with the poor and learn from them. As Joe Holland has pointed out, on the one hand, the middle class can look up to the rich and strive to be like them and therefore look down on the poor with fear and contempt. On the other hand, they can look downward and see themselves as closer to the poor and the oppressed. Then, disenfranchised with the poor, they need to join forces with the poor to effect change.[42]

In insisting on the centrality of these base communities as a strategy for transformation, I do not intend to play down the need of the institutional Church to continue its role as a public church and evangelizer. However, it is important to reflect on what should be the source of the vision proclaimed by the Church. There must be a reciprocal relationship between those who proclaim the Word and those who hear it, especially the poor and the oppressed. On the one hand, there must be the proclamation of the Gospel vision regarding the dignity of the human being, the principles of distributive justice, and the demands of love and justice and hope for the future. This vision plays an important role in the reflection process used by the base communities. On the other hand, the specific content of this Gospel vision must come from listening to the poor and the oppressed on a local and a global level.

Use of Media

In its role as public church and evangelizer the Church must use the media in all its dimensions. The media today has become the primary means by which values, cultures, outlooks, and perceptions of reality are communicated and handed on. In this process the media uses its own language and modes of communication and symbols. If the Church is to be effective in carrying out its mission, it must also be able to proclaim its message in the language of the media. Moreover, the Church must not see the media just as a tool to be used in its mission; it must also view the media as a system that needs to be transformed in light of Gospel values.

The Church Must Be Poor

Finally, if the Church in the United States hopes to be able to understand the meaning of the Gospel for today and to proclaim that Gospel in a credible fashion, the Church in the United States must become a Church of the poor and be poor itself. As was pointed out earlier, only to the extent that the Church identifies itself with the poor and the oppressed can it accomplish its prophetic function. It is only when the Church has nothing to lose or defend in the system that it can step back and take an honest look at the system. The institutional Church, then, must divest itself of its unneeded wealth. As long as the institutional Church maintains and manages wealth, it cannot be independent of the system. For many, the perceived wealth of the Church is a real impediment to their hearing what the Church has to say about the poor and justice. Further, the Church as an institution comes under the same demands of distributive justice as any other institution. When others lack the necessities of life, the Church loses its right to those goods it does not need to exist in dignity. Finally, the call of the Gospel to radical poverty for those who would be disciples of Jesus speaks also to the Church as an institution (see Mt 19:16–30; Lk 14:25–35).

Only by identifying with the poor in its midst and becoming poor with them will the Church come to understand and see even more clearly the system that oppresses. Even more important, by identifying with the poor, the Church may also learn from them what its real values should be, that is, its need for redemption, the need for dependence on God and one another, placing security in people rather than in things, the need of cooperation and patience, an openness to wherever the Gospel calls.

One final reflection on the Church becoming poor might be in order here. The Sermon on the Mount contains a call to total dependency on the Lord rather than on earthly treasure. As Matthew says,

> Do not store up for yourselves treasures on earth. . . . No one can serve two masters. . . . Do not worry about your life, what you will eat [or drink], or about your body, what you will wear. . . . Can any of you by worrying add a single moment to your life-span? . . . So do not worry. . . . But seek first the kingdom [of God] and his righteousness, and all these things will be given you besides. Do not worry about tomorrow; tomorrow will take care of itself. Sufficient for a day is its own evil. (Mt 6:19–34)

Matthew urges us to avoid useless worrying about our livelihood to the point of letting it affect our commitment to the Reign of God. Matthew is not issuing a call to irresponsibility, to an abandonment of working for what we need for life. Rather, Matthew recommends that our anxiety should not exceed the labor required to secure subsistence. It is not the use of the necessities of life that is discouraged, but the accumulation of goods as a means of security. In other words, if we get too wrapped up in earthly treasures as a source of security, then these treasures will become such a continuing source of concern that they will lead us away from a concern for the Reign.

Everyone knows from experience the wisdom of Matthew's observation. However, we also have experienced that Matthew's advice goes against our constant tendency to gather goods and lay up treasures to take care of ourselves at least in the lean times. Our tendency is to not want to depend on others so that we do not lose our freedom. This tendency can also be found in institutions—perhaps with even more force. In the institution the tendency to store up earthly treasures has its roots in the institution's responsibility to provide for its members. For this end, goods are necessary.

The issue, then, comes down to how an institution, such as a church organization, should go about acquiring the income it needs to take care of its members. Should the institution simply take it day by day, or should it accumulate treasures as a basis for a consistent, dependable income? In responding, we should keep in mind that no amount of storing up goods is going to prevent rough times when it is not clear how the bills can be paid.

In fact, our hoarding of goods as a way of seeking security creates another set of problems, such as fidelity to the will of donors, unwillingness to take risks if such risks could adversely affect our monetary situation, arguing over how to use the money stored up, and so forth. Also, we should keep in mind how most of the people in the United States (90 percent) live who have no investments. They are forced to live day by day and do what they can within their means. As a Church of the poor should not the Church approach life in the same way?

Finally, achieving the solidarity with the poor that is being called for here is difficult. People would much prefer simply to practice charity toward the poor. However, it is important to remember that Jesus saved us not by practicing charity toward us but by becoming one of us, entering into solidarity with us, suffering with us so that we could become enabled to take responsibility for ourselves. In the same way the United States as a country and the Church in the United States must enter into solidarity with the weak, the poor, and the powerless. We must become vulnerable with the poor and oppressed and suffer with them in order to empower them to gain economic and political freedom so that they can care for and assume responsibility for themselves.

NOTES

1. SOCIAL ANALYSIS: A TOOL FOR CHURCH PLANNING

1. What follows is almost totally drawn from Joe Holland and Peter Henriot, S.J., *Social Analysis* 2nd ed. (Maryknoll: Orbis Books/Center of Concern, 1983), chapter 1 and "Afterword." The material presented here is not meant to substitute for this excellent primer in the process of social analysis. Anyone or any group that is interested in using the process described here should begin by reading this book of Holland and Henriot.

2. Holland and Henriot, p. 14.

2. THE GLOBAL CONTEXT

1. For the following see Peter Steinfels, "The Foreign Policy Context of the Nuclear Debate," *Catholics and Nuclear War,* ed. Philip J. Murnion (New York: Crossroad, 1983), pp. 30–42.

2. See remarks of Secretary of State James A. Baker III as quoted in the March 31, 1990, edition of the *Chicago Tribune*, Section 1, p. 3. The article refers to a speech Secretary Baker made to the World Affairs Council of Dallas on March 30, 1990, which was intended as a benchmark address mapping the Bush administration's strategy for moving beyond the forty-year-old policy of containment of Soviet expansion.

3. Bill Moyers, *The Secret Government: The Constitution in Crisis* (Cabin John, MD: Seven Locks Press, 1988).

4. See quotation of Retired Admiral Gene LaRocque in Moyers, p. 35.

5. Moyers, p. 54.

6. Peter Steinfels, pp. 36–37.

7. Kevin Phillips, *The Politics of Rich and Poor* (New York: Random House: 1990), p. 133.

8. See chapter 3 for further development of this thesis.

9. See chapters by Marcus Cunliffe, Robert L. Beisner, and Robert N. Bellah in *American Character and Foreign Policy*, ed. Michael P. Hamilton (Grand Rapids: William B. Eerdmans, 1986).

10. John L. Gaddis, "The Modern World: World War I to 1984," *American Character and Foreign Policy*, p. 35.

11. It is estimated that in 1981 approximately $500 billion was spent by the superpowers and their partners in military spending and that 50 percent of all scientific research and personnel were involved in military projects.

12. Enrique Dussel, *Ethics and the Theology of Liberation* (Maryknoll, NY: Orbis, 1978), p. 10.

13. Barry Commoner, *Making Peace with the Planet* (New York: Pantheon Books, 1990), chapter 7.

14. Quotation of Dennis Robertson (30 years ago) in Richard N. Cooper, "The United States and the World Economy," in *The World Economic System: Performance and Prospects,* ed. Jacob A. Frenkel and Michael L. Mussa (Dover, MA: Auburn House, 1984), p. 2.

15. Penny Lernoux, "The Long Path to Puebla," in *Puebla and Beyond*, ed. John Eagleson and Philip Scharper (Maryknoll, NY: Orbis, 1979), pp. 8–9.

16. Phillips, p. 7.

17. See Phillips, p. 120f.

18. Commoner, p. 46.

19. This is a group of over four hundred people in the United States and elsewhere who are involved in research, public education, and advocacy regarding the problem of the debt crisis. See *Center Focus* 85 (July 1988): p. 4. (A newsletter published by the Center of Concern in Washington, D.C.)

20. *Oakland Tribune,* January 6, 1989.

21. Over the last decade a series of blue ribbon studies have called for basic changes in the world economic order, namely, the Club of Rome, New Futures, Brandt Commission, Global 2000, and the numerous special session reports of the United Nations. For specific references see Richard D. N. Dickinson, *Poor, Yet Making Many Rich: The Poor as Agents of Creative Justice* (Geneva: World Council of Churches, 1983), p. 3.

22. Dussel, p. 12.

23. Holland and Henriot, *Social Analysis*, pp. 46–51.

24. See Jagdish N. Bhagwati, "North-South Economic Relations: Then and Now" in *The World Economic System,* pp. 49–61.

25. Commoner, pp. 192–93.

26. Henry C. Wallich, "Institutional Cooperation in the World Economy," in *The World Economic System*, p. 85.

27. Wallich, p. 99.

28. Alvin Toffler, *The Third Wave* (New York: Bantam, 1984).

29. For the following discussion see: Joe Holland and Anne Barsanti, eds., *American and Catholic: The New Debate* (South Orange, NJ: Pillar Books, 1988), chapters 1 & 3; Robert A. Brungs, S.J., "Science and Technology," in *The Context of Our Ministries: Working Papers* (Washington: Jesuit Conference, 1981), pp. 58–59.

30. Holland and Barsanti, p. 21f.

31. Ibid., p. 27.

32. Peter J. Henriot, S.J., "International Dimension," in *The Context of Our Ministries: Working Papers*, p. 41.

33. See the following chapter.

34. Dickinson, p. 4.

3. THE NATIONAL CONTEXT

1. Robert N. Bellah, *The Broken Covenant: American Civil Religion in Time of Trial* (New York: Seabury Press, 1975), p. 3.

2. In the following discussion I will be primarily dependent upon Robert Bellah's book *The Broken Covenant*. For a fuller treatment of these myths the reader should consult this book.

3. Ibid., p. 5.

4. Ibid., p. 23.

5. Ibid.

6. James Sellers, *Public Ethics* (New York: Harper and Row, 1970), pp. 72–73, as quoted by Bellah, *Broken Covenant*, p. 24.

7. John A. Coleman, *An American Strategic Theology* (Mahwah, NJ: Paulist Press, 1982), p. 187.

8. Bellah, p. 27f.

9. Coleman, p. 190.

10. See further below.

11. William Lee Miller, *The First Liberty* (New York: Knopf, 1986), p. 209.

12. Herman Melville, quoted in Bellah, pp. 38–39.

13. Bellah, p. 37.

14. Ibid., p. 55.

15. See Bellah, chapter 3.

16. Quoted in Bellah, p. 115, from a 1946 statement by the National Association of Manufacturers.

17. Ibid., p. 124.

18. Miller, pp. 234–46.

19. Coleman, p. 66f.

20. John A. Coleman, S.J., "Social Issues," in *The Context of Our Ministries: Working Papers* (Washington: Jesuit Conference, 1981), p. 45.

21. Ibid., p. 44.

22. As quoted in Coleman, p. 46.

23. Robert N. Bellah, Richard Madsen, William M. Sullivan, Ann Swidler, and Stephen M. Tipton, *Habits of the Heart: Individualism and Commitment in American Life* (Berkeley: University of California Press, 1985), chapters 1, 2 and 6.

24. Miller, p. 206.

25. Ibid., p. 255.

26. Ibid., p. 264.

27. For the following discussion see Bellah et al., chapter 6.

28. Kevin Phillips, *The Politics of Rich and Poor* (New York: Random House, 1990) p. 14.

29. Ibid., p. 11.

30. Ibid., p. 166.

31. Ibid., pp. 8–11.

32. For more details regarding the impact of the 1980s on the poor, see Phillips, pp. 202–9.

33. See The Campaign for Human Development, *Poverty Profile USA: In the 'Eighties* (Washington: USCC, 1985), pp. 15–43.

34. Phillips, p. 20.

35. Ibid., p. 20.

36. See *Poverty Profile USA*, p. 18ff.

37. See Phillips, p. 167, Table 12.

38. Ibid., p. 204, Table 21.

39. *Poverty Profile USA*, p. 28.

40. Phillips, p. 15.

41. See Phillips, p. 204f.

42. Ibid., p. 22.

43. Ibid.

44. For the following discussion see Joe Holland and Peter Henriot's book *Social Analysis*, 2nd ed. (Maryknoll: Orbis, 1983), pp. 77–83.

45. Richard J. Barnet, "Profits at What Cost? America in the World Economy," in *American Character and Foreign Policy*, ed. Michael P. Hamilton (Grand Rapids: William B. Eerdmans, 1986), p. 73.

46. Barry Commoner, *Making Peace with the Planet* (New York: Pantheon, 1990), p. 46.

47. Ibid., pp. 46–47.

48. For the following see Robert L. Heilbroner and Lester C. Thurow, *Economics Explained*, 2nd ed. (New York: Simon & Schuster, 1987), chapter 13.

49. See Commoner, p. 85f.

50. See also Benjamin M. Friedman, *Day of Reckoning* (New York: Random House, 1988), pp. 198–203.

51. Phillips, pp. 91–101.

52. Friedman, pp. 204–6.

53. See below for more on this issue.

54. See Commoner, chapter 3.

55. John Naisbitt and Patricia Aburdene, *Re-inventing the Corporation* (New York: Warner Books; 1985), pp. 18–21.

56. Phillips, pp. 136–42.

57. See Heilbroner and Thurow, pp. 104–5; Thomas S. Johnson, "An Agenda for Economic Growth and Social Justice," in *The Catholic Challenge to the American Economy*, ed. Thomas M. Gannon, S.J. (New York: Macmillan Publishing Co., 1987), p. 190–91. See also Benjamin M. Friedman, *Day of Reckoning*, whose major thesis deals with the fact that America has thrown itself a party and billed the tab to the future.

58. Phillips, p. 127.

59. See *Time*, August 13, 1990, p. 50.

60. See the section below on the political context.

61. Phillips, pp. 87–88.

62. See Lester C. Thurow, "The Arms Race and the Economic Order," in *Catholics and Nuclear War* (New York: Crossroad, 1983), pp. 212–13.

63. Thurow, p. 205.

64. For the above data see Manuel G. Velasquez, "Ethics, Religion and the Modern Business Corporation," in *The Catholic Challenge to the American Economy*, p. 61.

65. Ibid., p. 66.

66. Bellah, *Broken Covenant*, pp. 130–38. See also Velasquez, pp. 70–75.

67. Bellah, p. 133.

68. Peter Henriot, "Political Order," in *The Context of Our Ministries* (Washington: Jesuit Conference, 1981), p. 36.

69. Bellah et al., p. 207.

70. Ibid., p. 207.

71. Henriot, p. 37.

72. Bellah et al., p. 200.

73. Henriot, p. 37.

74. See Bellah, p. 197.

75. John Naisbitt, *Megatrends: Ten New Directions Transforming Our Lives* (New York: Warner Books, 1984), chapter 7.

76. See Bellah et al., pp. 210–13 for the following discussion.

77. Phillips, *Politics of Rich & Poor,* p. 55.

78. Henriot, *Social Analysis*, p. 82.

79. See Phillips, chapter 7.

80. Phillips, p. 219.

81. See discussion in chapter 2.

82. Bill Moyers, *The Secret Government: The Constitution in Crisis* (Cabin John, MD: Seven Locks Press, 1988), p. 89.

83. Moyers, 117–18.

84. See Paul A. Soukup, S.J., "Communication and the Media," in *The Context of Our Ministries*, p. 67.

85. See Robert A. Brungs, S.J., "Science and Technology," in *The Context of Our Ministries*, pp. 59–61.

86. Naisbitt and Aburdene.

87. Naisbitt, p. 4.

88. Naisbitt and Aburdene, pp. 13–15.

89. Ibid., pp. 15–18.

90. Naisbitt, chapter 2.

91. Ibid., pp. 74–75.

92. See Brungs, pp. 62–64.

93. See Robert J. Schreiter, *Constructing Local Theologies* (Maryknoll: Orbis Books, 1985), p. 69.

94. Coleman, p. 191.

4. THE CHURCH IN THE UNITED STATES

1. Jay P. Dolan, *The American Catholic Experience* (Garden City: Doubleday and Co., 1985), p. 111.

2. Ibid., pp. 160–61.

3. George Gallup, Jr., and Jim Castelli, *The American Catholic People: Their Beliefs, Practices, and Values* (Garden City: Doubleday and Co., 1987), p. 2.

4. For these and the following figures see Gallup and Castelli, chapter 1.

5. Ibid., pp. 10, 24–25.

6. Ibid., pp. 42, 179.

7. Joseph Gremillion and Jim Castelli, *The Emerging Parish: The Notre Dame Study of Catholic Life since Vatican II* (San Francisco: Harper & Row, 1987), p. 30.

8. Gremillion and Castelli, p. 67.

9. Gallup and Castelli, p. 183.

10. Ibid., p. 44.

11. Ibid., pp. 46, 50.

12. Gremillion and Castelli, p. 58ff.

13. Gallup and Castelli, p. 47.

14. Ibid., pp. 47–48, 50, 184.

15. Gremillion and Castelli, pp. 188–90.

16. Gallup and Castelli, pp. 52–53. See also Gremillion and Castelli, p. 40.

17. While the Notre Dame Study supports the acceptance by "Core" Catholics of a married clergy, it showed that "Core" Catholics are decidedly uncomfortable

with the idea of a female clergy. The young and educated are far more likely to support this change. See Gremillion and Castelli, pp. 43 and 45.

18. Gallup and Castelli, pp. 53–57. See also Gremillion and Castelli, pp. 40–41.

19. See Gremillion and Castelli, chapter 6, for the findings of the Notre Dame study on lay leadership.

20. Ibid., p. 9.

21. Rembert G. Weakland, "The Church in Worldly Affairs: Tensions Between Laity and Clergy," *America* (October 18, 1986): 201f.

22. Gallup and Castelli, chapter 6.

23. Gremillion and Castelli, pp. 181–85.

24. While social action is seen as a proper activity for the Church and parish, it comes after more traditional parish programs, with only 4 percent of the parishioners being involved. The great majority of these are women. See Gremillion and Castelli, p. 68.

25. Ibid., p. 184.

26. Ibid., see chapter 7 and pp. 180–81. See also p. 190.

27. Ibid., p. 90.

28. Gallup and Castelli, chapter 9. See also Gremillion and Castelli, pp. 36–45.

29. Gallup and Castelli, pp. 188–91.

30. Ibid., p. 190.

31. Dolan, chapter 8.

32. See "Selective Catholicism" below.

33. Joe Holland, "Linking Social Analysis and Theological Reflection: The Place of Root Metaphors in Social and Religious Experience," in *Tracing the Spirit,* ed. James E. Hug, S.J. (Mahwah, NJ: Paulist Press, 1983), pp. 184–90.

34. Robert Gonzalez and Michael LaVelle, *The Hispanic Catholic in the United States: A Socio-Cultural and Religious Profile,* (New York: Northeast Pastoral Center for Hispanics, 1985).

35. Gremillion and Castelli, p. 75.

36. Ibid., chapter 5.

37. National Conference of Catholic Bishops, *The Hispanic Presence: Challenge and Commitment* (Washington: United States Catholic Conference, 1984).

38. Ibid., p. 7.

39. Gremillion and Castelli, p. 97.

40. Moises Sandoval, *On the Move: A History of the Hispanic Church in the United States* (Maryknoll: Orbis Books, 1990), p. 89.

41. What one sees as significant issues for the Church depends upon one's perspective, one's concerns at the moment. My concern is the mission of the Church in the United States. As was pointed out in the introduction I see the Church as being an instrument for transformation of society. Hence, what I see as significant issues for the Church flow from this perspective.

42. See Robert N. Bellah, Richard Madsen, William M. Sullivan, Ann Swidler, and Stephen M. Tipton, *Habits of the Heart: Individualism and Commitment in American Life* (Berkeley: University of California Press, 1985), pp. 220–23.

43. Ibid., p. 223.

44. Ibid., p. 227.

45. Ibid., p. 232.

46. Gremillion and Castelli, pp. 34–36.

47. Bellah et al., p. 270.

48. John A. Coleman, *An American Strategic Theology* (Mahwah, NJ: Paulist Press, 1982). See chapter 7 for this discussion.

49. Bryan Hehir, "Church-State and Church-World: The Ecclesiological Implications," *CTSA Proceedings* 41 (1986): 54–74.

50. Ibid., p. 64.

51. John T. Pawlikowski, O.S.M., "The American Catholic Church as a Public Church," *New Theology Review* 1(1988): 8–29.

52. See Pawlikowski article for general survey of issues.

53. See chapter 9.

54. J. Bryan Hehir, "A Public Church," *Origins* 14 (May 31, 1984): 41.

55. Pawlikowski, pp. 13–14.

56. Ibid., p. 26.

57. Coleman, p. 259.

58. Pawlikowski, pp. 15–17.

59. Ibid., p. 19. See also Coleman, p. 265.

60. As reported by Coleman, p. 179.

61. Dolan, p. 101.

62. Ibid., p. 111.

63. See Dolan, pp. 117–18 and James Hennesey, S.J., *American Catholics: A History of the Roman Catholic Community in the United States* (New York: Oxford University Press, 1981), p. 89.

64. Dolan, p. 308.

65. Quoted in Dolan, p. 309.

66. Ibid., pp. 310–11.

67. Ibid., p. 311.

68. Ibid., p. 316.

69. Hennesey, p. 203.

70. Dennis P. McCann, *New Experiment in Democracy* (Kansas City: Sheed and Ward, 1987), p. 13.

71. McCann, p. 319.

72. Dolan, p. 319.

73. McCann, chapter 2.

74. Coleman, pp. 180–81.

75. William McLoughlin, quoted in Coleman, p. 181.

76. Joe Holland, "Faith and Culture: A Historic Moment for the American Catholic Laity?" *American & Catholic: The New Debate* (South Orange, NJ: Pillar Books, 1988), p. 26.

77. Andrew Greeley, *American Catholics: A Social Portrait* (New York: Basic Books, 1977), p. 71.

78. Gremillion and Castelli, p. 37f.

79. Andrew Greeley, *American Catholics since the Council: An Unauthorized Report* (Chicago: Thomas More Press, 1985), pp. 58–69.

80. This would correlate with what I pointed out earlier in the discussion on the impact of individualism, namely, that people generally see their relationship to God as preceding involvement in a particular church.

81. Greeley, *American Catholics: A Social Portrait,* p. 272.

82. Coleman, p. 178.

83. Gallup and Castelli, p. 178.

84. August 1985. See Dean Hoge, *The Future of Catholic Leadership: Responses*

to the Priest Shortage (Kansas City: Sheed & Ward, 1987), Appendix A.

85. Katarina Schuth, O.S.F., *Reason for the Hope: The Futures of Roman Catholic Theologates* (Wilmington, DE: Michael Glazier, Inc., 1989), p. 111f.

86. Eugene F. Hemrick and Dean R. Hoge, *Seminarians in Theology: A National Profile* (Washington: USCC, 1986), and Raymond H. Potvin, *Seminarians of the Eighties: A National Survey* (Washington: NCEA, 1985).

87. Hoge, *The Future of Catholic Leadership,* Appendix A.

5. THEOLOGICAL REFLECTION: ANOTHER TOOL FOR CHURCH PLANNING

1. I am basically following Thomas H. Groome, *Christian Religious Education* (San Francisco: Harper & Row, 1980). See especially chapters 9 and 10.

2. Ibid., p. 192.

3. Ibid., p. 193.

4. Ibid., p. 194.

5. Ibid., p. 197.

6. BIBLICAL PERSPECTIVES ON LIFE

1. Walter Brueggemann, *The Bible Makes Sense*, (Winona, MN: St. Mary's Press, 1977).

2. While I have leaned heavily on Brueggemann's book in places, I take full responsibility for the perspective that follows. I hope that I have not done a disservice to a book that has been so helpful to me.

7. OUR LIVING FAITH

1. See Gerhard Von Rad, *Old Testament Theology,* 1 (New York: Harper & Row, 1962), p. 229f.

2. Roger Haight, S.J., *An Alternative Vision: An Interpretation of Liberation Theology* (Mahwah, NJ: Paulist Press, 1985), p. 33. Much of the following material is dependent upon Haight's synthesis of liberation theology.

3. Haight, p. 41.

4. Ibid., p. 134.

5. See above on "People of God."

6. EJ, Pastoral Message 14.

7. See the earlier discussion on salvation in the Old Testament.

8. See Albert Nolan, *Jesus Before Christianity* (Maryknoll: Orbis Books, 1978), p. 21.

9. Robert Gnuse, *You Shall Not Steal: Community and Property in the Biblical Tradition* (Maryknoll: Orbis Books, 1985), p. 10.

10. Gnuse, chapter 3.

11. For the following see Charles E. Curran, *Toward an American Catholic Moral Theology* (Notre Dame: University of Notre Dame Press, 1987), pp. 189–90.

12. For the following discussion see especially Charles E. Curran, *Directions in Catholic Social Ethics* (Notre Dame: University of Notre Dame Press, 1985), chapters 1 and 2.

13. Curran, *Toward an American Catholic Moral Theology* p. 189.

14. CP, 167–99. See Pope John Paul II, "Message to U.N. Special Session on Disarmament," 8 June 1982.

8. REFLECTIONS ON THE UNITED STATES

1. The term "Gospel" will be used throughout this chapter as a generic term to refer to both the biblical perspective on life and the material on the various "themes" developed in the previous two chapters.

2. Charles E. Curran, *Directions in Catholic Social Ethics* (Notre Dame: University of Notre Dame Press, 1985), p. 109.

3. See the previous chapter for a discussion of distributive justice.

4. Curran, p. 109.

5. John A. Coleman, *American Strategic Theology* (Mahwah, NJ: Paulist Press, 1982), p. 191.

6. See chapter 3.

7. John C. Murray, *We Hold These Truths* (Garden City: Image Books, 1964), p. 273.

8. See fuller discussion in chapter 3.

9. Manuel Velasquez, "Ethics, Religion and the Modern Business Corporation," in *The Catholic Challenge to the American Economy,* Thomas M. Gannon, S.J., ed. (New York: Macmillan Publishing Co., 1987), chapter 4.

10. Ibid., pp. 74–75.

11. Ibid., p. 75.

12. See the section on "Human Dignity and Human Rights," in chapter 7, pp. 127–29.

13. See Monica K. Hellwig, "Good News to the Poor: Do They Understand It Better?" in *Tracing the Spirit,* ed. James E. Hug, S.J. (Mahwah, NJ: Paulist Press, 1983), pp. 122–48.

9. THE CHURCH AND ITS MISSION

1. Pope Paul VI in his opening allocution at the second session of the Council (Sept. 29, 1963). See Walter M. Abbot, S. J., ed. *The Documents of Vatican II* (New York: America Press, 1966), p. 14, footnote 1.

2. John Coleman, *An American Strategic Theology* (Mahwah, NJ: Paulist Press, 1982), p. 2.

3. Richard P. McBrien, *Catholicism* (Minneapolis: Winston Press, 1980), pp. 715–16.

4. McBrien, pp. 718–19.

5. Leonardo Boff, *Ecclesiogenesis: The Base Communities Reinvent the Church,* (Maryknoll: Orbis Books, 1986), pp. 16–17.

6. Louis Bouyer, *The Church of God,* trans. Charles Underhill Quinn (Chicago: Franciscan Herald Press, 1982), p. 396, as quoted by Boff, p. 17.

7. Boff, p. 18.

8. Charles E. Curran, *Directions in Catholic Social Ethics* (Notre Dame: University of Notre Dame Press, 1985), pp. 120–21.

9. In dealing with this question John Coleman, for the sake of clarity, distinguishes three levels of Church: the Church as institution, para-ecclesial groups in the Church, and Christians as citizens. See *An American Strategic Theology,* p. 26. My concern is only with the Church as institution.

10. J. Bryan Hehir, "Church-State and Church-World: The Ecclesiological Implications," *CTSA Proceedings* 41 (1986): 57–58.

11. Ibid., p. 58.

12. Coleman, p. 27.

13. Ibid., p. 28.

14. Ibid.

15. Hehir, p. 69.

16. Ibid., p. 69.

17. Coleman, p. 30.

18. Coleman, pp. 30–31.

19. John Courtney Murray, S.J., *We Hold These Truths* (Garden City: Image Books, 1964), p. 272.

20. Charles Curran, *Toward an American Catholic Moral Theology* (Notre Dame: University of Notre Dame Press, 1987), p. 196.

21. For what follows see the footnote on this paragraph found in Walter M. Abbot, S.J., *The Documents of Vatican II*, pp. 685–87.

22. Murray, p. 272.

10. WHERE IS THE U.S. CHURCH GOING?

1. See discussion in chapter 4.

2. Paul G. King, Kent Maynard and David O. Woodyard, *Risking Liberation: Middle Class Powerlessness and Social Heroism* (Atlanta: John Knox Press, 1988), p. 40.

3. John Coleman, *An American Strategic Theology*, (Mahwah, NJ: Paulist Press, 1982).

4. Ibid., p. 80.

5. Ibid., pp. 270–72; and see p. 146.

6. See Ibid., p. 146.

7. Ibid., p. 146.

8. See earlier discussions on how far such statements should go in addressing specific issues and what U.S. Catholics will not accept (chapters 4 and 9).

9. See chapter 9.

10. Coleman, p. 145.

11. Ibid., p. 250.

12. Ibid., p. 251.

13. J. Bryan Hehir, "Church-State and Church-World: The Ecclesiological Implications," *CTSA Proceedings* 41(1986): 61–62.

14. See the discussion on this point in chapter 7.

15. Hehir, p. 62.

16. Coleman, pp. 258–66.

17. See section in chapter 9, "Intervention in Politics and Economics," pp. 174–77.

18. Coleman, p. 265.

19. For the following see especially Coleman, chapter 2.

20. Coleman, pp. 138–39.

21. Robert N. Bellah et al, *Habits of the Heart* (Berkeley: University of California Press, 1985), pp. 286–87.

22. Coleman, p. 241.

23. Ibid., p. 241.

24. Thomas H. Groome, *Christian Religious Education* (San Francisco: Harper & Row, 1980), pp. 198–201.

25. See chapter 5 for a discussion of Story.

26. Groome, p. 200.

27. See the prior discussion on the "public" Church in chapter 4.

28. Hehir, p. 64.

29. Ibid.

30. Ibid.

31. Coleman, p. 284.

32. Hehir, p. 73.

33. Dennis McCann, *New Experiment in Democracy: The Challenge for American Catholicism* (Kansas City: Sheed & Ward, 1987), chapters 5 and 6.

34. Sixty percent of ownership of the means of production is concentrated among 1 percent of the population and 90 percent of the population owns no such assets at all.

35. See King et al., chapters 2 and 3.

36. See King et al., chapter 3.

37. King et al., p. 58.

38. Coleman, p. 268.

39. Ibid., p. 269.

40. King et al., p. 88.

41. See especially Leonardo Boff, *Ecclesiogenesis: The Base Communities Reinvent the Church*, trans. Robert R. Barr (Maryknoll: Orbis Books, 1986).

42. Joseph Holland, "Linking Social Analysis and Theological Reflection: The Place of Root Metaphors in Social and Religious Experience," in *Tracing the Spirit*, ed. James E. Hug, S.J. (Mahwah, NJ: Paulist Press, 1983), p. 189.

Index